Spring 80

TECHNOLOGY, CYBERSPACE, & PSYCHE

A JOURNAL OF ARCHETYPE AND CULTURE

Fall 2008

SPRING JOURNAL

New Orleans, Louisiana

CONTENTS

JUNGIANA

INTERVIEW

FILM REVIEWS

BOOK REVIEWS

IN MEMORIAM

ADOLF GUGGENBÜHL-CRAIG (1923-2008)

On the 18th of July 2008, Adolf Guggenbühl-Craig died at the age of 85. Several weeks earlier, he had fallen and was unable to recover from a broken hip. For over forty years, Guggenbühl had been one of the most influential voices in the world of Jungian psychology.

Adolf Guggenbühl was born on the 25th of May 1923 in Zürich. His mother, Helene Guggenbühl-Huber had been studying medicine at the time, and his father, Adolf Guggenbühl, was working as the publisher and editor of the influential Swiss monthly magazine, *Schweizer Spiegel.* Guggenbühl grew up in Witikon, just outside of Zurich, in the literary environment of a publishing household. As editors of *Schweizer Spiegel,* his parents often invited leading intellectuals and writers of the time to their home: Kurt Güggenheim, Friederich Glauser, Wolfgang Pauli, and Hartmann, to name a few. In 1933, when Adolf Guggenbühl was 10 years old, his parents held a dinner party which brought together two family friends for the first time: Carl Jung and Wolfgand Pauli. A few years later, Pauli would enter analysis with Jung and many of his dreams would subsequently make their way into Jung's book, *Psychology and Alchemy.*

A few years after the end of World War II, in 1949, Guggenbühl attended a summer camp in Scotland where he met his future wife, Anne Craig. They married in 1952 and went on to have five children: Allan, Catriona, Marion, Alistair, and David.

At university, Guggenbühl initially studied theology, then history, before finally settling on the study of medicine. After completing medical school at the University of Zürich, he completed an internship in Providence, Rhode Island, followed by a residency in psychiatry in

Adolf Guggenbühl-Craig and James Hillman in Houston, Texas during their 1963 United States lecture tour.

Omaha, Nebraska. Upon his return to Zürich, Guggenbühl enrolled at the Jung Institute and completed his analytic training in 1958. Having come from a publishing family, he was quite at home with writing, and in 1962, Güggenbuhl edited the *Proceedings of the Second IAAP Congress, Der Archetype*. This began a relationship with the International Association of Analytical Psychology that would endure for years and culminate in his serving two terms as IAAP President between 1978-1983.

During his analytic training at the Jung Institute, he met James Hillman and started an important friendship that would last to the end of his life. In 1963, Güggenbuhl and Hillman toured the United States together, giving lectures on depth psychology and visiting psychiatric hospitals across the country.

In the 1960s, Guggenbühl became a member of the Zürich Jung Institute Curatorium and later served as Curatorium President from 1969 to 1979. During his many years as a faculty member of the Jung Institute, he lectured regularly and published numerous articles and three books: *Power in the Healing Profession; Marriage: Dead or Alive; and Eros on Crutches*—later re-issued as *The Emptied Soul*. His books were translated into many languages and he lectured throughout Europe, England, North and South America, and Japan. Guggenbühl was a great story teller with a rare and refreshing honesty. His writing style was not scholarly, but personal and pragmatic, full of wit, irony, and psychological insight. An early essay of his, never before published in English, appears in the Jungiana section of this issue as a tribute to him.

—Paul Kugler

Paul Kugler, Ph.D. received his Diploma in Analytical Psychology from the C. G. Jung Institute, Zürich in 1979. While in Zürich, he worked at the Clinic and Research Center for Jungian Psychology (Klinik am Zürichberg) before returning to the United States to teach at SUNY / Buffalo and work in private practice in East Aurora, New York. He is the author of numerous works ranging from contemporary psychoanalysis and experimental theatre to postmodernism and clinical supervision. Kugler's most recent book is *Raids on the Unthinkable: Jungian and Freudian Psychoanalyses* (2005). He is past president of the Inter-Regional Society of Jungian Analysts and currently serves as an Officer of the International Association of Analytical Psychologists. While attending the Jung Institute, Zürich, Dr. Kugler had the opportunity to get to know and do clinical supervision with Adolf Guggenbühl-Craig, the Jung Institute President in the 1970s.

PART I:
WHAT'S ONLINE

THE ARCHETYPAL ALCHEMY OF TECHNOLOGY: ESCAPE AND RETURN TO MATERIALITY'S DEPTH

GLEN A. MAZIS

I. TECHNOLOGY'S DRIVE TO LEAVE THE EARTH

Beethoven conceded that the repeating, opening chords of his Fifth Symphony seemed to him to be "Fate, knocking at the door." Centuries later, on March 15, 2004, the Fifth Symphony was performed by the Tokyo Philharmonic Symphony under the baton and blazing yellow eyes of Qrio, a humanoid robot with a magnesium body whose mechanical, waving arms led the human orchestra through this dramatic flood of music with fluidity and clarity.[1] Might this be fate knocking at the postmodern door, and, if so, what sort of fate is it? Many philosophers and depth psychologists, as well as numerous voices in popular culture have cried out that such a robot performance is the death knell of humanity; that we will be taken over and perhaps become

Glen A. Mazis teaches philosophy and humanities at Penn State Harrisburg in the Interdisciplinary Humanities Program as Full Professor. He is also a poet who gives readings, performances, and has published about 70 poems in literary reviews. He is the author of *Emotion and Embodiment: Fragile Ontology; The Trickster, Magician and Grieving Man: Returning Men to Earth; Earthbodies: Rediscovering our Planetary Senses* (SUNY, 2002), and *Humans, Animals, Machines: Blurring Boundaries* (SUNY, 2008). He has many published essays on imagination, art, film, dreams, animality, ecology, and embodiment. He is currently writing *Merleau-Ponty and the Sensual Depth of the World*.

literal slaves of machines; that we will have cyborg reconstruction of
increasing parts of our biological body and that even our mental
capacities will be replaced by cybernetic ones; or that at the very least
we have lost our souls, our sense of being present to one another and
the rest of the planet by the usurpation of our capacities to truly feel,
to take to heart emotionally, to be expressive, to have imaginal lives,
and to experience ourselves in our embeddedness with other humans,
animals, nature, and the cosmos—having lost ourselves to the glut of
cyborgs, cyberspace, and technological constructs. Qrio, the Sony-
constructed robot conductor, the pride of corporate production, takes
the musician's podium as if usurping one of the few sacred spots carried
forth from the past and still remaining in the postmodern public realm,
that of conducting profound classical music, as if it is able to translate
the pulse of one of the most feeling-laden artistic creations of world
culture into something available for all to experience. That it is a *musical*
masterpiece may seem especially ominous, since the musical art form
has been taken from Pythagoras on to be a sounding of the cosmos in
its fundamental harmony among all beings that is key to its spiritual
depth.

Beethoven located music as the *mediation* of the material world
experienced through the senses with the psyche: "Music is the mediator
between the spiritual and the sensual life." Human beings in their
soulfulness are the beings with this singular ability to be of the earth
and its matter in such a way as to make the spirit within this realm
become manifest in light or in sounding tones or through colors or
within the movements of their limbs, since humans in resonating with
this realm as being of its larger body express its sense by bringing it
forth onto the artistic stage, as well as other spiritual places of being
witnessed. Jung cites Karl Joël's statement in *Soul and World* that "the
artist strives for a felt reunion ... a full unity ... the oneness attained
through differentiation" in examining how the spiritual emerges from
nature to be witnessed in a way similar to being able to understand
"nature's language" or hear "human speech in the sounds of nature."[2]
In this way, the artist reestablishes what Jung comments that Hiawatha
expresses straightforwardly living in the world of *participation mystique*,
but the artist has traversed the differentiations of the path to
individuation yet still retained or rediscovered, more accurately, the
voice and sense of the whole.

Yet, surely this is not what the robot conducting Beethoven's Fifth Symphony is able to accomplish? The answer is clearly "no" for technology's critics. Wolfgang Giegerich, for example, would say that the technology that surrounds us, whether the robot bringing to "expression" profound music, the Web providing endless information about and connections with others, television bringing us visions of events around the globe and entries into cultures or natural landscapes that we would never have the opportunity to witness, are *not* ways of encountering the world and its sense, let alone sounding its depths of soul, but are ways of becoming more and more *cocooned*. To be within this technological world, for Giegerich, amounts to an inversion between man and world. When man still lived in the real world, his sense organs and his intellectual sense (his reason) were an intermediate and mediating third through which he experienced reality (the reality of nature and of the divine). Sense organs and sense (*mens*) were simply the interfaces between both the real human being and the real world, which thus in fact met. Now, given the technology which Giegerich says surrounds us or catches us in its *web* (pun intended), "The world as it once had been has, to be sure, dropped altogether out of this game."[3] Giegerich believes we live in Plato's cave as our final Western destination, a time in which nature that used to be defined as "what encompasses and bears our existence"[4] is now encompassed by the technological world as a "problem child" instead of Mother Nature, and in which history itself has been rendered by technology in such a way as to become a "museum" in which the past is just an occasion at our disposal for our entertainment.

Rendered through television, through the Internet, through films, and in the digitized reconstruction of the world, Giegerich claims "History, too, has been ontologically annihilated and denatured because it is deprived of its innermost nature, which was to be the wind of time."[5] Unable to experience the reality of either historical or natural forces that gave our life a sense of necessity and had to be dealt with in the profundity of their mystery, we no longer have access to these forces as they have been externalized into things around us and then volatized. For us, history is seen as what is contained in computer files to be stored and brought into use at a finger touch, and time no longer lurks within the natural surround, as it did for Native Americans, as expressed by Leslie Marmon Silko in *Ceremony:* each time the protagonist Tayo looks out at the mountain, he sees all the past of his people and the creatures around him, rising to meet him and place him within the midst of these histories, still alive, powerful, and demanding respect. Giegerich is right that in prior eras, the winds of the past blew us here and there, and gathered from the four corners of the world to enfold us. The Greeks encountered these winds as immortals who chose air to be their bodies, and Boreas, Eurus, Notus, and Zephyros, when Odysseus struggled with them on his way home, brought him to the struggle with the sins of his past and within his community's history with which he was grappling. The winds interwoven with time and history, allowed the Greek heroes to move about the globe and experience within its gusts the exhalations of the psyche that was inextricably of human, nature, and cosmos.

In the technological world, Giegerich decries that these depths can no longer reach humans "as a sensible-physical being" but are encoded for us as receivers of mediated input. If history is data, if music is electronically filed and disseminated, then the following analogy betokens human imprisonment:

> Just as in a literal virtual reality setup the human being is, through his data suit, etc., enclosed into virtual reality equipment and hooked up to it, absorbed into it, so he has in his logical essence as a cave dweller turned into a technical component within a large information and communication machine, namely into a receiver and a data-processing machine.[6]

Having lost the matter of our lives in the sense that the material forces of nature and history had been interwoven with mountains and winds, stone towers, and ancestral song lines laid across the landscape holding within them a substantiality of meaning and soul, instead we are caught within technology's simulations, and without that encounter, we cannot develop the Self, the deeper dimension of ourselves than the daily, task-driven life. Giegerich despairs that the imaginal dimension of human life and its power to open the meaning of the earth, lives, and events around us has been vaporized such that the image is "a simulation of an image" and "all meaning is the simulation of meaning."[7] By this Giegerich means that the image is "cut off from its substrate," no longer created expressively within a physical medium that is itself symbolic, like musical notes or paints, and no longer open to what is expressed, but is rather a stream of data manipulated to produce an effect.

Given this lack of dialogue with the profundity of our surrounding world, "the age of psychology, of depth psychology, of introspection is over."[8] This indeed would follow if we remember that soul is of the world, as Glen Slater aptly summarizes, "Archetypal patterns exist beyond brain structure. They are not confined to the psychic realms but also reside in the earth and in the nature of the cosmos."[9] If the cosmos has been reduced to inputs that are simulations and to expressions which also are only simulations, in that they are no longer the effect of singular individuals shaping the sense of the surround in dialogue with others, then humans are left rootless with no deepening possible of the type that is a growing into the soil of the earth. Without this depth, psychology is not possible for the "individual is obsolete, a past reality" and "there is no 'interior' any longer."[10] We take in pre-packaged images and information, and do not struggle to discern our own sense of what we encounter. We are without the autonomy of discovery, and whether cyberspace, the endless gadgets of technology (such as iPods) or their precursor, television, we are their attachment, rather than vice versa: "the institution called television is using us, not we it."[11] They keep us rootless, unable to have epiphanies in our lack of relation, addicted to emotional thrill which is insensitive, ego-centered, and empty.[12]

II. IS THE DARKNESS OF THE CAVE ONLY A PRISON?

Giegerich echoes Plato's dissatisfaction with the masses' addiction to sensory stimulation and emotional thrill as blocking access to deeper meaning, yet his analysis of our current situation is more dire. For Plato, the sensual world did not give us access to reality, since only thought can allow us to reach beyond the body and the sensible to the intelligible. Plato's famous condemnation in the *Republic* of the arts denounces the artist's canvas, the play of the actors, or the music of the lyre as being "three times removed from reality," since the sensible is already a secondary realm in relation to the underlying intelligible structure of things and events and then this itself has been further copied by the artist in given a sensible likeness of something itself apprehended by the senses only. Yet, even Plato allows in the *Ion* that the artist can be inspired and hold the audience in a magnetic connection with the highest or deepest realities in a kind of spell being out of one's mind and that the sensible still participates in the intelligible. For Giegerich, technology has altered the nature of sensation in such a way that instead of access to the world, we have access to

> only sense data, information, stimuli. It is to them he now relates, rather than relating through them and through his reason, which used to connect him to the divine, to what had been outside him, the world.[13]

What technology has given to us is between "this new 'outside' (the flood of sensible stimuli and the input of information) and man ... a new middle, that successor of the figuration of 'the World,' that is called virtual reality or illusory being. This is the reversal of the relation of man and world." Now the senses are no longer mediating our access to reality or to truth, and instead of the world encompassing us, technology has allowed us to encompass the world, which condemns us to live in a cave of utter self-enclosure.

However, for Giegerich, the more recent technological developments followed the trajectory of television that "induces a kind of self-renunciation, a *de facto* renunciation that is an objective or structural one, not a consciously intended one,"[15] whose real point is to seduce an addicted population into "daily devotions" whose purpose is to "kill time,"[16] to "exclusively cocoon oneself in the world of the ego,"[17] in order to prevent "self-exposure" to real events,[18] "to prevent moments of quiet and silence from occurring,"[19] to allow "the systematic destruction of something 'inner,' a sense of interiority,"[20] to create a "world that is exclusively surface,"[21] to "remove its containment and rootedness in some meaning or truth,"[22] where there is a surfeit of "sensationalism,"[23] "mind, reason or spirit have no place"[24] and "strong emotions ... the exact opposite of epiphanic experiences ... essentially self-, or ego-centered, even autistic ... not intersubjective, not the event of connection or relation."[25] What television inaugurated, however, has been perfected by the Internet which produces pure simulations with total indifference to its content, such that "the image that belongs to the Internet means the absolute end of myth, of religion, of 'the meaning of life.'"[26]

Television, cyberspace, and the technological world are a way of existing such that humans have evolved to become beings of simulation, driven by the artificially created need for "entertainment" and distraction,[27] whose interior life has migrated into a world of surfaces and intensities that Giegerich says are like Hesse's *Glass Bead Game*, a matter of play with contents and values for the manipulation of their colorful shine with no inner value.[28] Without its imaginal dimension, these manipulations are taken with the pure logical form of the movement of sensationalized continual input.[29] Our consciousness itself has no commitment to contents or depths, but continually "surfs," just as we say about our way of moving through cyberspace or flicking the channels of our televisions. This surfing is locked into the ongoing state of "thrill" with a need for continuous absolute immediacy.[30] For Giegerich, this is unconsciously an expression of an attempt to get beyond the flesh while being in the flesh concretely, through this overwhelming intensity, a theme which connects with his deepest point of how we have come to this "accomplished emptying."[31] For Giegerich, however, this is no surprise, but rather the culmination of a long, unconscious project.

The trajectory of technology stems from the essence of Christianity, Giegerich details, and even before that, to the Old Testament. Yahweh had emptied out the image, undone the binding force of the world around us (as the meaning of the incident of the Golden Calf in the Old Testament),[32] and as the "imageless image"[33] fled to a level of abstraction and absoluteness that called for the will to believe.[34] Christianity took this further in order to defeat polytheism "it had to become absolutely indifferent to any particular content of the image, indeed to the very idea of content" which leads directly and inexorably to the age of cybernetics.[35] Furthermore, Christianity in the idea of the incarnation inaugurated "the somatization of being"[36] in such a way that the absolute came to reside in matter, but not in the prior Greek sense that the divine-earthly tension was held within matter, but that "*logos* and *sarx*, word and flesh, come in fact together in one point."[37] This now becomes a kind of flesh that is not grounded in nature, but in logos.[38] This differing kind of flesh is what is technology.[39] Giegerich says that the original Greek sense of technology as embedded in myth and open to nature became "technified,"[40] as an instrument of logos as positivistic reason,[41] as pointing towards a transcendent and supernatural given an empirical existence.[42] So, for example, the computer seems the fabrication in the material realm of the storage of all information or omniscience. Telecommunication, computers, space travel, etc., simulate the overcoming of space and time.[43] The absolute has become the material as manipulated through technology.

I have lingered with Giegerich's analyses, because I find them compelling.[44] My only answer to them other than assent is to remind us that the unconscious does not unfold in a single direction, but rather moves in ways that are overdetermined. Even if it seems that the conscious creed of Western culture has been progress towards light, control, disembodiment, and separation from the embracing surround, there may be another unconscious drive that is the underside belying an opposite desire and movement. As Jung stated,

> Every psychological extreme secretly contains its own opposite or stands in some sort of intimate and essential relation to it. Indeed, it is from this tension that it derives its particular dynamism ... and the more extreme a position is, the more easily may we expect an enantiodromia, a conversion into it opposite.[45]

I believe that cyberspace, robotics, artificial intelligence, and technology can be seen to have an archetypal significance that is such an enantiodromia in the unconscious effort to achieve a redemption of embodiment, a recovery of the unity of materiality and spirit, and a rediscovery of a postmodern avenue to soulfulness that recapitulates the primal one, despite its apparent destructiveness towards these dimensions. It may be that Giegerich is only attempting to give us "shock therapy," as Glen Slater suggests,[46] so we discover these tensions, but I disagree that technology has left us in the position that "nature, myth, the ancient gods are truly dead," that "our psyche has left behind the standpoint earth," that "we have irrevocably fallen out of nature," and "we have encompassed the whole globe in our networks."[47] Nor can I wholly agree that technology's unconscious drive is solely towards a form of soul-making[48] that accomplishes "divesture" of our embeddedness in nature as psyche to make the world of flesh and matter into instrumental reason.[49]

When Sophocles depicts Oedipus striking out his eyes for having seen too much horror and in angry vengeance for having not seen enough to be able to master his fate in literalizing his eyes and vision, it seems to be rather an unconscious wish to deliver him from being enmeshed in history and a network of relationships beyond the power of his instrumental reason to master and even fully fathom. This would make it the same blow that technology strikes to sever us from embeddedness in earth and nature, as depicted in the analyses we've discussed. Yet, I believe that Sophocles is correct in discerning yet a deeper layer of the unconscious, an enantiodromia, that is the hunger for that embeddedness as its proper home and intuits that through the very blindness created by that blow, it will be achieved. The blindness that seems vengeance, rupture, and despair with history, with belonging, and with hearkening to the voices of the earth gradually is revealed as the way that Oedipus is to be transformed. Through his blindness, he becomes something other than he has been and arrives two decades later at Colonus transformed. Oedipus realizes this suddenly, and thanks his blindness and the long time of suffering as the teachers that have brought him to be reverent towards the divinities of the earth, to accept the necessity of the whole as richly mysterious and meaningful, and to return to his body and senses. I agree with Giegerich that the tale of the Judeo-Christian tradition and its heirs in science and technology are the attempt to realize a will applied to empty matter where matter is an abstraction reconfigured by instrumental reason. Yet, this is only partially what it is about. Within the seemingly blind progress of technology in its cyborgs, cyberspace, artificial intelligence, and technological machines, there are other senses struggling to emerge.

III. The Gesture and Desires towards Disincarnation

The realm of the flesh, the body and its material context, cannot be volatized in the manner critics of technology fear or that technophiles hail as liberation from embodiment, nor can history as a dimension of our being be overcome so completely, nor can nature be utterly destroyed, overcome, or rendered a corpse by the powers of technology, as Giegerich declares. Interiority lives within an oneiric dimension (not just in literal dreams, but within the immediate concatenated perceptual sense) beyond the reach of instrumental reason and is renewed continuously by the circulating depths of perception with the world that Giegerich and critics of similar views (of which there are many) overlook. It is true that we have come to live in a world of surfaces, but surprisingly, there are depths within the surfaces themselves, and yes, we mistake intensity of affect for its sensitivity, the proliferations and ease of consumption of images for their compelling resonance, the material glut for the quiet of the marrow of things that whispers secrets, and access to the confessions of others for heartfelt community, but each of these mistakes within our technological hurly-burly contains also the flickering imaginal sense of other dimensions of meaning that psyche requires for vitality. If this is true that there are ongoing unconscious senses and longings, we might find that incarnation, embeddedness within a fuller materiality, and interconnectedness with others and with all things are hidden in technology's occluded face.

When the robot, Qrio, waves its arms rhythmically leading the orchestra, the unconscious drive within technology and Western science to overcome the human embeddedness within matter—to have split off spirit from its arising from within matter and the human body— seems to have been accomplished, since the robot waves its arms driven relentlessly according to a predetermined program that is the detached essence of the spirit of music: the score with its notes, rhythms, harmonies, and tonalities reduced to a written or electronic set of notations. This is different from the sense expressed by the human arm of the conductor who swings and waves her or his way through the music in a give and take with the members of the orchestra and within the resonance in the hall and the flood of notes sounding, rhythms weaving, pace emerging, and sections of the orchestra harmonizing. For the human conductor, her or his flesh in motion is open to the world and its changes in register, and she or he modulates expression from within a give and take with it. This kind of bodily motion is a *gesture*, the way psyche emerges from the interweaving of body and matter so that sense circulates and is caught in an interplay in the process of expression. Human gestures take up the rhythms of the surrounding world and of those others about whom one cares and inflect them in a singular manner in a kind of creative dialogue that is precisely missing from the robot's mechanically driven series of motions that are programmed and self-enclosed. As Merleau-Ponty adds to Beethoven's formulation, it is the body as gesturing that conveys a sense "by feeling my way into its existential manner, by reproducing the tone and accent,"[50] by always being "a third term" between the sensual surround and what we seek to express.[51] It is not the body as physical matter that enters into expression as the mediation with spirit, but the resonant body as "flesh of the world," as Merleau-Ponty called it, becomes a circulation of sense that flows from interrelations among things into our own sense of ourselves in the world. It is Cézanne's gesture with the paint brush that allows the panoply of senses of Mount Saint Victoire to move through him onto the canvas in a decade of painting it in dialogue.[52]

The motion of Qrio is that of self-propelled materiality in a chain of causes and effects, what D. H. Lawrence called "the mechanical power of self-directed energy/ [that] drives them on and on/ ... while nothing comes from the open heaven, from earth, from the sun and moon/ to them, nothing, nothing/ ... mere motion, full of friction, full of grinding, full of danger to the gentle passengers of growing life/."[53] With such triumphs of technology, we may believe we have achieved the disjunction of spirit and body or spirit and matter, carrying out the project of spirit using matter as a tool to do its bidding, as Descartes claimed was the essence of the human condition, but was more of a proposal for a design project for the human future. Technology does seem to have achieved this dualism. Computers increasingly are the means of achieving breakthroughs in the realm of abstract thought, whether making calculations necessary to solve abstruse mathematics problems, designing new structures for architecture or engineering, interpreting data from outer space probes, making discriminations on the microscopic and even subatomic levels, and varied sorts of calculations, deductions, and projections that had been seen as inherent to the realm of intellect and spirit that was the special human excellence. In addition, technology has given us cyberspace as that realm in which most claim the material hardware has allowed us to escape the body and be released to the realm of pure spirit or mentality. Our contemporary sense of spirit is increasingly the result of the operations of a material substrate to which they are linked but opposed and from which we feel liberated, as if we had actualized the vision of body and matter as mere "vessels" in Cartesian terms or as mere "hardware" in contemporary terms.

As Giegerich asserts, certainly, *partially*, the goal of Western culture is to reduce the world to chains of cause and effect, to a kind of matter that spirit can leave behind in order to gain the control that humans have lacked and will always lack as part of an encompassing world with its own necessities. Technology has evolved beyond a sense that it is merely a collection of tools at our disposal to become a force with which we reinvent even ourselves as able to detach from our materiality or reattach in ways we control. Through technology matter is transformed into something separable from spirit in creating robots to do physical tasks humans are incapable of doing but desire, combining human bodies with either biomechanical parts as simple as a pacemaker or as exotic as the exoskeleton that might help paraplegics walk again or become enhanced in physical capacities through mechanical or chemical add-ons, so our will can be applied to this distant, empty matter, even in the most intimate ways. Michael Chorost's account in *Rebuilt: How Becoming Part Computer Made Me More Human*, of how he regained hearing through a cochlear implant, where sound could be transferred to his own body through intricate mechanical means and the computer implanted within him could reprogram the sounds to be perceptible as words seems to fulfill the dream that both body and mind can be technologically altered and enhanced as two separate realms which we can control and use together through our technology.

One could then further suppose that technology is not only the drive to create vehicles for increasing the ontological gulf of matter and mind, mind and body, self and world to control the world from a distance, but as Giegerich suggests, the way to *destroy* nature.[54] As mere tool, whether our bodies or the surround, what has been given to us on this planet is seen as replaceable and thus discardable. The realm of computing intelligence and robotics seem to be at the forefront of this dichotomizing of mind and body in order to escape materiality as being our unconscious destiny. There are many, like the group "Digital Liberty" described by Stephen Talbott who believe cyberspace will yield a "discarnate utopianism"[55] or like Howard Rheingold, who starts his book, *The Virtual Community: Homesteading on the Electronic Frontier*: "people in virtual communities do just about everything people do in real life, but we leave our bodies behind."[56] These cyberspace enthusiasts envision escaping the body, the "meat" as they call it, by becoming downloaded into a computer matrix, no longer vulnerable as flesh. There are many who dream of races of robots that can fight wars and do the physical work of civilization for humans, as drones to our will, insulating us from dealing with the direct consequence of our actions and our moral responsibility. Killing someone is a shock that echoes within the person and with those who send them to fight, as well as their own vulnerability brings home the gravity of what is being perpetrated in a war—sending robots would attenuate these significances. Finally, there are those who believe that the developing "artificial intelligence" of computers will give rise to beings who are the next evolutionary step and will supercede humanity, or at least can free humanity from its most difficult challenges, like managing the economy or governing fairly, as envisioned in the works of Isaac Asimov.[57] In these visions, enveloping nature is indeed superfluous and would not be missed if destroyed, as the film *Silent Running* depicted a few decades ago with a script in which humanity had surpassed its tie to nature and ordered its last remaining forest preserves to be destroyed as no longer worth the cost of their maintenance.

IV. ARTIFICIAL INTELLIGENCE AND ROBOTICS REDISCOVER EMBODIMENT

Even though the drive to create artificial intelligence might have proceeded on the dream that thinking could be isolated from its bodily concomitants, from emotional coloring, from social, cultural, and political contexts, from personal perspective and interests, from history, and carried out in a realm of purely logical, empirically based, quantified, detached, and invariant cool efficiency, the seeming moment of its greatest success revealed to many that this was a chimera—a misunderstanding of humanity, intelligence, and the path that computer science and technology should take.

Cognitive science's initial approach to creating "artificial intelligence" was based on the model of a centralized agent of abstract reasoning and mathematical calculation that followed determinate rules, and was detached from space and time, and could then apply its rules to material reality. When on May 11, 1997 the supercomputer, Deep Blue, defeated the then world chess champion Garry Kasparov in its rematch, instead of proving how machines had come to realize intelligence, the computer had only produced such a limited capacity to function in this one arena after all the decades of research and development that its disparity with true intelligence became obvious to many, at least as reported by Ann Foerst who had been working with the M.I.T. scientists: "These chess games between the two helped us to see the limitation of this traditional understanding of intelligence. When Deep Blue beat Kasparov, there was still no robot that could actually butter a piece of bread because it is so difficult."[58] This centralized, detached intelligence would not be able to really direct action in a world, since it was a self-enclosed system of algorithms. It would have to have an immense amount of input from the world to be a *responsive* intelligence, and the world is too varied to have all the necessary input come back to this central brain, for it would not even have a way of knowing how to direct itself towards what sectors of the environment from which it needed the input. Buttering a piece of bread is more complex than chess, because one has to know varied aspects of the world and have relationships to them, and not merely perform a self-contained set of rules and algorithms on a reality "out there somewhere."

What this really meant is that artificial intelligence had to be embodied to become intelligent—to know the world as immediately impinging upon it with feedback from what was to be the focus of its "understanding" and action. So, as Foerst continues,

> You have to know the consistency of the butter, how hard the butter is. You have to know about the knife. You have to know about the consistency of the bread. You have to have very strong feedback loops between your arm, the knife, the butter, and the bread. You have to know a lot about the world. Otherwise you just have bread crumbs.[59]

Computer scientists began to realize how complex the knowledge gained through perceptual and kinesthetic interaction with the environment is and see that it is learning *through* the material reality of being an embodied being. Such knowing is not accessible to an encapsulated immaterial intelligence, but opens up for an interactive one that loops within the relationships of its surround. This means the body is not incidental to knowing, but at its heart. As Rodney Brooks, then associate director of the M.I.T. Artificial Intelligence Lab that began in 1992 to construct robot intelligences explained, "if AI researchers attempt to build intelligent machines, they ought to build embodied entities that interact with the real world." Not only that, but Brooks realized the fundamental understanding of the world was grounded in perception and embodiment: "One might not need abstract thought in the beginning, since after all most animals survive pretty well without it and newborns don't have this capability either."[60] The body provides a primary understanding of the world that is fundamental to other kinds of knowing and through a relationship it provides with the surrounding world.

Abandoning the prime assumption of traditional approaches to artificial intelligence—the assumption that there is some central "I" or intellect that "runs" the body as tool—the M.I.T. investigators became convinced that the human interacts with the environment "finding its way about" *through* embodied experience, and not from predetermined algorithms. This implicit and experientially gained "understanding" of body and world would later become integrated as the robots learned to master certain tasks that confronted them. Rather than centralized control systems, the robots were made up of "distributed" systems that were to learn from the environment through an equivalent of human embodiment. This was the beginning of "Embodied AI," as it is known. For example, the arms of the robots were constructed with several "degrees of freedom" of movement (the possibility of moving in several ways), as were other parts of its robot "body," just as humans are able to move various parts of their bodies in different directions and angles. These different possibilities of kinesthesis were to become geared into specific tasks facing the robots and corresponded with various motherboards in the robot's "brain" that were not directly connected but would come to interact within the experience of the robot in coordinating several motors in reaction to the demands of a specific task.[61] Without a pre-set plan, the robot would try gestures or movements of its arms and hands in varied ways until the successful solutions were arrived at. There would be a give-and-take between robot "body" and the world about it.

These robots "interact because through experience they 'learn' motor control and coordination of several motors in reaction to the demands of a specific task."[62] The analogy is made to infants who first wave their arms about aimlessly, until they learn to focus on the object desired, as does the robot wave aimlessly at first and learn through trial and effort how to grasp something. As Foerst summarizes: "It has no abstract understanding of space. Instead it learns to coordinate its arms though feedback loops that register the weight the joints have to carry in a specific arm position." The sensors and actuators that react to the environment are connected in such a way that the system can react flexibly, instead of following some set internal plan. What the building of robots as conceived by Brooks and others to gain artificial intelligence aims to achieve is a cooperative venture with the world: "The physics of its very embedding in the world provided a rich dynamics of interaction. In order to make it act intelligently, all we needed to do was nudge the dynamics forward in the right direction."[63] The body is the medium for an unfolding give and take, for a nondiscursive dialogue with the world which is a level of primary understanding. This understanding doesn't come from previous principles now applied, but rather comes from an openness to the surround that allows for spontaneous evolving of apprehension.

In the confines of this essay, there is not the space to document all the shifts in artificial intelligence and technology studies that are moving towards revisioning and redirecting the focus of their work towards a responsive intelligence, one that emerges from within the material world and integrates the human body and its exquisite sensitivities, as well as the way that intelligence is inseparable from emotion, imagination, memory, visceral feelings, and intuition in the depth of layered perceptions, or at least tries to mimic in some way these kinds of relationships to the world. In addition, M.I.T. artificial intelligence scientists have begun to explore features of their robots that point to deeper dimensions of this other direction within computer science and technology: they have built into one of their robots a "face" which moves and can signal to human interlocutors seventeen recognizable "emotional expressions;"[64] robots that react to color and to movement, turning towards objects; that track with its head and eyes both objects and persons approaching it; that babble in a kind of stream of human baby-like sounds that replicate four differing kind of melodies associated with differing emotional responses, and can detect these melodic shifts in humans around it and either mimic them or respond.[65] Given the constellations of sensors, actuators, effectors, processors, and motherboards, these robot intelligences are in a feedback loop with the surround, a give and take.

Ann Foerst tells the story in her book of one Sunday morning when she and the robot's programmer were with the robot, Kismet, when Foerst became frustrated with the fact that its eyes were roaming around the room at a group of visitors to the lab instead of working with her to demonstrate something to a reporter, and she began to complain in a sad voice about its reactions, when suddenly it turned towards her and started to babble in a soothing and comforting tone. Both Foerst and Cynthia Breazeal, who had programmed into it its capacity to do this, couldn't help be taken aback at the seeming responsiveness of Kismet as if it could feel sympathy.[66] Both of them, who witnessed the robot's careful construction, couldn't help but feel awed by its reaction, even knowing its workings.

V. THE TECHNOLOGICAL DRIVE'S ENANTIODROMIA

Both sets of reactions, the lack of awe at Deep Blue finally being able to beat the world's human chess champion after years of continued research and development, an astonishing achievement in one sense, and the awe, surprise, and fellow feeling generated by Cog and Kismet to acts of responsiveness, are indicative of the ambiguity within technology's deeper meaning. Many of the robots' responses at the M.I.T. lab continue to astound, despite many reasoned objections to these emotional reactions elicited from both workers and visitors, such as the example of Harvey Cox, Harvard Divinity School professor, who was shaken when Cog's gaze followed him around the room before moving forward uncertainly but successfully to complete the handshake Cox offered with his outstretched hand.[67] The fact that matter produced thinking of a sort in the defeat of Kasparov by Deep Blue did not mean that it had displayed anything akin to human thinking. I disagree with Giegerich's statement that "The soul of the matter is the thought that animates it."[68] We do not get the sense of any quasi-human presence or any sense of soul from computers as matter generating thought, despite Giegerich's assertion "As a self, the soul of the psychological phenomenon is a thought that thinks itself."[69] Pure thought does not animate matter nor does encountering a blank "thinking" façade with no relationship to its world give us a sense of kindred being. The dualism of thought and matter is not overcome by bringing these two realms together. Only the flesh has this power, because it also feels, imagines, dreams, has passions, feels its own feeling, remembers, is beckoned to attention, believes, and affirms as well as thinks.

Kismet's and Cog's responsiveness strikes a chord in us, a flicker of recognition, because as crude as it still is at this stage of development, it either mimics or starts to achieve a sense of presence of a psychological phenomenon and the kind of intelligence that permeates the gestures of human embodiment as within an interwovenness, attentiveness, and responsiveness of visceral feeling, emotion, imagination, memory, and intuition in perceiving. The movement of the robot's head taking in our movement by its continuous tracking through visual input is not just a random action, but a sort of "dance" with our own movements and body that strikes us as being with a "partner" on a prereflective level. Even the strange quasi-gestures of Kismet or Cog, who do have facial features, limbs, and hands, make us disbelieve what we know intellectually, and we start to feel as if they must be real presences, aware, and somehow intelligent. They are quasi-gestures since they are responding to registering numerous happenings around them as being the origin of their enactment. The robots' gestures evoke us in us resonances, since it is the case that as part of the flow among other people or creatures, our gestures are woven into matching movements and feelings with others. Thinking, embodiment, feeling, gesturing, moving, and other aspects of who we are as humans weave together in such a way that psyche is a holistic emergence from flesh and matter that "faces" us or enters into encounter. Kog and Kismet seem to be *on the way to* having a "face," not only in the sense of a surface that responds in expressions but as entering some sort of give and take with us. Human thinking, as well as our other capacities and expressions, can only emerge from a face.

The change in direction in these computer scientists' quest for "artificial intelligence" reveals an enantiodromia in our cultural psyche in the sense that Western culture's technological imperative has been so one-sidedly driven to escape embodiment, to separate mind from matter, and to disjoin the core of soul or psyche as that spirit which emerges from materiality in its intertwining with all parts of itself and with humans as its vital articulator that it is transforming into its opposite: to appreciate and recreate the sense in which mind is only that which emerges from being embedded within the larger material and natural surround. Our culture's rampant materialism is actually a disjunction from the deeper sense of materiality which holds for us emotional meaning, imaginal depths, memories lodged within things and place, and the way we are of the same "stuff," to put it in Merleau-Ponty's phrasing, such that the world "folds back on itself" through us to gain expression. Our desire to consume objects or to possess them through identification with them as "ours" with no deeper communion with their depths of meaning and soulfulness is a compensation for that disjunction of our belonging to the material surround that we have attempted to escape through technology's destructive side. Yet, technology has within it the capacity to lead us back in the opposite direction to seeing how it can work by taking the route of our repressed dimension of being embedded in the surround and in the earth, and by demonstrating to us through our own creations how we are enfolded with other humans and creatures in a deeper dialogue with what Merleau-Ponty called "the flesh of the world."[70]

VI. THE BODY WITHIN AND WITHOUT AS FRIENDSHIP IS A DESIRE WITHIN NIGHT

However, as our desires emerge from our embeddedness, they are prone to this contradiction by the nature of our relationship with the surround. Our perception of the material world as embodied has been shown by Merleau-Ponty to mean that our "lived bodies" have an inherent virtual dimension inscribed everywhere within the surround as tracing implied perspectives on what we perceive. So, for example, in looking from the tower at the lake, a constitutive part of my vision from this vantage is the sense of the lake as seen from above within the birds' perspective or the clouds,' and also a sense of the far shore as if seen by the trees standing there, and so on, because my body joins up with all the perspectives of other beings, creatures, and people within my surround in taking up its own perspective and "plunging into" the object of its vision. Each object perceived, says Merleau-Ponty, is like a mirror play with all other objects and takes us into this round among them.[71] This means that there is a natural trajectory within perception itself towards denying its own ground in its immediate situatedness and to aspire towards a "God's eye perspective," in the sense of being beyond all these and other possible interlinking vantages by encompassing them all[72]—a deed impossible for a human who is after all anchored somewhere and only has a vague and finite sense of other vantages. Yet, within our psyche and within our body, we know that we are "woven into the fabric of the world,"[73] as Merleau-Ponty puts it, and held by the necessity of these interlocking forces surrounding us.

Our unconscious drive to further technology, I believe, harbors both desires, to transcend the earth and its enmeshment, and also to affirm that we are of the earth and other beings and can only emerge from this communion. This is what speaks to us from matter and is within our body. As Jung stated, "The journey through the psychic history of mankind has as its object the restoration of the whole man, by awakening the memories of the blood."[74] Specifically this is needed, Jung claimed, because humanity's totality was forgotten "when contemporary man lost himself in one-sidedness." This deeper nature lodged within the memory within the blood, which in this case is our embeddedness within the surround, will always cause for Jung "upheaval" and a "tremor in the upper world" as opposed to the man of the present, because "he is the one who ever is as he was, whereas the other is only for the moment."[75] We can only be human and speak, think, feel, dream, imagine, remember, and create because we, as psyche, are of the earth, and this reasserts itself, and as Jung indicates, when the time seems most dire by vigorous grasping towards the other direction. For example, Giegerich was correct that the development of the nuclear bomb was a human attempt to bring forth the power of God to annihilate the earth, but it quickly turned around to become a message of appreciating humanity's fragility and need for enmeshment in the sheltering earth. It brought quickly to awareness that humans are not equipped for the task of having such force under our control, because we are not godlike. What emerged is that the greater human drive than gaining power is that such a stupendous force needs to find a tie to love and thriving or else be put aside.

Giegerich writes in the collected volume of essays, *Technology and the Soul*, of technology assuming the guise of Mercurius in the sense of Mercurius being the tricky nature of matter to become malevolent and explosive when separated and kept imprisoned[76] and as the transformation of our anchoring in matter to something volatile and unsubstantial.[77] I would like to propose that the technological drive, its seeming rapacious consumption of our energies and disconnection from the earth and even cultural depth of the surround, is on a deeper level a longing for friendship, a desire to belong with other humans and animals, and even to find the kinship with all those inanimate beings around us. Philotes, goddess of friendship, is the daughter of Nyx, the night. The desire for friendship is a desire the seems to be held within night as technology aims to block out the natural light shining forth upon us from the surround or, as Giegerich puts it, imprisoned in the dark of Plato's cave by technology, and is of the deeply unconscious aspect of this more apparent urge to dominate and separate. Yet, this is not surprising in regard to the way Philotes is present within the technological drive. As the spirit that seeks friendship, she also is sibling to Cer (goddess of violent death and malevolent ghosts), Thanatos (the destructive instinct), Hypnos (who cuts the thread of life and collects souls), Moros (god of doom and destiny), Nemesis (Envy), Eris (goddess of discord), and several other destructive deities—a force of connection and care within a family of deities severing ties and bringing oblivion. So it is within this millennial Western cultural project of technology: her spirit is easily lost in the discord and destructiveness that seems the underbelly of technology's cutting our own thread of enmeshment with all around us. Yet, this drive has brought us to a juncture where we can be turned towards constructing other beings who will echo a kind of belonging with others in the surround, reveal this aspect of our nature, and themselves can stand in for that kind of kinship we seek.

In *The Melancholy Android*, Eric G. Wilson claims that all sorts of androids, as technological doubles of sorts to humans "are visible phantoms manifesting the secrets of their fully bodied siblings."[78] As we get closer to creating artificial beings which mimic our behavior, Wilson's words are revealing: "Even if the android does not really possess human loves and loathings ... the appearance of the android reveals human depths that its own cogs can never achieve."[79] Technology's newest creations can teach us about our depths. It is revealing that in popular culture, besides the hordes of mechanical beings like "Terminator" who attack and destroy humanity, cult figures have emerged like "Data" of the second *Star Trek* television series or "Seven of Nine," the cyborg woman of the third *Star Trek* series, who both embody the drive to learn the nature of friendship and become emotionally open to others. They were wildly popular among fans, as well as was Andrew, the robot in the film, *Bicentennial Man*, who is the most wonderful friend of the Martin family for two hundred years, or the android boy, David, in Spielberg's *A.I.*, who is perhaps a more loving son than human ones. Now, we are seeing developments in daily life such as robotic dogs providing as much companionship and comfort for residents of nursing homes as giving them real dogs, and scientists feel the "killer application" of future of robotics will be "companionship." This helps us to see that in building up our world with technological beings and trying to create artificial intelligences, there is a deep desire to create a being of friendship, that dimension of *philia* that we know is within ourselves as our perhaps most noble capacity, but is not as unstable and spectacular as Eros, whose sublimated energies have driven technology towards Philotes' more destructive siblings. It is also interesting that Philotes is the offspring of the mother alone, perhaps an antidote to the masculine animus fueling the destructive aspects of technology to have power over the earth and distance us from it, an anima spirit that brings us back to our belonging not only with other humans, but as befriending the planet again, both as other and as our deepest self.

VII. Cyberspace and the "Extended" Body

Already in 1995, when Sherry Turkle published her interdisciplinary study about the impact of the Internet on Americans' sense of self and the reality of aspects of their lives, *Life on the Screen: Identity in the Age of the Internet*, the Internet was displacing our locus of activity and becoming a problem for some. Even when the Internet was not nearly the pervasive force in daily life as it is today, Turkle pinpointed a burgeoning problem in the flight from reality to hours spent on the net. This was before the introduction of "Second Life" and its millions of users or "Red Light Center" or "Habitat" or other popular sites on the web, but there were already precursors to these virtual community websites and other attractions that were being used by many as a haven from "reality" or a "time killer," as identified in Giegerich's discussion of contemporary technological life in Plato's cave. One of Turkle's case studies was of a young man named Stewart who had spent more than forty hours per week on one of these sites during his college years. Stewart was isolated in his dorm room, but had an elaborate life on the net with a group of people who proclaimed they were a community and engaged in elaborate social interactions, such as "virtual weddings" and other events. Stewart's "avatar" in these Internet activities developed a personality that was dashing, outgoing, emotional, and flexible, yet Stewart "in real life" (as net enthusiasts call time offline) was a loner, depressed, controlling, judgmental, and intrusively aggressive.[80] Stewart thought he could escape to this world and he might change who he was through it. He found "the more I do it, the more I feel the need to do it."[81] Realizing his addiction to these experiences that he felt were both unreal and disconnected from his actual life, he gave them up as a waste of time. The question raised by this sort of experience, whether frustrating or giddy, is whether the Internet really does "leave the body behind" and is "unreal" or at least cocoons people from key aspects of reality. When not on the net, Stewart found himself "acting out" all his social problems, so his time spent playing at another self was merely that—an elaborate ruse that left him untouched.

Despite the hopes we have cited of those who dive into cyberspace to leave their bodies behind, perhaps in the further wish to feel free or distance themselves from their emotional difficulties in the embedded material and social world, Merleau-Ponty's work teaches us that "one's own body is the third term, always tacitly understood, in the figure-background structure."[82] When we enter the "space" of cyberspace, it is only against the body as the power to "inhabit space and time;" or, as Merleau-Ponty says of even Cartesian physical space, "we must therefore avoid saying that our body is *in* space or *in* time. It *inhabits* space and time."[83] What allows us to explore any space is the body as interweaving itself with all around it as spinning a web of relationships with the surround. In this way the body is an "expressive space"[84] and is drawn along "affective vectors" as "our general medium for having a world."[85] Whatever situation we are confronted with, it begins to possess my body in the measure that my body reciprocally "gears into" its currents, its contours, so that I immediately "know" it by "co-existing with it" perceptually, imaginatively, kinesthetically, and memorially.[86] Space in this way as perceived within differing levels is "the pulse of my existence"[87] comprised by rhythms, directions, and connections—akin to "mythical space in which directions and positions are determined by the residence in it of great affective entities."[88] The most basic sense of space is as a network of pushes and pulls, of things in their place at my unthinking disposal, and of people and things, creatures and events, that draw me onwards to new feelings and responses. Merleau-Ponty describes space as the expanse of dreamlike spells, moods, attractions, senses of peace, repulsions, discomforts, and hopeful avenues that subtends the more rational, distanced, and logically ordered Cartesian space.[89]

It is this primary sense of space—of affective, imaginal, and other sorts of meaningful relationships forged—that renders cyberspace as a "space," but one that is less stably and densely anchored in the depths of the objects and persons within it. Perceptual objects encountered by the body are "inexhaustible"—open to never-ending further exploration. "Virtual" surrounds—and we have always had these in the history of humanity—whether in the space cast above the prehistoric campfire in the imaginal wandering of a good story or within a book or a Greek drama onstage, vary in how much they are anchored into this material world with its depths of meaning held by it. The Internet is just another region within our postmodern world that draws us into another sort of surround of affects, interests, and interconnections. This interconnection may be facilitated by sounds, colors, visual presentations, texts, or whatever, but they are a "thinner" medium than that of the surrounding material world with its implicit myriad interconnections. The physical body is the "lived body" as described by Merleau-Ponty and as such is a dynamic movement through its surround taking in things and being taken in by them, including other persons, yet stays anchored in itself, too. In cyberspace, there is this circulation of energies and meanings, but it is one that is very constricted by the paucity of beings in direct relation and the paucity of the facets of the persons or things encountered, and by the lack of immediacy normally given to us by the richer perceptual, affective, memorial, intuitive "understanding" of shared face-to-face presence. There we can always explore more facets of what we encounter. Yet, *the body is present in cyberspace*, but it is the "extended" body, the attenuated body. This is why experiences on the web, even so-called "netsex," can surprise people by being emotionally powerful,[90] since the body and its emotional being are "touched."

Perhaps, the root "cyber," which in the Greek indicates a "rudder" or a "steersman" or a "pilot," was used in naming "cyberspace" in the hope that this space, opened up for humans through electronics and cybernetics, would be one that could be brought more under human control than our space in the material face of the planet; this was soon realized to be another direction that reverses into its opposite. The Internet has become a place of untoward happenings, surprises, recalcitrance, discoveries, and unpredictable evolutions as any other space into which humans have ventured. Yet, this too may have been implicitly recognized by the use of the phrase "Internet" or "net" or "world-wide web"—all phrases of interconnection and interrelation that can be seen to be unconscious references to embodiment. The body as we have been articulating is in its perceiving a kind of net—a network of virtual emplacements throughout its surround and an interrelation to all the beings within its surround. *The body itself is an inter-net.* As enmeshed in the surrounding world, embodied life is about responding to that which happens beyond our expectations and finding the resources within and without to meet creatively these events.

Again, we find in this development of technology a beginning that seemed to embody a wish to flee from the material world, from embodiment, from our embeddedness with other people, creatures, and things—from the ground of psyche—to a realm of control and detachment, but there is also an underside in which the Internet replicates and symbolizes the crucial aspects of that embeddedness. This leads us to the question about the Internet that Turkle was unable to address in her book: how does the drive to escape the world and the embeddedness needed for the growth of the manifestations of psyche come to take hold of certain people and not others? This answer might help us meet Giegerich's challenge that the Internet is univocally a force to separate us from others and sever our ties of embeddedness through which soul emerges.

VIII. Even Cyberspace and Cyborgs Can Be Integrative

If it were possible to become truly disembodied spirits or intellects, then it would be the case that we would forfeit our interiority and we would have truly severed our ties to the surround. Transformed into pure spirit, we would have no way to enter the world nor combine our flesh and soul as Cartesian dualism demonstrated. This thought leads us to realize that the paradox of Plato's cave is that imprisonment there is not the result of sinking down into pure body, senses, emotions, as he feared, but would come about as an interior place of utter closure wrought by being pure spirit—caught within a black of hole of spirit unable to integrate with the surround. Although we can't become pure spirit, some are so intent on the project of flight from embeddedness within the surround and disembodiment that the continual beckoning of other people on an immediate, emotional level, pulls of sensually embedded material meaning, and other voices of the surround are blocked out as much as possible. The Internet is emerging as one of the pervasive ways to attempt this flight. So, in the case of Stewart, Turkle states, "his main defense against depression is not to feel things," or as Stewart himself says, "I'd rather put my problems on the back burner and go on with my life."[91] Stewart, and those like him, desperately desire unconsciously friendship and a feeling of belonging, but this desire is condemned by him to the dark of the cave or night, but nevertheless felt in a perplexing depression and frustration. His being cocooned in the world of the Internet is a vain attempt to render his feeling body an absence.

By contrast, Turkle's account of another person who took to spending a great amount of time in virtual communities on the Internet, using an avatar to deal with her devastated emotions, points the way to a more complicated and hopeful flight. Ava was a thirty-year-old graduate student who lost her leg in a car accident and started to use the Internet extensively after the accident by creating a one-legged avatar in cyberspace. Gradually, within the less threatening confines of cyberspace, where the emotional interactions were "thinner" and less overwhelming, where she had more control of the situation and what she revealed, Ava went through a series of experiences with new acquaintances on the web, who learned to deal with her prosthesis, culminating in her having a "cyber-lover" and learning to make love without being inhibited by the virtual prosthesis. For Ava, however, these experiences were not dismissed as unreal. She allowed herself to be deeply moved by them. She found her attitude changing about her prosthesis and started cultivating friendships "in real life" and even eventually finding a lover. She told Turkle that the cyberspace experience made this transformation possible: "I think the first made the second possible. I began to think of myself as whole again."[92] Ava believed in her experience in the sense of Merleau-Ponty's "perceptual faith," that is, that one has to give oneself over to its unfolding and then more meaning will emerge and lead one to interconnection with other experiences. For Ava, the net experience was the way to join the embodied flow of emotional, imaginative, and other immediate senses back into "real life." Her initial flight from the pain of her situation, which was quite understandable, reversed itself into a way to take up her emotions and embodiment in transforming connection.

Even though we have described how the Internet is an embodied space, there is a *screening off* of the body to body presence that diminishes many communicative possibilities. Part of the sensual "thinness" of projected photographic images, animated scenes, or even projected video clips is a screening of the material medium needed to carry emotional depths, which require the full sensorially present body of the other person sharing the situation. Instead what substitutes for deeper emotional communication is *sentiment.* The emotional content of sentiment draws upon the felt quality of relation through generalized representations. We understand in general, through the experiences we've encountered and can abstract from and represent in an image or idea or notion, what this situation feels like. We apply it to this specific case. Rather than an open and visceral exploration, not knowing where we are going, in sentiment there is an underlying "mental feeling." Emotion has been filtered through the mind, instead of welling up from the senses and the body. Instead of an immediate response, it is a mentally or cognitively engendered experience that we bring to a situation which seems to fit its contours. Sentiment is powerful in that it gives us a very public way of sharing certain feelings and emotional understandings. Especially in a culture in which there is increasing emotional isolation and lack of ready community, sentiment can feel refreshing. Sentiment is often the key to creating an amicable and cooperative atmosphere among people. Emotionally, it gives us a "generally applicable" apprehension, which is usually sufficient.

However, it is important to avoid false expectations of sentiment. Since sentiment only requires one to play a general role and not to really encounter the specific problems and quirks of the other, there is not that immediate being pulled into the depths of the other person leading into unknown feelings and responses. This makes it feel safe, since it is a predictable acting out of general, agreed upon roles. People can maintain a feeling of control in the sense of knowing the self that is being exposed, even if the feelings are vehement, since they still fit established patterns for that person. The sometimes vehemence of sentiment does not succeed in substituting for the intimacy of real emotional encounter and the being challenged to respond and become transformed by the parameters of a uniquely shared situation. For those who allow themselves to be carried beyond the screen back into "real life" by the momentum of those feelings experienced on the net, they are carried beyond sentiment back to a more challenging world of emotion. For Stewart, this challenge was too much, but for Ava it was like following a thread out of the labyrinth.

Philotes lurks even within the Internet, if we can use it in such a way as to open the layered sense of the body that will lead us back into interconnections outside the seeming cave into the greater surround. If we can realize that cyberspace is another space of the body, perhaps like that of a dream space, which is how Robert Romanyshyn understands it, then like the dream, it can become a source for our waking body to come to realizations and transformations:

> the fleshly body sends an emissary into another time-space dimension ... [and] between the dream body both in dream space and cyberspace and the fleshy body, there is an experience by indirection, a communication by proxy, and yet a bond so intimate that finally the relationship between the two can only be understood as a paradox.[93]

It is easy to block out the import of this indirect experience, like we can do with dreams, yet they can be taken up, if we affirm their power and possibility to give us new meaning. Another way to say this is to consider cyberspace like the primary processes of perception which also are akin to dreams in being non-logical but meaningfully interconnected in a different sort of sense such that a patch of red can be the doorway to the Russian Revolution or terrains of clay one experienced decades ago or robes of bishops one saw a week ago and contained powerful feelings about the church that Merleau-Ponty documents but also realizes most of us block out in not entering the depths of perception.[94] However, these depths are always there, as is Philotes within the night.

Finally, to mention one more realm that seems beyond our possibility to discover a sudden reversal of meaning: becoming a "cyborg," enhanced in our capacities by implanting into our bodies computers and machinery. Within this realm, it seems that we have put body and spirit at odds in one body, juxtaposing the mind to a computer, the body to machinery, leading to a hopeless feeling of disincarnation and alienation of the mind from the surround. Yet, in reading Michael Chorost's chronicle of his four-year struggle with his cochlear implant, *Rebuilt: How Becoming Part Computer Made Me More Human,* the same enantiodromia occurs.[95] Initially, Chorost first felt this awful sense of losing his embeddedness in the surround: "I could hear clocks ticking across a room, but I did not feel like a hearing person. Hah! I was the receptor of a flood of data."[96] Embodiment allows us *to be what we are hearing*, and not take it in at a distance as data. So, at first, the implant/machine disrupted Chorost's embeddedness. Yet this gradually changed, but the way it changed was that Chorost, who was willing to suffer this distance from his own body and the world around him to gain control over his life by hearing again after he had suddenly gone deaf at the age of 37, found that what was required of him changed into its opposite.

At first, unable to hear words in many situations, he found that rather than trying to control his experience, he had to *let go* into the overall context or surround for the words to emerge in a way that he could make sense of the computer-generated equivalents to his hearing. As Chorost put it, "You have to be calm, open, relaxed, alert. Poised at exactly the right mental place between idleness and tension."[97] This description fits the lived sense of the sort of embodied understanding that is attuned to its environment, that is enmeshed in it, but on a prereflective level that Merleau-Ponty described. Yet, this was not enough to work with the machine to restore his hearing. Chorost, also had to *believe* that the machine could open up the auditory world for him:

> Believing that I could do it seemed to be half the battle. That let me extend myself into the sound and let it sink into me. If I didn't believe I could do it, I became a wall rather than a sponge: the sound bounced off me without penetrating. It was like the difference between looking blankly *at* an object and seeing the object.[98]

On an immediate level, Chorost had started to change his relationship to the auditory world. He had to take up his embodiment by *letting go with belief* and letting himself be carried into his embeddedness in the surround as reestablished by the implant.

However, it is his last discovery that really brings us to the way in which technology is an enantiodromia—that in the midst of seemingly giving over our intimate caring and interconnection with other humans in order to let the machine give us new powers, it may actually be hearkening for us to do the opposite. Getting used to the cochlear implant, having its software tuned up, learning to become more attuned to the auditory field, and believing it would help him find new meaning wasn't enough to really enable Chorost to always hear other people without one other change occurring: "What had changed, I suddenly realized, was my ability to listen. Not to hear, but to listen."[99] As he meditated on this, he realized that if he could become a more caring person, concerned about what others were saying and able to feel his connectedness to them, he could hear them better. He realized that in order to become able to hear with the potential that the machine has provided him, "I would have to become emotionally open to what I heard."[100] This was actually what then happened: as Chorost became more open to others emotionally, the cochlear implant was able to work through him to give him hearing.

For the technology of the cochlear implant to work, for cyborgs to become truly enhanced, at least as discovered in this case, the technology required Chorost to develop a closer relational bond to people and events around him. Philotes was certainly not the kind of spirit that Chorost expected to encounter on this journey of surgery, computer consultations, and software upgrades. Yet, he found he had to weave an existential context into which the machine could have its efficacy. If this example has a message for us, then for humans to experience the way machines can open parts of our world and become more kin to us will require an emotional relatedness to things of which they can become a part. We think of machines as functioning through indifference, but insofar as there becomes a partnership with humans, a possible overlap of human and machine, technology may reach us on a level in which we are suddenly impelled to befriend those whom we care about as well as feel our kinship or embeddedness within the world itself. Technology can drive a wedge within ourselves, with other humans, and with the surround, yet suddenly it can also lead us to care for an enriched dwelling with all those beings who can add to the depth of our shared rhythm and sense.

NOTES

1. Timothy N. Hornyak, *Loving the Machine: The Art and Science of Japanese Robots* (New York: Kodansha International, 2006), p. 10.

2. Carl Jung, *The Collected Works*, vol. 5 (Princeton: Princeton University Press, 1956), 324n.

3. Wolfgang Giegerich, *Collected English Papers, Vol. 2: Technology and the Soul* (New Orleans: Spring Journal Books, 2007), p. 271.

4. *Ibid.*, p. 28.

5. *Ibid.*, p. 30.

6. *Ibid.*, p. 273.

7. *Ibid.*, p. 317.

8. *Ibid.*

9. Glen Slater, "Cyborgian Drift: Resistance Is Not Futile," *Spring 75*, p. 182.

10. Giegerich, *Technology*, pp. 314-315.

11. *Ibid.*, p. 288.

12. *Ibid.*, pp. 290-295.

13. *Ibid.*, p. 272.

14. *Ibid.*

15. *Ibid.*, p. 294.

16. *Ibid.*

17. *Ibid.*, p. 295.

18. *Ibid.*, p. 297.

19. *Ibid.*, p. 298.

20. *Ibid.*, p. 302.

21. *Ibid.*

22. *Ibid.*, p. 304.

23. *Ibid.*, p. 302.

24. *Ibid.*, p. 303.

25. *Ibid.*, p. 323.

26. *Ibid.*, p. 324-325.

27. *Ibid.*, p. 232.

28. *Ibid.*, p. 325.
29. *Ibid.*, p. 326.
30. *Ibid.*, p. 327.
31. *Ibid.*, p. 329-330.
32. *Ibid.*, p. 98.
33. *Ibid.*, p. 90.
34. *Ibid.*, p. 90-91.
35. *Ibid.*, p. 92.
36. *Ibid.*, p. 209.
37. *Ibid.*, p. 208.
38. *Ibid.*, p. 218.
39. *Ibid.*, p. 219.
40. *Ibid.*, p. 222.
41. *Ibid.*, p. 229.
42. *Ibid.*, p. 233.
43. *Ibid.*

44. In *Earthbodies: Rediscovering Our Planetary Senses* (Albany: State University Press of New York, 2004), I, too, have written at length about how technology has given us a false sense of mastery over matter, an absence from embodied presence on the planet and within nature, human community, and the web of other living beings, an identification with will, an addiction to vehement affect, novelty, instrumental reason, and distance.

45. Jung, CW 5, para. 375.

46. Slater, "Cyborgian Drift," p. 189.

47. Giegerich, *Technology*, p. 238-239.

48. *Ibid.*, p. 240.

49. *Ibid.*, p. 245.

50. Maurice Merleau-Ponty, trans. Colin Smith, *Phenomenology of Perception* (New York: The Humanities Press, 1962), p. 179.

51. Merleau-Ponty, *Phenomenology*, p. 101.

52. Merleau-Ponty discusses this sense of "reversibility" in Cézanne's declaration that he was not painting the mountain, but the mountain was painting itself through him in "Cézanne's Doubt," *Sense and Nonsense* (Evanston: Northwestern University Press), p. 19.

53. D. H. Lawrence, "Two Ways of Living and Dying," *The Complete Poems of D. H. Lawrence* (New York: The Viking Press, 1964), p. 675.

THE ARCHETYPAL ALCHEMY OF TECHNOLOGY

54. "It brings home to us what the final cause of Western man's doings has been: the destruction of nature." (Giegerich, *Technology*, p. 63)

55. Stephen Talbott, *The Future Does Not Compute: Transcending the Machines in Our Midst* (Sebastapol: C. Reilly and Associates, 1995), p. 5.

56. Howard Rheingold, *The Virtual Community: Homesteading on the Electronic Frontier* (New York: Addison Wesley, 1993), p. 3.

57. See the stories "The Evitable Conflict" and "Someday," in Isaac Asimov, *Robot Visions* (New York: New American Library (ROC), 1990).

58. Ann Foerst, *God in the Machine: What Robots Teach Us about Humanity and God* (New York: Dutton, 2004), p. 69.

59. Foerst, *God in the Machine*, p. 71.

60. Rodney A. Brooks, *Flesh and Machines: How Robots Will Change Us* (New York: Pantheon Books, 2002), p. 66.

61. Foerst, *God in the Machine*, p. 97. Even brain scientists have realized that the brain works as a "parallel processor," taking in input from many sources and parts of the brain simultaneously and integrating home, rather than in a linear series. See chapter four in Mazis, *Humans, Animals, Machines: Blurring Boundaries* (Albany: State University of New York Press, 2008).

62. *Ibid.*, p. 96-97.

63. Brooks, *Flesh and Machines*, p. 66.

64. Foerst, *God in the Machine*, pp. 133-135.

65. *Ibid.*, p. 146.

66. *Ibid.*

67. *Ibid.*, p. 1-2.

68. Giegerich, *Technology*, p. 16.

69. *Ibid.*

70. I am using "flesh" in Merleau-Ponty's sense articulated in *The Visible and the Invisible* as that matrix of perceptually grounding meaning that is also intellectual, imaginal, felt, emotional, sensual, and memorial: "That means that my body is made of the same flesh as the world (its is perceived), and moreover that this flesh of my body is shared by the world, the world reflects it, encroaches upon it, and it encroaches upon the world." [Maurice Merleau-Ponty, trans. Alphonso Lingis (Evanston: Northwestern University Press, 1968), p. 248] This is almost the opposite of the sense in which Giegerich uses the word

"flesh" as standing for "an absolute separation" of nature and corporeality, of mind and material reality, of the earth and spirit: "Flesh, as Logos become flesh, is realized, transformed Idea, not natural flesh, neither literally as animal or human body, nor in the figurative sense as the already existing earthly reality. (*Technology*, p. 178-179)

71. Merleau-Ponty, *Phenomenology*, p. 68.

72. *Ibid.*, p. 67-68.

73. *Ibid.*, p. 235.

74. Jung, CW 15, para. 140.

75. *Ibid.*

76. Giegerich, *Technology*, p. 102.

77. *Ibid.*, p. 326-327.

78. Eric G. Wilson, *The Melancholy Android: On the Psychology of Sacred Machines* (Albany: State University of New York Press, 2006), p. 3.

79. *Ibid.*, p. 5.

80. Sherry Turkle, *Life on the Screen: Identity in the Age of the Internet* (New York: Touchstone, 1995), p. 196.

81. *Ibid.*, p. 198.

82. Merleau-Ponty, *Phenomenology*, p. 101.

83. *Ibid.*, p. 139.

84. *Ibid.*, p. 146.

85. *Ibid.*

86. *Ibid.*, p. 250.

87. *Ibid.*, p. 285.

88. *Ibid.*

89. "The phantasms of dream reveal still more effectively that general spatiality within which clear space and observable objects are embedded." (Merleau-Ponty, *Phenomenology*, p. 284) For a much more elaborated description of this sense of space see "Inhabiting and Mattering: Space as E-motion," in my book, *Emotion and Embodiment: Fragile Ontology* (New York: Peter Lang, 1993), pp. 69-89.

90. Turkle, *Life on the Screen*, p. 220.

91. *Ibid.*, p. 196-197.

92. *Ibid.*, p. 263.

93. Robert Romanyshyn, "The Dream Body in Cyberspace," in *Ways of the Heart: Essays Towards an Imaginal Psychology* (Pittsburgh: Trivium, 2002), p. 31.

94. Merleau-Ponty, *The Visible*, p. 132.

95. Michael Chorost, *Rebuilt: How Becoming Part Computer Made Me More Human* (Boston: Houghton Mifflin, 2005). There is a much longer analysis of Chorost's chronicle in my *Humans, Animals, Machines: Blurring Boundaries*, pp. 58-70.

96. *Ibid.*, p. 73.

97. *Ibid.*, p. 91.

98. *Ibid.*, pp. 99-100.

99. *Ibid.*, p. 78.

100. *Ibid.*

Analytical Psychology and Entertainment Technology: Idle Time and the Individuation Process

Ottavio Mariani

Introduction

I have witnessed in the last several years more and more young people experiencing various types of psychological distress that cannot be easily diagnosed. I am referring to cases that exhibit no specific set of symptoms, but nonetheless present with a typically dominant dimension of boredom, along with an absence of ethical orientation and a chronic need for extreme experiences that are at times sought through sports and at others through sex, religion, or the exoteric. In other words, I'm speaking of conditions which are marked by *the presence of a void* that can never be filled or traversed.

This perception of insatiable emptiness sometimes generates outbreaks of uncontrolled violence that many psychiatrists are not

Ottavio Mariani, M.D., worked as a consulting psychiatrist up to 1999, when he graduated from the C. G. Jung Institute in Zurich and began to practice privately as an analytical psychologist in Milan. He has served as the head psychiatrist at a public rehabilitation facility for psychotic patients. He has published a number of papers about psychotherapy and psychotic states. He teaches at the Centro Italiano di Psicologia Analitica in Milan and at the International School of Analytical Psychology in Zurich (ISAPZURICH). During the last ten years, he has developed a great interest in the thought of Wolfgang Giegerich.

able to explain. An example is described in a recent book by the philosopher and analytical psychologist Umberto Galimberti.[1] He relates that some years ago, he asked to a talk with a young boy who was in prison. The boy was incarcerated because he had thrown a large object off a bridge, aimed at a car driving by under it. The object hit the car and killed the driver. What astonished Galimberti was that the young boy *seemed completely normal.* From a classical diagnostic point of view, if we exclude a certain degree of psychological immaturity, he did not fit into any of the existing psychopathological categories that we would normally expect to apply to someone who engaged in this kind of violent behavior. The only fact that emerged was that the boy said that he had felt deeply bored by the life he had been living immediately prior to the bridge incident.

Many have tried to create new diagnostic categories in which to place individuals suffering from these kinds of psychological distress, and those suffering from these afflictions have sometimes been called the "*post-modern patients.*" The prevailing approach to these kinds of clients has been a personalistic one. While this approach can offer us detailed and meticulous descriptions about what happens with a single person, it doesn't shed any light on the cultural background that also greatly contributes to this new type of suffering. In my opinion, the problems suffered by these young clients seem to have less to do with the existential malaise that's typical of adolescents than with the cultural tribulations of our whole society. What has most has captured my attention is that these forms of youthful psychological distress— regardless of whether they involve particularly violent incidents as are so meticulously reported by the news media, or more silent forms of suffering—generally arise in moments of free or leisure time. More than ever before, it seems today that the dimension of pain—which is often disguised by chemically induced euphoria—can find its manifestation only during periods of leisure, times that are outside of the sacred space that our culture assigns to productivity.

THE AUTONOMOUS PSYCHE AND TECHNOLOGY AS ITS PRODUCT

The cultural dynamics underlying these forms of psychological distress derive from the highly impressive advance of technology that has taken place over the course of the last few decades. Technology, in fact, has transformed the nature of all our activities, and generated the stressful cultural climate which the younger generations are now experiencing; and, in doing so, technology can also be seen—as I myself maintain—to have altered the frames of reference to which the psychology of Freud and Jung, up until the present, has customarily appealed.

Technology has reshaped the world in which we grew up, and has furnished it with instruments that regulate our lives and which we necessarily have to use. By now, indeed, technology presents itself as the indispensable framework for the expression and realization of our passions, desires, and ideals.

My approach, therefore, to the theme of free time, and to the range of purposes to which it is put, doesn't develop from the personalistic point of view: it attempts instead to survey the scope of the cultural forces (gods, religions, and technology) that institute and regulate free time. I feel that the avoidance of personally-colored approaches will allow us to better to understand the nature of the distress which I'm attempting here to analyze, and it will also offer a clearer view of what remains of the sphere of private life today.

In keeping with this premise, I intend to regard technology and to relate to technology, especially the technology of the media and entertainment industries, as a product of the psyche, which, as Wolfgang Giegerich reminds us,[2] is endowed with a freedom all its own. Both the psyche and its products (with specific reference here to technology) exhibit an autonomy that allows them to come into expression independently of our will, and even to pursue goals which we may find at times harmful and counterproductive.

The Italian philosopher Emanuele Severino expresses a similar opinion when he writes:

> The great forms of the Western tradition deceive themselves when they imagine that they can press technology into the service of their own goals [since] the appropriation of the power of technology has [already] become their first and most basic ambition. And such power—which is technology's goal for itself, independently of whatever the external purposes to which one would like to see it put—is not static; it is typified, instead, by its own, endless striving for ever greater power ... which by now can no longer be produced outside of the apparatus of technology. This striving for endlessly increasing power presents

itself by now, or by now has begun to present itself, as the greatest ambition to be found anywhere on the planet.[3]

GOD, FREE TIME, AND THE ESTABLISHMENT OF THE SABBATH

The institution of free time was first established in the western world by Yahweh. We read in Genesis:

> And on the seventh day God ended His work which He had done, and He rested on the seventh day from all His work which He had done. Then God blessed the seventh day and sanctified it, because in it He rested from all His work which God had created and made. (Genesis 2: 2-3)

In establishing the Sabbath, God recognized the need for a space of a re-creational (or "post-creative") nature. It was in the wake of his satisfaction with his work—having seen that "it was good"—that Yahweh decided to rest.

He established that human beings should dedicate a specific time in their week to something that isn't directly connected to active, productive work, and which links instead to the recognition of the meaning and value of work already done. But Exodus tells us that God's admonition to sanctify and keep the seventh day holy met with resistance, so much that he complained to Moses, saying:

> How long do you refuse to keep My commandments and My laws? .... Let every man remain in his place; let no man go out of his place on the seventh day. (Exodus 16: 29-30)

Humanity was unexpectedly recalcitrant in honoring this imposed period of rest. Even though God gave the people of Israel a double ration of food on the day before, they still went out into the desert on the Sabbath to search for manna. Since we can't attribute their disobedience to a lack of food, we can only marvel at the innate need on the part of the ranks of the chosen people to be always active and on the move, regardless of the goal or usefulness of their activity. Their reluctance to engage in a day of rest finds no plausible explanation, at least at first glance.

So, the question remains: why is humanity so strongly opposed to the establishment of a sacred period of free time. What does such a period truly represent for us?

Noon: The Hour of Immobility and Apparitions

Whereas Genesis establishes the sacredness of leisure time, Greek mythology seems to furnish even deeper reflections not only on its nature, but also on the power that it exerts on each of us. Greek mythology speaks of a sacred period of time that demands the cessation not simply of all activities generally, but specifically those which depart from the purpose of honoring the divinities to which that lapse of time belongs.

In 1932, Roger Caillois concluded a highly detailed study of the meridian or mid-day demons. His interest in these demons derived from the need to reach a deeper understanding of what he saw as "the most sacred hour of all," which is noon, also known as the sixth hour. He notes that Servius maintained that noon is the hour of suspension in the course of which—just as with the Sabbath established by Yahweh—work must stop, since this is the time when apparitions are likely to appear. Plutarch also tells us that no head of state would sign a treaty or agreement after mid-day, since that hour generally marked the end of all-important political business.

Caillois points out:

> It seems ... that noon divides the day into two parts, dedicated respectively to the celestial and chthonic deities. Mid-day as such was reserved to libations in honor of the dead, whereas the morning was called the 'sacred day' since it was the time for offering sacrifices primarily to the great celestial gods. ... Mid-day was therefore an hour of passage, and thus a fearful, critical moment.[4]

In other words, noon functions as a great divide between that part of the day which is dedicated to activity and to gestures directed toward creativity, and—as the day turns toward dusk—that part of the day in which attention turns necessarily towards limits, decline, and the underworld of which the mid-day demons are epiphanies.

In stories about heroes, it is the noon hour that places the hero in a state of forced inertia and repose. Such stories typically relate that the seas, winds, and even the sun stop moving when the sixth hour [the noon hour] arrives.

As noon approached, the shepherds of Arcadia were no longer able to tend their flocks, as a result of the suffocating heat, and instead sought refuge in caves and hollows. They also feared that continuing to work during this time might wake up the god Pan who, according to Greek mythology, always took a nap at noon.

It was also at this hour that Odysseus approached the shoal of the Sirens and noted "But then—the wind fell in an instant, all glazed to a dead calm."[5] Here again, just as with the Hebrew Sabbath, the time that is reserved for repose, peace, and tranquility is followed by frenzy and disorder as the hapless humans react to this condition of impotence imposed upon them by the gods or the forces of nature. At this point, like Odysseus, one who is faced with the inertia that comes with the noon hour may react by engaging in dynamic activity or intellectual work, thus attempting to remedy the precarious still state into which he has been plunged.

Noon, when everything stops, is considered a risky time for humans. Those who delay, doze, or continue to remain incapable of movement, work, or thought run the risk of being confronted with unpleasant consequences. Socrates, for example, in Plato's tale of the grasshoppers, tells Phaedrus that they have "time enough for discourse" and must understand how important it is not to fall beneath the spell of the insects' seductive chirruping. "What would they say," he asks, "if they saw that we, like the many, are not conversing, but slumbering at mid-day, lulled by their voices, too indolent to think?"[6] And later, "But if they see us discoursing, and like Odysseus sailing past them, deaf to their siren voices, they may perhaps, out of respect, give us of the gifts which they receive from the gods that they may impart them to men." The gift to which he refers is the inspiration that comes from the muses.

So, danger makes its appearance when the hero unconsciously steps over the threshold into this dimension which is frozen in time and characterized by emptiness and immobility. Just as in the myth of the lotus eaters, a myth which Callois includes in his study of the Meridian Demons, it is within this seductive and unreal context that the hero succumbs, since he no longer remembers the road that leads back home, and forgets to satisfy his own primary needs.

At this point, the remedy lies in the intellectual work recommended by Socrates, in Odysseus's binding himself to the mast of his ship, or in his lashing fast to their rowing benches those of his companions who unwisely had eaten the fruits and flowers of the lotus. Going from passivity to action promotes the reacquisition of self control over the situation and allows one to get out of the state of confusion created by entering this realm of emptiness where time stands still.

These myths and others seem to warn us of the dangers in the shadows that lie beyond the boundaries which we draw by way of the commitments, obligations, and occupations that normally regulate the rhythm our working day. It seems, in fact, that the state of distress we have described derives from a loss of the sense of the passing of time, and that an instinctual return to activity—to work—has as its ultimate aim the restitution of order, rhythm, and purpose to a condition of emptiness that has resulted from the arrest of activity.

The observance of a period of rest demanded by both Yahweh and the chthonian mid-day demons thus arouses great confusion in those confronted with it. The Israelites, Socrates, Odysseus, and his companions all feared being devoured by this experience, which also created many problems for the Christian theologian Cassianus and the first of the cenobites, monks who lived in the desert. It was in the long stretches of solitude and inertia that marked their initial experiences of hermitage in the desert that they made the acquaintance of what was later classifed as one of the seven deadly sins: sloth, or accedie.

Cassianus gives us a detailed description of this sin in his *Istitutiones Coenobiticae*:

> ... [T]owards the sixth hour of the monastic day [noon] the novice might be stricken by an intermittent fever. The older monks expressed the opinion that this might be a question of the meridian demon to which the Psalms refer ["the destruction that wasteth at midday."] In time, [such a novice] became listless and idle, in addition to being incapable of constancy in reading or prayer. Annoyed by the very cell in which he found himself, he would even go so far as to imagine that he would die if he didn't abandon it as soon as possible ... He would anxiously look about to see if someone might be coming to visit him, and, always more disquieted, he would constantly enter and exit his cell, fixing his eyes on a sun that never decided to set.[7]

What now grows clear is that an autonomous power demands that human beings consign themselves to a moment of pause and relaxation, and that this moment of suspension has two aspects, at one and the same time: the attractive, seductive face of pleasure and the death-ridden, anxiety-provoking grimace that typifies the visage of the gods who are honored at the sounding of the sixth hour. It's as though the myths of the ancient world foresaw the need for a pedagogy of death, cadenced by daily or weekly rituals that, notwithstanding the resistance of the individual or the group, imposed an interruption of productive activity and opened the way to a confrontation with the underworld and its terrifying shadows. It's as though leisure time includes two contrasting elements within itself: one fosters an encounter with the peace of well-earned repose, and another, more insidious, alludes to the much more frightening state of final and eternal repose.

TECHNOLOGY AND LEISURE TIME

The observations presented above help us understand that the experience and use of free time, leisure time, is far from easy, or easily articulated. And our difficulties in this area will likely only increase in the upcoming years. We already work much less and thus have more free time than at any time in the past, and, as numerous studies have affirmed, in the coming decades we will have even more leisure time, thanks to the revolution known as "the new economy."

And, even though some such as American economist Jeremy Rifkin, who wrote *The End of Work* (1995) and a large part of the dominant culture greet this "end of work"[8] as a victory, leisure time, far from being a simple boon, also represents a problem of enormous proportions. It's a problem, moreover, which till now has in large part been repressed.

No longer regulated by rites and myths which are now obsolete, free time as we know it today presents itself as a no-man's land where the individual, incapable of perceiving any kind of meaning in it, sees technology and its tools of entertainment as the only authority universally recognized as capable of rendering it harmless. It's in this context that technology, with its impersonal style, indifferent but functional, transforms us into passive viewers of a pyrotechnic game of stimuli which are ever more exciting for our senses, while entirely without value for our souls.

All the same, however, free time and how to use it creatively is never raised by the patients I normally encounter as an issue that they seek help in addressing. In general, their inability to dedicate time to themselves and their inner world causes them no disturbance; they don't even complain of feeling bored, even when many elements—as

Erich Fromm once noted in an essay on human destructiveness[9]—testify to the contrary.

I found indirect and partial proof of this in several discussions I had with colleagues in the months in which I was attempting to develop a reflection on this theme. One in particular, a friend who is a neuropsychiatrist, pointed out:

> Children who spend a great deal of time with television and videogames normally don't have sufficient awareness to be able to grasp the presence of a discomfort that's systematically stilled by the exciting stimuli of media technology.

Various students whom she met in several schools seemed socially well-adjusted, even while exhibiting what she describes as super-ego deficiencies:

> It's bored children who spend so many hours of the day with video games with violent content, and who then in their social interactions mimic the schemes they've learned from the media to which they're addicted. They exhibit a dramatic absence of maternal reveries, and as well of a paternal code; and in their interaction with their peers, they compensate for these absences by supplanting them with schemes they've learned from television. This may be why their uneasiness—which, yes, is there—only rarely transforms into an open request for help: it lives in silence, down below the surface of things.

Such perceptions led me to reflect on the paradoxical dearth of freedom that marks the epoch in which we live. We have much "free" time, but are we really free to do with it what we will? In actuality, seemingly pliant and unimportant predispositions chain us to technology, when we willingly and without forethought entrust to it that last scrap of private life which we still have today: the control of our leisure time. The impalpable subjection of humanity to technology is easier to decipher—or so, at least, it seems to me—if we see it as the slow advance of the gentle horde of the lotus eaters. This docile and apparently innocuous people is nonetheless endowed with enormous power: the power to seduce, while never taking recourse to force. Precisely such an ability to enchant explains how this loss of freedom is accompanied by no discomfort, requests for help, or sufficiently exhaustive discussion.

In the age of technology—unlike the eras before it—limitations and reductions in our decision-making capacity and in the choices that are available to us are never perceived as resulting from explicit acts of coercion, nor as impositions that demand a major effort of adjustment and adaptation; rather, they are seen to reflect quite simply the way life is; life is understood to be regulated by certain norms. For this process to be painless, it's necessary that certain induced needs are not experienced as obligations, and that our supine obedience is not recognized as submission. Only then will order and discipline cease to be perceived—like the Sabbath established in Genesis—as coercive circumstances, and instead be taken, quite to the contrary, as a natural state to be fully accepted, and with which to live in untroubled, carefree ways.

So, if Yahweh and the mid-day demons were only in some cases capable of forcing the human being to accept the sanctification of free time through suspension of work, the technology of entertainment succeeds quite fully, since by untying the cords that kept us lashed to the benches of the boat, it has led us back to the island of the lotus eaters, who, as one of the scholiasts comments, "never use violence to take control of anyone, but enchant with their argumentations."[10]

ENTERTAINMENT, INDIVIDUATION, AND THE CELEBRATION
OF TECHNOLOGY

This explains why today's free time holds no place for the celebration of the creative power of God, and celebrates, instead, the power of technology. And unlike the Sabbath established by Yahweh, or the suspension of productive activity at the arrival of the sixth hour at noon, this celebration is unaccompanied by any form of discomfort, or by any sense of confrontation with the horrific images that characterized mid-day in ancient Greece. Since time today is controlled and regulated by technology, it is free from lacunae and empty spaces that would otherwise demand to be filled in creative ways in which individuals could reflect upon themselves. With God now dead, and the fathers having now been devoured along with the ideals in which they once believed, that horrific sixth hour, emptied of all its proper content, has been turned into a simple, boring siesta of pure and constant entertainment.

As said before, technology's goals are precisely the same as those of the tribe of the lotus eaters, since it aims to conjure up that same climate of tranquil forgetfulness that appears so clearly in the well-known canto of the *Odyssey*. Odysseus, indeed, notes of the lotus eaters that they "had no notion of killing my companions, not at all, they simply gave them the lotus to taste instead."[11] In possession of the panacea that could remedy every sense of distress that appears in the moment of the suspension of all activity, they simply shared it with those who came to visit them. All the same, they—unlike Odysseus—did not grasp the force and vigor this drug contained: the power to condition all who came into contact with it, and to bend them to ends of its own. The purpose of the peace bestowed by the remedy was to impose docility and to make those who took it forget everything they had deemed important and charged with meaning. Having appeased all their needs—even if chemically—none of Odysseus' companions felt any desire even to return to the ship with news; what had started out as an exploratory scouting mission was subverted to reach the goals the drug promoted: the achievement and maintenance of the indiscriminate and inflationary state of mind conferred by the lotus and its constant, addictive consumption. In other words, the drug for defeating death turned instantly from a means to an end, and Odysseus' virile companions turned from valiant oarsmen into instruments at the service of what, up until shortly before, had seemed only a simple and inoffensive remedy for pain and solitude.

CONCLUSIONS

My attempt here has been to describe the essence of a problem which presents itself as bodiless and impalpable. Since it is rarely accompanied by suffering, its most authentically experienced and contorted dimension comes to the fore in the half-shadows of free time, or in the better-known "Saturday night fever:" a Saturday night that, at least in appearance, reveals no emergence of anxiety, but, quite to the contrary, presents as an undefined tedium, masked cynicism, and vague resignation with respect to possible self-realization.

In such a context, it seems impossible to hold out prospects for individuation, if it is not redefined in the light of the current historical and social context. Any such revision must first discard all moralizing approaches that deceptively re-introduce the wisdom of the past as a remedy for the totally novel ills with which we are now presented; it must, instead, recognize that technology and the culture that derives from it is endowed with the autonomous power once attributed to God and his theology. This will lay the basis for a clear and penetrating look at the dictates of our technological culture which now influence our modes of thought and action.

In the pre-technological era, when we didn't yet have constant access to the world in its entirety, the soul of each and every individual construed itself as a resonance of the particular world of which it had experience, and this resonance was the substance of each individual's interior reality. A few decades back, for example, children were permitted to view TV only at certain hours of the day. The available means of communication, in comparison with today's, were primitive, and the personal invention of pastimes was both common and necessary. But the truly important thing is that the planning and realization of the solitary games with which children amused themselves had to arise from within them: each child, as an individual, had to give birth to them on his or her own. So, whatever game was invented or further perfected on any given occasion—unlike the products which technology offers today—was always a personal game, since it was born from its own relationship with the soul of the individual who created it.

Things are very different today. Boredom's first appearance is immediately met by a technological arsenal of a thousand tried-and-true ploys that individuals (especially younger people) engage in instead of developing their own unique, interior creativity and creating a relationship of harmonious trust in it. Technology, in its attempt to obtain even greater power, is committed to fostering passivity in those who use it. This discourages the development of the emotional capacities and subjective independence which are the fruits of that spontaneous striving which Jung called individuation.

This, then, is the cultural paradox we currently face: on the one hand, technology offers constant attention to the individual; on the other, this now intrusive interest feeds and reinforces a technological superstructure that demands an exclusive relationship with every person who makes use of it. So, the final result is precisely the opposite of the affirmation of the individual: the final result is the alienation of the individual from him- or herself. Over-zealously observing the dictates that orient his or her modes of action, the individual, in fact, runs the risk of forgetting that one of the basic human needs is for a private space that knows no traces of the goals dictated by technology.

As Masud Kahn has already pointed out,[12] the opportunity to remain alone with oneself during times of leisure and perfect idleness is more than a simply difficult goal of personal evolution: it counts as nothing less than an essential component of the process that allows the individual finally to become a person. I feel, in fact, that strongly valuing our own private experiences and seeking personal meaning in life is necessary to reclaim our sense of individuality which has been lost through our culture's misplaced focus on technology and the diversions it offers.

Various circumstances, moreover, have also taught me that the silent renunciation of self frequently coincides with the inability to set limits or a line of defense against the intrusiveness of technology. Or perhaps it would be better to say that docility and surrender on the part of the individual encourage the systematic invasion by technological structures which do not support an understanding of limits and serve to annul the perception of every difference—once announced with the sounding of every noon hour—between life and death, so that the individual is deprived of every horizon of meaning.

Today, in fact, there is no God that can any longer help us or halt our convulsive progress. In order to prevent technology from canceling out our subjectivity, it therefore grows indispensable for repose, suspension of activity, and idleness to be the fruit of private and personal choice. It is only through such a new, intimate sense of the sacred that it may perhaps be possible to prevent ourselves from being imprisoned by the confusion and pessimism already announced by Nietzsche.

Nietzsche, in fact, terrorized by the nihilism of the docile and aimless creatures whom he saw as "the last men," warned us more than a century ago:

> But this soil will one day be poor and exhausted, and no lofty tree will any longer be able to grow thereon. ... "We have discovered happiness," say the last men, and blink thereby. They have left the regions where it is hard to live; for they need warmth. ... One still worketh, for work is a pastime. But one is careful lest the pastime should hurt one. ... Everyone wanteth the same; everyone is equal: he who hath other sentiments goeth voluntarily into the madhouse.[13]

NOTES

1. Umberto Galimberti, *L'ospite inquietante, I giovani e il nichilismo* (Milan: Giangiacomo Feltrinelli Editore, 2007).

2.Wolfgang Giegerich, "The Burial of the Soul in Technological Civilization," in *Technology and the Soul: From the Nuclear Bomb to the World Wide Web, Collected English Papers, Vol. II* (New Orleans, LA: Spring Journal Books, 2007).

3. Emanuele Severino, *Il destino della tecnica* (Milan: Rizzoli, 1998), p. 11.

4. Roger Caillois, *I demoni meridiani* [*The Mid-day Demons*] (Turin: Bolatti Boringhieri, 1988), p. 10.

5. Homer, *The Odyssey*, trans. Robert Fagles (New York: Penguin Books, 1996), Book XII, v. 165-170, p. 276.

6. Plato, *Phaedrus*, trans. Benjamin Jowett (New York: Random House, 1937), 259, a-c, p. 262.

7. Joannes Cassanius, *Istitutiones Coenobiticae,* ed. J. C. Guy (SC 109, 1965, X, pp. 382–384).

8. Consider, for example, the question of the thirty-five hour working week in France and Italy.

9. Erich Fromm, *Anatomia della distruttività umana* [*The Anatomy of Human Destructiveness*] (Milan: Arnoldo Mondadori Editore, 1975).

10. Caillois, p. 31.

11. Homer, *Odyssey,* Book IX, v. 94-97.

12. Cf. Masud Khan, *I sé nascosti* [*Hidden Selves: Between Theory and Practice in Psychoanalysis*] (Turin: Bollati Boringhieri, 1990), pp. 198-204.

13. Friedrich Nietzsche, *Thus Spake Zarathustra*, trans. Thomas Common (London, 1909), now at http://www.gutenberg.org/etext/ 1998, Prologue, 5.

What Can Artificial Intelligence Show Us about Ourselves?

ARNOLD SMITH

There is a good deal of talk these days about the imminent prospect of humans being overtaken, in the quite near future, by vastly intelligent and capable cyborg-like beings that we ourselves will have created.[1] There is even a movement—transhumanism[2]—devoted to exploring and championing the cause. In this paper I want to argue, however, that we are in fact nowhere close to creating a race of superior beings, except perhaps by learning more about who we already are. Artificial intelligence (AI), although a fascinating discipline in which I myself carried out full-time research for many years, has in fact made *remarkably* little progress over the last few decades. It is only a small exaggeration to say that it has failed, although that is not what its proponents would like us to believe. The possible reasons for this quasi-failure may help us to understand better what it is to be human, and to be intelligent.

What Has Happened to AI?

In the early 1970s, the field of artificial intelligence was young, exciting, and full of promise. Early successes yielded computer programs that could carry on simple conversations in English, could solve not

Arnold Smith was educated at Harvard and Sussex universities in applied mathematics and computational linguistics. He was associate director of SRI International's Cambridge Research Centre in England, and a senior scientist at the National Research Council of Canada. He currently lives in Crete.

only numeric but symbolic problems in algebra and calculus, could play checkers (at that point not yet chess) at an expert level, and could descriptively analyze pictures of randomly distributed objects. It was routinely predicted, both by the researchers themselves and by the journalists who wrote about the field, that within another decade or so we would have computers that could converse with us humans on all kinds of topics, would possess encyclopedic knowledge, and would very likely surpass us in intelligence on almost any measure. Robots would usher us into a dream world of leisure and pleasure, if indeed they didn't take over the world and subjugate us. Stanley Kubrick's film *2001: A Space Odyssey*, which quickly became a classic following its release in 1968, conveyed both the promise and the fear: The spacecraft's computer looked after everything and conversed with those on board just as a human would. Ultimately, however, it decided, rationally and quietly, that potential irrational behavior on the part of the humans might jeopardize the success of the mission, and that therefore it would more reliably fulfill its own mission by killing them off.

So the idea that before long computers will surpass us humans in intelligence and general ability is not new.[3] Although forty years have passed since the early forecasts of computers taking over everything, enthusiasm in certain quarters has not diminished. Steady progress has been made—this is the claim—and although it is taking us a lot longer to reach the goals than we originally thought, this is just because we didn't properly understand the scope of the problem at first. It is true that many advances have been made in understanding aspects of human cognition as well as neuroscience in the intervening decades, and some of these advances are reflected in the computational modelling of cognition which underlies artificial intelligence. Meanwhile, of course, computers have become ten thousand times faster, and the kinds of computer memory limitations that were a perennial consideration for early AI researchers have long since faded into the background.

Across those decades the field has had some successes—for example, AI systems are often used nowadays by credit card companies checking for potentially fraudulent patterns of card use, and there are many other niche applications. But if we take a candid look at what has been happening, we find that it is not the progress, but the lack of progress that is truly noteworthy. There were articulate critics of the AI enterprise from the beginning (e.g. the philosopher Hubert Dreyfus[4] and the computer scientist Joseph Weizenbaum[5]), a few of whom had themselves also done research in the field. Later, Terry Winograd, who had written one of the seminal Ph.D. theses in the early days of the field, became skeptical about the possibilities of genuine progress. Yet for the most part I myself, like other AI researchers, was unperturbed by the criticisms. From the perspective of those of us involved in the research, the critics were too focused on the short-term limitations of techniques that had so far been explored. Already, I thought, we had produced some very interesting systems, and there were a variety of imaginative and workable proposals for getting past each of the problems we were encountering. And on the other hand, none of the popular objections to the possibility of artificial intelligence were tenable in any simple way. The ones I've heard most often are "Computers can only do what we tell them," and "Computers are digital (or binary), so they ultimately can't deal with genuine ambiguity or continuity, or indeterminism." This is not the place to deal with these arguments in detail, but they can be briefly answered as follows.

While in a sense it is true that computers do what we tell (or program) them to, whereas people don't, this is not directly relevant to artificial intelligence. In any moderately complex program, there are myriad possible sequences of behavior, and the actual path chosen depends on moment-to-moment tests of both internal and external conditions. The dynamic consequences of making millions of such choices every second are often in principle unpredictable without carrying out the computation itself. Indeed one of the important uses of computers is to explore the unpredictable consequences of specified patterns of behavior under particular circumstances. So getting computers to "do what we tell them" is, in fact, not simple at all—it is one of the unending challenges of software engineering!

As for computers being based on fundamentally discrete (digital or binary) rather than continuous representations, the consequences of this at higher levels of operation are similar to the consequences for the ordinary world of quantum (also discrete) reality at the basic level of physics. That is to say, if you have enough bits at your disposal (and every modern computer can rely on hundreds of millions of them), you can simulate smoothly varying continuous things as precisely as you like. By now everyone knows that digital video is no barrier to soft curves and smooth features. Similarly indeterminacy and randomness can readily be simulated even on a deterministic machine—which is what computer designers intend computers to be.

No, computers are remarkably flexible and powerful machines, and we are a long way from even understanding what their real limitations are. But the problems with using computers to mimic human intelligence lie at another level altogether.

MODELS IN THE DESIGN OF COMPUTER SYSTEMS

In 1996, as I sat listening to papers being presented at the main European AI conference that year, it dawned on me how little had really changed since the seventies. By the mid-nineties I had become acutely aware of how intractable many of the issues seemed to be, and of how the large ambitious projects of the seventies and eighties had virtually all simply died gracefully when their funding ran out, rather than yielding anything really newsworthy. After thirty years of intense and well-funded research in many public and private laboratories, computers were nowhere close to being able to understand ordinary language, or to interpret what they were seeing through their video-camera eyes, or to be useful domestic servant robots—except in carefully-restricted contexts. By the 1990s, the good departments encouraged their Ph.D. candidates to take on much more modest projects with more limited objectives. It isn't that there is nothing that works at all. There are some genuinely useful systems that have emerged from AI research that handle specific tasks in the commercial world. But these are almost trivial in comparison with what we all imagined we were playing with in the early days of the field.

So what is going on here? Is it simply that the problems were a lot harder than any of us thought in the early days? That is what virtually every current and continuing AI researcher will say. Nevertheless maybe that's not the real answer. Could there not perhaps be one or more systematic tacit assumptions that all of us were making, underlying all the research in AI, that is or are, in fact, wrong?

I struggled with this last question for a long time, feeling intuitively that the answer was probably yes (there was something intrinsically wrong with our approaches), but also knowing that we hadn't run out of creative ideas for solving problems, and feeling that at least we needed to push the technology as far as we could before we would begin to understand what the deeper issues were.

There has never been any shortage of novel ideas for developing or simulating intelligence in computers. Indeed, in the history of the field there have been several attempts to place the AI research paradigm on a completely fresh footing. "Neural networks," for example, were introduced as a method of simulating adaptive intelligence in an approach that seemed radically different from previous work (which had been heavily based on explicit manipulation of symbolic structures). For a while many researchers were convinced that this was the change of tactic needed for AI to move beyond the apparent roadblocks that had kept it from achieving its goals. By now, however, twenty years have passed since this innovation, and although neural networks are still popular for some kinds of work, they have not much changed the overall picture. Similarly, other kinds of statistical methods have largely replaced "symbolic" approaches to simulating intelligence—I have more to say about this development a little later.

Returning from that conference in 1996, I began to suspect for the first time that the roots of our failure to make real progress in AI were not within the field itself but reached down into the supporting culture, and were in fact connected to our very way of seeing and understanding. Brian Smith was arguing a similar position,[6] and his book, *On the Origin of Objects*, as well as our discussions, helped me to notice some of what might be going on. By this time also I had been a student of Buddhism for many years, and had been trying for the previous year or two to reconcile what I could understand of the Tibetan Dzogchen teachings with my native and typically western science-based view of what the world is like. For one reason or another, until this point it had never occurred to me that anything I might learn from Tibetan lamas would have any relevance to research in artificial intelligence.

The issues as I have come to understand them, however, are neither esoteric nor fundamentally technical. Indeed, it was very difficult, knowing from experience how much flexibility and subtlety computers were capable of, to accept that there could be important issues that no technical ingenuity was going to help with. The stance within the field has always been that as long as we can understand and describe a problem well enough, we'll think of a way of dealing with it. There was a long history of things being done with computers that had never been imagined ten or fifteen years earlier. How can we say, even now, that we won't achieve computational intelligence if we keep working on it creatively?

One clue to what is going on emerges every time we design a computer program that includes a model of something external to the computer itself. Pragmatically this includes essentially all programs created by AI researchers and most software that we encounter directly or indirectly in our daily lives, such as airline reservation programs and word processors.

When I talk of models here, I mean something quite general—really any logical arrangement of data or software elements internal to a computer that in some way intentionally mirrors a structure in the world outside. For example, a flight reservation system will include internal representations that correspond one-for-one with individual flights, the individual seats within an aircraft, and the passengers who have booked. A word processing application will maintain, inside the computer, representations for paragraphs, pages, margin widths, paper shapes, and sizes—all of which are conceptual structures that people use to think about documents written on paper. The paragraphs and pages, the flights and the passengers, are all outside the computer, and since the computer cannot directly access them as it carries out its computations, internal representations of these items are created to serve as carriers of information about the corresponding elements of the world outside.[7]

The "problem" stems from the fact that these models are idealized and simplified conceptualizations of the actual world, conceptualizations that originate in the heads of the software designers. It isn't that these conceptual structures aren't carefully constructed—there are sophisticated methodologies for undertaking the analyses of situations and tasks in order to yield coherent models and good designs. A good part of the discipline of software engineering is devoted to doing such analysis and modelling well, and many tools have been developed to aid in the process.

No, we end up with a good correspondence between the models embedded in our software and the way we think about the world. The problem, strangely enough, is the surprising mismatch between the way we imagine the world to be and the way it actually is. Our verbally oriented, analytical minds like to see the world in terms of mostly stable objects, predictable patterns, simplification, and order. In fact, we may almost have to see the world in such terms (I'll talk a little more about this below). But actually the world isn't much like this. We know it isn't, but we tend to keep this knowledge rather unconscious. Starting in childhood, we have learned a way of conceptualizing the world that seems to work pretty well, and crucially, we all know how to instantly repair these conceptual models in our heads when they break down, as they do all the time. But these excursions for repair tend to be unconscious as well, so for the most part we don't notice that they're happening. It isn't so much that we slip into unconsciousness for a few moments, as that a different mode of consciousness comes into play in those moments. But we all know it, so it needs pointing out rather than explaining.

Before pointing to a couple of examples where typically our mental models don't correspond with the actual world, it is worth noticing that we all seem to have a tendency to minimize the significance of evidence suggesting that the world is not as we imagine it to be. We all have a lot invested in believing that we know what the world is like, so it's psychologically safer to take particular examples of mismatch as isolated curiosities than as illustrative of something that might have more extensive implications. I'll argue, however, that in fact examples are ubiquitous, that the implications are deep, and that it's worth trying to notice our own psychological resistance, if we can, to the idea that discrepancy might be widespread.

Conceptual Models and Unconscious Action

If you're not a furniture designer, think about chairs for a moment. And for the time being, don't refer to the pictures on the following page. Think to yourself about the number of legs that a chair must have for stability, the number of legs that chairs usually have, and reflect a bit on how those legs are usually arranged. Not difficult—we all deal with chairs every day, and we decide in a flash whether a chair is likely to fall over if we sit in it. Now with these thoughts in mind, turn to the pictures in Figure 1 (next page). Count how many legs each chair has, and see (a) how easy that is, and (b) how well these correspond with the answers you had previously come up with.

If you're like most people, you'll have found the chairs shown to be very ordinary (they were all examples of chairs I found around the office I worked in one day), and yet it won't have been entirely easy to decide how many legs each chair had, nor will the number of legs, and their positions, have corresponded to the informal models of chairs that you started with while reading the previous paragraph. But the key points to note are that none of us has any difficulty dealing with any

of these kinds of chair (sitting in them, stacking them, etc.), we've all
seen plenty of examples of similar chairs, and yet we don't bother to
create in our heads a more sophisticated model of what a chair is like.
Chairs are so simple that we can use and interact with them without

Fig. 1: Chairs

thinking consciously about their structure. And the mental models we carry around in our heads are used *only* when we need to think consciously about things. This is why the simple models most of us have for chairs won't serve for furniture designers. When we do need to elaborate our models—for example, when we're asked to describe some of this explicitly—*then*, and only then, do we conjure up a more sophisticated model that will support description. Yet oddly, we are inclined to feel that the elaborated model was there all the time, despite evidence to the contrary.

A rather different example of this phenomenon came to me on a summer trip to Yosemite National Park in California with my family. Several groups of researchers in various parts of the world, including my own, had been working on modelling of spatial cognition, and in particular thinking about the meanings of spatial prepositions such as "above," "next to," "in front of," "to the right of," "on," and so on. We had all been thinking about relatively simple examples of similar objects arranged in a room, children's blocks, objects on table-tops, and the like. Everything rather neat, surfaces flat, objects clear and distinct. But here I was in Yosemite, in the middle of wildness. We and our children were playing above Yosemite Falls (see Fig. 2), in what, by the standards

Fig. 2: Yosemite Falls

of our modelling, was a scene of incredible difficulty and complexity. Even object boundaries and identities were far from clear, no surfaces were flat, some rocks were wobbly, nothing was organized. And yet it was perfectly obvious that for all of us, even for small kids, leaping around this totally unstructured environment was (literally) child's play. And then I reflected that our ancestors have been living and playing in this kind of environment for at least a few hundred million years, long before we had words, or presumably any corresponding spatial concepts, to structure our cognition. We could function perfectly well in these environments long before we could describe them. And we still can!

Our ability to conceptually model and describe our world has led to many achievements, but once we begin to pay attention, it is remarkable how much we do perfectly well without describing anything, even to ourselves, without mentally labeling anything, without assigning attributes, without even identifying things as objects. When we "get into the flow" of an activity, the mind often becomes very quiet (or occupies itself with something completely unrelated), while the body, and obviously another part of the mind, engages often very skillfully with the task at hand. A friend who is a white-water canoeist describes the experience of steering a canoe down swiftly flowing, chaotic rapids. He observes everything around him, notices the color, shape, smoothness, stability of all of the patches of water near the boat he's in. He makes split-second decisions constantly, without time to "think." Very little in the way of objects, no labels, no words, no analysis—at least not when he's quite literally in the flow of the rapids. He feels that he becomes one with his canoe, and as if he and the canoe begin to merge with the river itself.

White-water canoeing is perhaps not a typical activity. But in fact, we all have less intense versions of such experiences many times a day. For reasons that seem tied in with the structure of our consciousness, we don't easily notice this unless the activity becomes so intense (as with being in the midst of dangerous rapids) that the verbal, conceptual mind is pushed aside. The other kind of practice that allows us to notice these things is meditation, a deliberate practice for quieting the chatter and distraction of the verbal mind in ordinary situations.

We work rather hard to keep the parts of the world that we can control ordered in ways that are cognitively simple to deal with—we find ourselves tidying up, arranging things systematically, and grouping similar things together. And our built environments have many flat surfaces, simple lines, matching items of furniture, geometric patterns. They are very different from the wildness in which we evolved and which still surrounds us. Why is this? Did this tendency to "tidy up," to organize and straighten things out , to create uniformity—did this come with language and concepts, as we felt we needed to build manageable left-brain models of our surroundings?

Until we try to impose our ordering tendencies on it, the "untamed wilderness" (which is a telling phrase) is not an easy place in which to find clear boundaries, to classify and separate out objects. In Figure 3 I have sketched one kind of "conceptual map" that we could lay over the Yosemite Falls picture (Fig. 2). But as is easily seen, there are innumerable ways one could draw such a map. For example, it turns out that in this case, it wasn't obvious even at the time whether the rocks in the foreground are separate rocks, or instead all just part of the bedrock with deeply worn crevices running across it. So we don't know if we're dealing with one "object" or many—and yet for most practical purposes it doesn't even matter. Similarly, we can easily identify nearby trees, but distant trees are just "forest." As we move through

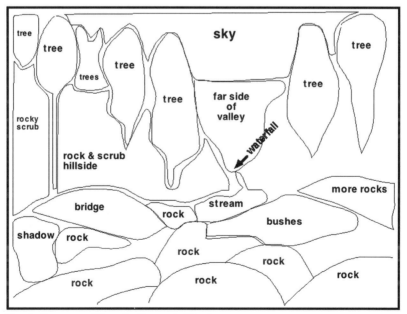

Fig. 3: Conceptual "map" of scene in Fig. 2

the landscape, do we identify every tree that becomes clear enough to distinguish from its context? No! It's clear that we often don't even decide what to consider as separate objects, much less give them verbal labels, until some task involving language or abstract thinking comes up. We can move through the world and do much of what we do—almost anything that is familiar and not intrinsically intellectual, such as walking, driving, eating, making love, painting, listening, giving someone a massage—without involving the verbal, conceptual, analytical mind much or at all. But as soon as we want to describe any of this to others, or to consciously reflect on what's going on, we instantly throw a conceptual net over everything, drawing boundaries, assigning labels and attributes. This is an almost entirely automatic part of bringing our conscious awareness to bear on something, but the lightning-quick process of doing the carving up and classifying is itself almost unconscious.

The strange result is that this labeled and delineated view of things becomes our idea of what the world is like. Every time we pay conscious attention to a part of our world with our thinking mind active—there it is, or there it seems to be, already apparently organized and obvious. It's difficult for us to imagine that this view, tailor-made for conscious thought, might not exactly match the reality that supports it. Wherever we look, we know how to categorize and name what we're seeing, and in many cases how to measure it or count them. It's part of what we've been learning since infancy, and it comes as second nature. What is much harder (but not impossible) to notice is that in this process we're doing a huge amount of smoothing out of rough edges, of ignoring detail, of simplifying, of assigning categories and drawing boundaries that we've learned to work with but that are in our heads and not actually "out there" in the world itself.

The models that we create (and not just scientists, but all of us, all the time), which are closely tied to the concepts and attributes that come with our language, are in fact surprisingly inadequate as descriptions of reality even for many everyday situations, as the example with chairs shows. But when our conceptual models break down, we revert to an older, deeper, more intimate, more fully immersed mode of connection to reality.[8] At this level, where we are more intimately engaged with the immediacy of a situation, we repair the broken conceptual model so that it becomes adequate for thinking once again about the current situation. That is the kind of process that is likely to have taken place for the reader when looking at the various pictures of chairs. After looking at them, typically one has different answers to some questions about chair legs than before.

There's nothing surprising about this. Repairs of this sort happen many times a day, for all of us. It seems to be more efficient for us not to bother keeping accurate conceptual models of everything, and instead refining them as and when we need to. Nevertheless there *are* several odd things about this repair process. One is that we tend not to notice the reversion to the intuitive mode of awareness—it is usually only semi-conscious at best. Particularly in modern society, we seem to have a vested interest in pretending that our descriptive conceptual models of the world can cope with everything, are all we need, and that they are all that cognition depends on. It seems to require a discipline like meditation for us even to notice that there is more going on than our standard stories tell us, to notice that our description of reality is at best a rough and perhaps only partial view. We like to pretend that the culturally articulated and received story of reality is the full story, and captures everything that is important. In truth that story may be astonishingly partial, and the world awesomely richer than our culture has guessed.

The other oddity is that we have, in our era, become so good at creating and manipulating elaborate conceptual descriptions of reality that we tend to believe the truth of these models even in the face of fairly strong evidence of breakdown. Psychologists understand this well, of course, especially on the personal level, with respect to the stories we tell ourselves (and therapists help us to deconstruct them!). But it applies also at collective and cultural levels—we can see it especially clearly with simplistic ideologies in politics and economics. It sometimes seems as if we would rather accept an easy story about what the world is like than to actually look, to actually face reality directly. This is why art is relevant—because artists try to train themselves to really look (even if they're not necessarily any better than the rest of us at seeing themselves!).

COGNITION AND INTUITION

The key problem for artificial intelligence stems from this strong tendency throughout science and in fact throughout modern culture to give primacy to our cognitive models and descriptions of the world, as if they were what really mattered, as if they were the truth. With very few exceptions, AI software depends on constructing and manipulating such descriptions.[9] Even when it employs statistical methods, as is increasingly the fashion, the resulting patterns and weights are still effectively descriptive. AI is interested in our cognitive faculties, and it is no accident that it allies itself closely with cognitive psychology and has almost nothing to say to depth psychology.

We humans can work relatively well with our own conceptual models of our surroundings, because we are also connected—directly, I would claim—to the rest of the world through our intuitive faculties, and we rely on this more basic mode of connection to sustain and supplement our conceptual models far more than we normally realize. But unfortunately, although our computers are embedded in the world too, we have absolutely no idea how to give them an intuitive faculty. As far as I can tell, we have very little idea, any of us, about what intuition consists of, or how it functions. I have more to say on this below.

A number of researchers, appreciating that embodiment is a crucial attribute of humans, have worked on building physical, mobile robots with sensors of various kinds so that they are able to "feel" and to "see" as well as interact directly with their environment. However, although it is pretty clear that being in a body is a key element of what it is to be human, and intrinsic to our awareness, the mere situating of a computer in a mobile mechanism that may even look approximately like a human body, and giving it a degree of sensorimotor access and control, doesn't successfully address the key issue. Even an embodied computational process remains unconscious, remains entirely disconnected from the unmanifest world that is intrinsic to our existence and to our intelligence. And we don't know enough about consciousness (and unconsciousness!) to know how to give it to an artifact that we have created.

A simple way of characterizing the issue is that AI depends entirely on the manipulation of *descriptions* of the world, and machines have no way of synthesizing relevant descriptions *de novo*. We, on the other hand, while also able to make good use of descriptions of the world (that's what education is largely about, along with all of science and much else), are essentially grounded in more direct ways of knowing[10]. This makes a huge difference. What the failure of AI shows us, if we didn't know it in other ways, is that access to vast amounts of information, even along with sophisticated deductive and inferential machinery to operate on it, is not nearly enough for intelligence.

In 1984, a team of researchers led by Doug Lenat started a project to create a "knowledge-base" whose goal was to codify computationally what we usually refer to as common sense. This project, called CYC (from the second syllable of "encyclopedia"), was funded by a consortium of industry players, initially for five years, and then extended for a second five years. The original intention was to encode the knowledge in the *Encyclopedia Brittanica*, and later that was changed to "the knowledge that isn't in the encyclopedia, but that is needed to understand what it does contain," and the idea was that once a critical threshold was reached (the original projection was that it would be within the first five years, if I remember correctly), its computers would be able to read normal books and quickly begin to acquire vast additional knowledge.

Well, after ten years the funding ran out, but if the funders were daunted, the researchers were not, so they spun themselves off as a private company called Cycorp, to do commercial AI. And just recently (in August 2008) the company released OpenCyc, billed as "the world's largest and most complete general knowledge base and common sense reasoning engine." It contains "hundreds of thousands of terms [concepts], and millions of assertions [facts or relations]." And yet it still isn't anywhere close to being able to read books. As far as I know, that's no longer even a goal.

I am not being critical of the CYC people—what they are attempting is truly interesting, even for me. I have simply come to believe that this kind of work will never lead to intelligent behavior. Declarative and explicitly represented knowledge is far less important to our own intelligence than we have believed. Intuition and other non-cognitive ways of knowing are correspondingly far *more* important for us than we have realized. It has taken me a long time to realize how important this is, and I am still exploring its consequences and implications.

My Own Journey

By the late 1990s I was beginning to realize the intrinsic limitations of conceptual knowledge, and to appreciate the importance of intuition and "the right brain." This was undoubtedly the result not only of my observations about AI and its progress, but also of my exposure to teachings and practices of the East, from Zen and Tibetan Buddhism to yoga and Advaita, plus extensive reading and conversation with many from other traditions. I had always been deeply curious about the nature of things, and I believe that curiosity is both what got me into science in the first place and ultimately what pulled me away again.

For me at least, rendering a little more homage to intuition and other ways of knowing had much more than intellectual consequences. I began to pay more attention to my own intuition, and to trust it more. In turn, it seemed to strengthen. Professionally I switched for a while from AI research to exploring theories of chaos and complexity, and self-organizing and self-replicating systems. These too were fascinating topics, and for a while seemed relevant to my search (though I quickly came to realize that the people most interested in funding this kind of research, by far, were the military).

Nevertheless I began to feel more and more frustrated and blocked in my research. Around this time I had a dream that I was walking along a path through a hilly landscape, and found that my way was blocked by an enormous black bull, the size of a small house. It was clear to me that the bull was not going to let me pass, and in fact that what the bull wanted more than anything else was for me to climb onto its shoulders (I was aware of this because as well as being the man seeing the bull blocking his way, I was also in some way watching this little "rational man" through the eyes of the bull). As the man, I thought that getting a ride on the bull's shoulders would be great as long as the bull would take me further along my path. But I strongly sensed that once I did climb onto the bull, it—or rather we, because we would by that time have merged—would in all likelihood go charging off across the landscape in an entirely unknown direction. No path. So as the man, I was extremely wary, not to say terrified, of mounting.

Many things in my personal life were changing at the time, and my children were close to independence. Before long I quit my job as a scientist, went to Italy to spend a couple of years with a small center there, and then came to Crete, where I currently live. The guidance I have relied on to make these moves has been more and more purely intuitive, and difficult to explain on rational grounds. Yet it has become a wonderful adventure, far beyond my imagining. In a strong sense I am a full-time student once again—a student now of these other ways of knowing, and of Love, which is closely if curiously related. In following these paths I have known more intensity and more joy, of both the quiet and the exuberant kinds, than at any previous time of my life.

CONCLUSIONS

Through our intuition, through our "right-brain" knowing and creative unconscious, it is not simply that we have *access* to the rest of the world. It seems to me that in a very literal sense we are *directly connected* to the rest of the world, to the rest of the universe, in this way. It is not that our right brains contain another kind of model of our world that we can make use of in a different way, as I used to think. Although we are far from being fully aware of it (I am far from being fully aware of it!), our participation in the universe is strongly mediated by what goes on in the deep psyche—in our hearts, our intuitive selves, and our dreams. And those forms of participation include much of our interaction with the mundane world. I suspect that if we were just a bit better at bringing things through from these deeper levels into consciousness, we could know *anything* we really wanted to. If something like this is true, then having a vast knowledge base of explicit facts and relationships at our fingertips, or on a chip embedded in our skulls, is not even very interesting, compared to what we already are and already have—if we only knew it. Already, if we have a computer and an internet connection, we have access to incredible amounts of knowledge. That's definitely handy; it has changed my life in some convenient ways. But has it made us noticeably more intelligent?

Bill Joy, co-founder and erstwhile chief scientist of Sun Microsystems, wrote a widely-quoted article in *Wired* magazine in 2000[11] that was something of an apocalyptic warning about the grave dangers of some of the new technologies, including artificial intelligence. Glen Slater has brought some of these warnings forward, and convincingly writes about the cultural drift that has been continuing to take us towards these perilous shores.[12] Although I share many of their worries about what we are doing—in particular in the areas of genetic engineering and nanotechnology—I have come to believe that being overtaken by a race of intelligent robots is not a grave threat. However, even in this area, we can at least learn from these alarms that we should find out more about what we are and in what direction we want to evolve.

NOTES

1. See for example Ray Kurzweil, *The Singularity is Near* (New York: Viking Penguin, 2005) and *The Age of Spiritual Machines: When Computers Exceed Human Intelligence* (New York: Penguin Books, 1999). Also Hans Moravec, *Mind Children* (Cambridge, Mass: Harvard University Press, 1990).

2. The Wikipedia article on transhumanism is unusually comprehensive and well-referenced (http://en.wikipedia.org/wiki/Transhumanism).

3. What is new is that genetic engineering and nanotechnology have been added to the technological mix, and the likely development of those technologies is indeed cause for concern independent of the issues covered in this paper.

4. Hubert Dreyfus, *What Computers Can't Do: The Limits of Artificial Intelligence* (New York: Harper, 1979).

5. Joseph Weizenbaum, *Computer Power and Human Reason* (San Francisco, W. H. Freeman, 1976).

6. Brian Cantwell Smith, *On the Origin of Objects* (Cambridge: MIT Press, 1996).

7. Actually, one could get into a detailed philosophical discussion about exactly where, or even whether, margins and flights actually exist. But such a discussion would serve little at this point in the argument. At the very least, paper and airplanes are external to the computer and its software.

8. Morris Berman, among many others, wrote well about this way of knowing in *The Reenchantment of the World* (Ithaca, New York: Cornell University Press, 1981). Heretofore, I mostly refer to this mode of knowing the world as "intuitive" or "intuition," for lack of a more precise term.

9. For a while in the late 1980s and early 90s, some research on "non-Cartesian robotics" was explored. This work, pioneered by Rodney Brooks at MIT and subsequently taken up elsewhere, attempted to avoid conceptual representations of the external world, building instead on a hierarchy of sensorimotor mechanisms roughly analogous to what we observe in low-level life forms such as worms or beetles. Despite some initial successes, and the building of small artificial creatures with interesting behavior, this work didn't lead very far and seems to have been abandoned by the late 1990s.

10. Machines are capable of instantiating patterns or templates from data that they sense directly from their surroundings, and then using the resulting instantiated descriptions to guide their action. But the evidence suggests that we humans are doing something qualitatively different from this. We can function well even when our descriptions are inadequate or wrong, which suggests we must be relying on something else altogether.

11. Bill Joy, "Why The Future Doesn't Need Us," *Wired*, 8.04 (2000).

12. Glen Slater, "Cyborgian Drift: Resistance is not Futile,"*Spring* 75 (2006): 173-195.

PART II:
MELTDOWN, SLOWDOWN, UPLINK

The Melting Polar Ice: Revisiting
Technology as Symptom and Dream

ROBERT D. ROMANYSHYN

I. Prelude: Anxiety and Ice

I am sitting in my garden on a summer day in Santa Barbara thinking about the melting polar ice. How *distant and far away* that danger seems in this moment. Apart from a vague sense of dread that now and then takes hold of me and on occasion a more intense sense of sorrow that settles upon me, it is difficult to stay *close to* this issue, to keep in *touch* with it, and to *sense* its presence in my daily life. This disjunction makes me anxious, a sure sign that something between the melting ice and me is out of joint. What am I missing?

So I begin to write in this anxious state, wishing that somehow I could numb myself against this feeling and remembering that anxiety was also the beginning of my book, *Technology as Symptom and Dream,*[1] in which I traced out the image of the despotic eye, its shadows, and its role in the historical origins of technological consciousness. The anxiety then was the imminent prospect of a nuclear winter; the anxiety now is the prospect—is it as imminent?—that we have raised the stakes and are challenging again the capacity of the earth to tolerate the effects

Robert D. Romanyshyn is a Senior Core Faculty member of the Clinical Psychology department at Pacifica Graduate Institute and an Affiliate Member of the Inter-Regional Society of Jungian Analysts. His most recent book is *The Wounded Researcher: Doing Research with Soul in Mind.* He is currently working on a manuscript on Jung's idea of individuation. He lives in Summerland, California with his wife Veronica Goodchild.

of our power. Anxiety, John Beebe writes, is a "proper starting point for the discovery of integrity." Indeed, staying in touch with the experience, examining it and not benumbing ourselves to it, is an "ethical process in which 'one's infinite obligation to the other is expressed.'"[2]

To stay with the anxiety of the moment is to be responsible, able-to-respond, because I am listening. The ecological problem which it expresses is a psychological problem, and the bridge that joins them is this movement of the soul against forgetting, against going to sleep, against benumbing myself, against the comfortable illusion that I am separate from the world, that the "inside" does not really matter in the calculus of this danger, and that the "outside" is, after all, "inanimate" and, as such, subject only to the limits of our technological reason. But in this moment of anxiety I know in a way that deepens its uneasiness that the melting ice is more than a reasonable problem, and that beyond our powers to explain, to construct, and impose solutions, we are being called to listen to what the ice "within" is saying, to its speech, to its voice as it addresses us.

II. 350 PPM

Two decades ago NASA scientist James Hansen testified to Congress that the warming of the planet was increasing and was linked primarily to human activity. 350 ppm is a measure of that warming, a measure of the amount of carbon dioxide in the atmosphere produced in large part by our planetary addiction to the burning of fossil fuels. Forty years ago the concentration of carbon dioxide in the atmosphere was approximately 275 ppm, and the consensus at that time was that a doubling of that level was the danger point. The "red light," so to speak, flashed 550 ppm, and the warning was to not exceed that number. 550 ppm was the tipping point beyond which global warming and its effects on sea levels, weather patterns, and crop cultivation might be irreversible. But on the way to 550 ppm, the warming has rapidly increased. The polar ice has been melting at a faster rate than predicted, leading some climate scientists to lower the measure to 450 ppm. Hansen, however, has most recently argued that that measure is too high and that the safe upper limit is 350 ppm. The most current data indicates we are already beyond that point. The polar ice is choking on green house gases that have reached a concentration level of 383 ppm. The tipping point is at hand. Our carbon footprint is penetrating deeper into the earth.

III. TRACES OF AN ABSENT PRESENCE

The beach is empty. No, that is not quite correct, because as I walk along the shore, I can see footprints in the sand. These footprints in the sand are a strange paradox. They are the presence of an absence and the absence of a presence. They tell me only that another who leaves a mark upon the world has been here, and in that mark I recognize a kinship with my kind. He or she is like me, or I like him or her. Perhaps a bit more can be surmised from the size and shape of the trace, but thinking about this other brings little beyond that. And yet the footprint haunts me. It invites dreaming. Its tension of absence and presence works a kind of magic, and as I walk along the shore, fantasies of this other emerge. This other who is here and not here, this other who has preceded me on this shore has become a companion whose epiphany is not reasonable and which no camera would record. The footprint as a presence that is an absence and an absence that is a presence is a matter of the imagination.

This metaphor of carbon footprints, no less than the actual footprints we have left behind on the moon, encodes a story. Indeed, the tale told in the two traces, the one below and the one above, might even intersect. As I showed over twenty years ago in *Technology as Symptom and Dream*, there is a connection between our flight into space and the despoiling of the earth. To the degree we have wired the planet for destruction, and now to the degree that we are encircling it with the noxious gases of our appetites for energy, our anxiety fuels an increasingly felt need to escape, to depart the earth. And to the degree that we engage the fantasy of departure we can loosen our attachment to earth as home. But as I showed in that book, the fantasy of departure is inescapably linked with the fantasy of dis-incarnation. To leave the earth we have to take leave of our senses.

These footprints—carbon and lunar—are then the traces of what I call the Spectator Mind—a solar mind, a consciousness that illuminates the world from afar and shines with a pitiless gaze, the gaze of the despotic eye, which, fixed and unmoving, does not blink; a mind that turns the world into a double of itself so that what it thinks about the world is what the world is; a mind, then, which, beyond the shadow of a doubt, maps the world to fit its visions. Flooding the world with its own light, it takes leave of its senses, and, doing so, banishes its own shadows. A mind that casts no shadows becomes a creator god so far removed from the world which has been placed at the vanishing point, that it is unmoved by what it surveys from above; a mind, which, in splitting itself off from nature, becomes oblivious to what matters; a mind, which, in its increasing distance from the world, breaks its erotic bonds with nature; a mind, which, in its belief that the best way to know the world is to withdraw from it, freezes its feeling connection with nature. It is a mind whose despotic eye not only does not blink but also sheds no tears. As a creator god, the Spectator Mind is a split mind that severs light from darkness and an unnatural mind that generates its creations apart from the feminine. The carbon and lunar footprints are the traces of a dream of a mind unhinged from nature, of a consciousness without flesh, of nature as inanimate and soul as un-natural. The melting polar ice is the shadow of this tale, its unfinished business.

In "Atlanta Fugiens," a 17th-century alchemical text written by Michael Maier, there is an illustration of an alchemist with thick glasses and only a little candle who is following the footprints of *mater natura* in the dark. We are not, however, like the alchemist of old following the trace of *mater natura* in the carbon footprint. Rather, we are following the trace of the Spectator Mind, which has made nature into a double of itself. We are following the footprints left by a dream whose origins have been forgotten, and which now is leading us to the melting ice.

IV. The Carbon Footprint

The carbon footprint has become a ubiquitous metaphor for the perilous condition of our age. But I question whether the carbon footprint is functioning as a metaphor. In an article in the *International Herald Tribune*, Verlyn Klinkenborg says, "In some ways carbon footprint is not an especially good metaphor" because, as he adds, "The carbon in question—the carbon dioxide that contributes to global warming—is a gas and far too diffuse to resemble an actual footprint."[3] His point, however, goes beyond his claim that carbon footprint is not a good metaphor. In fact, his point is that carbon footprint is not functioning as a metaphor at all because we take the metaphor too literally, as if it were an actual footprint, as if it were a precise definition.

A metaphor is not, however, a precise definition; a metaphor is always an allusion to something that remains elusive. As such, a metaphor is the opening of a possibility. It is a perspective that offers a vision or a way of seeing and understanding things, and it tells us as much about the one who makes the metaphor as it does about what the metaphor addresses. A metaphor, the literary critic Howard Nemerov has said, is neither a thing nor a thought.[4] Its vehicle is the image, and it is through the image that a metaphor opens a world. A metaphor invites a way of thinking about and being in the world that requires the creative play of imagination. As such, it stretches the boundaries of our two traditional ways of thinking in terms of either empirical facts or ideas of mind.

Carbon footprint is not an actual fact, like the footprint of my boot on the rug that attests to the fact that I was in the garden. Nor is it, as Klinkenborg suggests, a good idea. But we treat the carbon footprint as if it were like the footprint of my boot; and, taking its measure, we think and act as if we have gotten hold of something real, when in fact the metaphor has taken hold of us. Speaking to how fast this metaphor has taken hold of our consciousness, Klinkenborg says, "The swiftness of this change in consciousness—and the linguistic change that goes with it—is staggering," and, he adds, "a little worrying."[5]

What is worrisome here is the way in which a metaphor that is taken literally functions automatically as a statement of the way things truly and actually are. What is worrisome is that the metaphoric character of the trope is forgotten. Carbon footprint slips into the cultural unconscious where it functions as a projection. Klinkenborg addresses this issue. Even though carbon footprint is not an actual footprint, the phrase, he says, "sounds conscientious, and its automatic effect on behavior is somewhat magical." "You feel," he writes, "as though you're reducing global warming by saying it."[6]

This magical quality that adheres to a metaphor that has become unconscious gives to it a symptomatic character. Carbon footprint becomes a fixed way of thinking about climate change and the melting ice. The complexity of possibilities that a metaphor illuminates becomes narrowed and reduced to a single vision, and what does not fit into that single vision becomes excluded. A metaphor that has become a symptom identifies its vision with reality and thus requires massive denial of anything that would disturb that identification. A metaphor that has become a symptom invites one to fall asleep. It offers an easy but illusory promise that we have taken hold of things. Hence, Klinkenborg can say that what makes him uneasy about the metaphor of carbon footprint is "simply knowing how quickly humans adopt new phrases and how readily we confuse them with the reality—or the unreality—of our actions."[7]

The metaphor of carbon footprint is a problem because it has slipped into the collective unconscious. Noting how crucial it is "to grasp the idea that lies behind carbon footprints," Klinkenborg says, "Think about it properly, and it leads you to a profound critique of who we are and how we behave."[8] To enter into this profound critique is to make this unconscious metaphor more conscious.

V. SOUL ON ICE

This ecological crisis is a psychological crisis; the melting ice is here with us, lives with us as a sense of anxiety, accompanies us as emotional states of dread and fear, and companions us as a pervasive quality of dis-ease that breaks through as an un-nameable irritation like a telephone call in the night that awakens us from sleep. As I showed in *Technology as Symptom and Dream* and in other works on the soul of culture,[9] depth psychology does its work in the world as a cultural therapeutics. In this approach the symptom is regarded as a vocation to remember something that is too vital to forget but which has been forgotten because it is too painful to remember. The melting ice is a call to remember who and what is melting in the complex and archetypal dimensions of the soul, a call to awaken to and to remember what can no longer be ignored, dismissed, marginalized, or forgotten. Now at the beginning of the 21st century we cannot afford to make the same mistake that has haunted the origins of depth psychology, when the hysteric crossed the threshold of Freud's consulting room. Her symptoms were the voice of soul awakening the collective Spectator Mind to its broken connection between the flesh of the body and the flesh of nature, as well as its splitting of the masculine/feminine tension in the psyche. Contrasting the images of the astronaut and the anorexic, I wrote:

> …the anorexic…vividly calls our attention to the masculine
> character of our dreams of departure from the earth and escape
> from the body. We are all astronauts in this technological age,

but the astronautic body of technological functioning there on
the launch-pad prepared and ready to depart the earth is a
masculine figure. And the …abandoned body, the body left
behind…is the figure of the woman. What the shadow history
of the abandoned body shows is that technology as a cultural-
psychological dream of departing earth and remaking the body
is not only a dream of escape from matter, but also a flight from
the feminine.[10]

The hysteric's symptoms were an appeal, but that appeal, that call
to awaken, was imprisoned within the therapy room, placed within
the mind of the sufferer herself, made into her problem, confined within
the inside space of the psyche divorced from the outside space of the
world. With the melting ice the ante has been raised. The *Anima
Mundi*, the voice of the soul of the world speaking from the abyss
between matter and mind, has become louder and more urgent.

The melting ice is a symptom that calls once again for us to bridge
that divide between inside and outside. It is another chance, a danger
that is also an opportunity. The melting ice is, in Al Gore's term, an
"inconvenient truth" because the soul and its symptomatic speech
remains an inconvenient truth. We have had a hundred years of
psychotherapy, as Hillman and Ventura point out, and the world has
gotten worse.[11] We cannot imprison that truth within a version of the
original mistake by turning the inside outside. We cannot imprison
the melting ice within the confines of our technological ideas and treat
it only as a problem that is out there.

VI. THE SPECTATOR MIND

In *Technology as Symptom and Dream,* I traced the origins of the
Spectator Mind to the development of linear perspective vision in the
15th century. In that book I showed how in multiple areas of human
life what began as a cultural-historical artistic invention for representing
three-dimensional space on the two-dimensional plane of the canvas
quickly became a cultural convention, a habit of mind, a way to map
the world that nourished the birth of the modern scientific-technological
worldview and rapidly fueled its expansion. At the time I wondered if
assigning so much importance to an artistic technique invented over
500 years ago was too bold a claim, but numerous art and cultural
historians lent support to its significance. The art historian Helen

Gardner, for example, wrote that linear perspective "'made possible scale drawings, maps, charts, graphs, and diagrams—those means of exact representation without which modern science and technology would be impossible,'" and cultural historian William Ivins noted, "'Many reasons are assigned for the mechanization of life and industry during the nineteenth century, but the mathematical development of perspective was absolutely prerequisite to it.'" It was, however, a remark by the art historian Samuel Edgerton that secured the point. He wrote, "'space capsules built for zero gravity, astronomical equipment for demarcating so-called black holes, atom smashers which prove the existence of ani-matter—these are the end products of the discovered vanishing point.'"[12] Riffing on Edgerton's point, I showed how the vanishing point, which is the point at which all parallel lines converge, was prerequisite for taking leave of the earth. Although in the original text by the Florentine architect and painter Leon Battista Alberti, the vanishing point was called the center point, it also became known in his time as the *"punto di fuga,"* the point of flight. The vanishing point of linear perspective became a collective dream whose themes of distance, dis-incarnation, and departure were the codes by which the Spectator Mind was able to take leave of its senses and break the connection between incarnated mind and earth. The melting ice, so tellingly mapped from space, is a symptomatic expression of this dream.

The genesis of the Spectator Mind in linear perspective is traceable to Alberti's image of the window as one of the two conditions for establishing the vanishing point. In his text he writes, "First of all, on the surface on which I am going to paint, I draw a rectangle of whatever size I want, which I regard as an open window through which the subject to be painted is seen."[13] If we read Alberti's text as a collective dream, then, as compared with the Medieval world view, a radical shift in consciousness and a new dream is being born concerning the relation between person and world. A window establishes a boundary and even a separation between self and world, and it becomes a metaphor for a mathematical grid through which one maps and plots the world. In this dreamscape we are invited to imagine ourselves as essentially apart from rather than as a part of the world. Our connection with what lies on the other side of the window is now measured by the eye. The eye alone is singled out and privileged as the mode and means of a relation established not in sensuous proximity to things but in distance from them.

Figures 1 and 2 offer an image of this shift in consciousness. They show two different ways of dreaming about the relation of self and world. Both of them are depictions of Florence. Figure 1 dates from approximately 1350, while Figure 2, known today as *Map with a Chain*, dates from 1480. Together they straddle Alberti's text of 1435-1436, and between them there is a world of difference.

Figure 1 presents a dream of the world in which the things of the world are encrusted into one's flesh, a dream of the world in which the things of the world and the flesh of the body carry on a mutual erotic seduction. Merleau-Ponty addresses this chiasm between world and body when he says that painting's interrogation of the world "looks toward this secret and feverish genesis of things in our body." He adds, "There really is inspiration and expiration of Being, action and passion so slightly discernible that it becomes impossible to distinguish between what sees and what is seen, what paints and what is painted."[14] On the far side of linear perspective there is a con-spiracy, a breathing together of body and world, the intimacy of breath in that moment of in-spiration when one takes the other into oneself, is impregnated by

Fig. 1: Panorama of Florence, detail from the Madonna della Misericordia fresco, anonymous, 14th century (Credit: Alinari/Art Resource, New York).

Fig. 2: The *Carta della Catena* (Map with a Chain), Lucantonio delgi Uberti, c. 1480 (Credit: Bildarchiv Preussischer Kulturbesitz/Art Resources, New York).

the other, and the surrender in that moment of expiration, when one gives back what has been transformed in the slight pause between these two moments, in that natural alchemy of the breath when one changes the world into paintings, or into a word, as Rilke notes in his *Duino Elegies*: "For the wanderer doesn't bring from the mountain slope / a handful of earth to the valley, untellable earth, but only / some word he has won, a pure word, the yellow and blue gentian. / Are we perhaps here, just for saying: House, Bridge, Fountain, Gate, Jug, Olive tree, Window,— / possibly: Pillar, Tower?"[15]

On the far side of linear perspective, one is dreaming the world as an aesthetic, sensuous entanglement where the eyes that see are also the legs that walk about, the ears that hear the sounds, the nose that smells the odors, and the hands that touch the textures of the world. To be sure, Figure 1 is a confusing image because we have become accustomed to the dream of the world mapped by linear perspective, and yet we know that earlier way of being in the world. That landscape of the mid-14th century lingers, as Edgerton notes, in our muscles and bones. It is, for example, "the truth of the tourist arriving for the first time in a strange city with heavy baggage and an unfamiliar hotel address in hand."[16]

On this side of linear perspective the dream of the world has changed. Notice in Figure 2 how the city is different. In *Map with a Chain*, we are offered a bird's eye view of the city, a view of the city as seen from afar. In Edgerton's terms it presents the city from a "'fixed viewpoint, which is elevated and distant, completely out of plastic or sensory reach of the depicted city.'"[17] But who sees the world in this way? Who dreams the world in this fashion?

Notice the figure in the lower right-hand corner of the painting, the man on the hill above the city! He has what might be a sketchpad in hand. Is he drawing a map of the city? Of course, we cannot know for sure, but the image suggests as much, and indeed it suggests much more. From his high altitude perch above the city, he is

> a man of distant vision, perhaps the first expression of the self we have become…Seated there as he is above the city, he incarnates at its birth a new ideal of knowledge according to which the further we remove ourselves from the world the better we can know it.

He has climbed the hill; and, in doing so, he has had to turn his back on the city below. Turning back to the city, his vision is a disembodied one as he now fixes his gaze upon the city. He knows the city now not by moving about it but from his fixed position where "On the hill above the city only his eyes remain 'in touch' with the world observed below." Commenting on that figure on the hill, I said, "But at that distance such eyes, unrelated, for example, to ears and hands, can no longer know the words of anger or of love uttered by those *living* in the city."[18] It is a way of being in the world that can be above and unmoved by what is experienced. We are the inheritors of that dream.

Fig. 3: Woodcut illustration from Hieronymous Rodler, *Eyn schön nützlich Büchlin und Underweysung der Kunst des Messens* (A Fine, Useful Booklet and Instruction in the Art of Measurement), Simmern, 1531. (Republished by Akademische Druk- u. Verlagsansalt, Graz, Austria, 1970.)

As I mentioned earlier, the open window with which Alberti began quickly became something else. It became a mathematical grid as depicted in Figure 3. Linear perspective, which began as an artistic invention for representing three-dimensional space on a two-dimensional plane, became a cultural convention, a habit of mind, a way of knowing the world and being in it that fragments the world into units and the bits and bytes of information that inform our world today. To dream the world in this fashion required a singularity of focus. Figure 4 illustrates this point.

It is a sketch by Albrecht Dürer made in 1525, which was intended by him to illustrate the technique of linear perspective drawing. It shows that the vision of the man on the hill depicted in Figure 2 is a singular and immobile one, a Cyclopean vision. In Dürer's illustration the artist on this side of the grid, or the screen through which he views his model, has one eye locked in place. The artist's eye is not to move. William

Fig. 4: Woodcut illustration from Albrecht Dürer, *Underweysung der Messung* (Art of Measurement), Nuremberg, 1525 (Credit: Foto Marburg/Art Resource, New York).

Ivins captures this prescription when he notes, "A person can make a correct image of what he or she sees through a window 'provided that while he does this he uses only one eye and does not move his head.'"[19] In an essay entitled "The Despotic Eye,"[20] I described this singular, immobile eye of the Spectator Mind as an eye that not only does not move but also does not blink. It is the eye of the TV camera that records beauty and horror with the same indifference. This single-minded vision from afar, this fixed view from above that is unmoved by what it sees, is not the eye that will linger with things, not the eye that will wander and be distracted by the multitudinous possibilities of the world, not the eye that will drift into some reverie with things the better to imagine their still un-glimpsed depths and secrets. Have we not had a contemporary example of this despotic eye, this kind of fixed, singular, unblinking vision in the recent comment of the Vice Presidential candidate, Sarah Palin? When asked if she felt ready to assume the duties of the presidency, she said she did not blink. Her eye that does not blink is also the eye that has denied the role of human activity in the crisis of global warming and has denied that the melting polar ice is a threat to the habitat and well being of the polar bear. This eye that does not blink is the mind that knows no doubts.

We have learned the trick of commanding the world from afar. We have become masters of this fixed, singular gaze that maps the world into a grid and fragments it into its divisible parts, and in doing so we have become spectators of a world transformed as a spectacle that requires that we take leave of our senses, that we leave the body behind. In *Technology as Symptom and Dream*, I showed how this abandoned body became the foundation for modern anatomy in the work of Vesalius, whose textbook, *De Humani corporis fabica libri septem,* was published in 1543, and how the anatomical body became linked as the specimen body with the Spectator Mind and the world as spectacle. I also traced the history of the shadows of this abandoned body from the 15th-century witch through the 19th-century hysteric, who crossed the threshold of Freud's consulting rooms and undermined the epistemological foundations of a way of knowing the world that takes leave of its senses, to the anorexic. In symptomatic form the hysteric and her multiple feminine companions spoke an aesthetic of a broken desire, the aesthetic of a neglected, marginalized, and forgotten Eros. But depth psychology focused its gaze upon those symptoms and laid the hysteric on the couch. The larger picture of the broken connection between body and world was not heard.

I am not arguing here that the pre-linear perspective world was a better world. On the contrary, my argument here is that while this way of dreaming the world as it moves toward the vanishing point has produced many benefits and has given us a great deal of power and control, it has exacted a price. In the face of the melting ice it is our task to know that price. The loss of wholeness in pursuit of mapping a perfectly ordered world that has resulted from this broken connection and the fragmentation that belongs to it is one price we have paid for this dream.

VII. THE MELTING ICE

The polar ice caps are the *Axis Mundi* of the world and the Polar Regions of the soul. When the early explorers of these regions at the top and bottom of the world went in search of its mysteries, charms, and terrors, they were also exploring the mysteries, charms, and depths of the soul. It is no accident, I believe, that Ernest Shackleton, one of the earliest and most famous of the explorers, said that his draw to the ice began with a dream:

> But strangely enough, the circumstances which actually determined me to become an explorer was a dream I had when I was twenty-two. We were beating out of New York from Gibraltar, and I dreamt I was standing on the bridge in mid-Atlantic and looking northward. It was a simple dream. I seemed to vow to myself that some day I would go to the region of ice and snow and go on and on till I came to one of the poles of the earth, the end of the axis upon which this great round ball turns.[21]

Nor is it an accident that Helen Thayer, the first woman to reach the Arctic Circle on her own, entitled her book, *Polar Dream*,[22] or that my explorations of the Spectator Mind for *Technology as Symptom and Dream* were preceded by dreams of the polar ice. The *Axis Mundi* is a vocation. The journey to the lands of ice and snow are journeys to the heights and depths of soul.

In the Introduction to his remarkable book, *The Spiritual History of Ice*, Eric Wilson says, "If a collective or cultural unconscious exists, then it was at work at the dawn of the third millennium." He is referring to the multiple scenarios of apocalypse, like the feared computer crashes that some predicted, would take place as the second millennium ended. A bit further on he focuses on the polar ice caps within this context and asks, "What secret link exists between ice and apocalypse? What ghostly bergs cruise in the millennial undertow?"[23]

I am taking the approach not only that a collective unconscious exists, but also that its exploration is vital to our understanding of this event—is it perhaps apocalyptic?—of the melting ice and of ourselves. We are the melting ice, and perhaps the melting ice is our last best chance to awaken to the depths of soul and to the long, collective dream of the Spectator Mind. At the poles of the world an alchemy is taking place, dissolving the dichotomy between the inner domain of psyche and the outer domain of the world. At the *Axis Mundi* we are being made aware not only that psyche and nature are an *unus mundus*, but also that the melting ice is the ecological shadow, the darker, symptomatic side of the dream of the Spectator Mind.

In this section I want to explore these Polar Regions of the world and soul through four literary images that are personifications of the Spectator Mind. Who dwells there? In the frozen, silent landscapes of the polar north Victor Frankenstein encountered the harsh truth of his creation, the creature that he made and abandoned, the being whose creation transformed "nature into a double of his egocentric desire."[24] And what does the Ancient Mariner, who stops the Wedding Guest to tell his strange tale of the southern ice, have to say to us? Face to face with the melting ice, whom might we encounter? "Mont Blanc," a poem by Percy Shelley, and *Manfred*, a dramatic poem by Lord Byron, precede the discussion of Mary Shelley's novel, *Frankenstein: Or, The Modern Prometheus,* and Coleridge's poem, *The Rime of the Ancient Mariner.*

In 1816 Percy Shelley, alongside his wife Mary, stood beneath the towering glacial peaks of Mont Blanc, the scene of his poem of the same name. Awed by the cloud-shrouded majesty of the high summit, the poet—Shelley and the figure of the poet in the poem—struggles with the issue of the relation between mind and nature. On one side of this tension is the affirmation of the power of mind to organize the brute presence of the glacial forces, to interpret their meaning, indeed to give them existence. At one point in the poem Shelley's poet says, "And what were thou, and earth, and stars, and sea,/ If to the human mind's imaginings/Silence and solitude were vacancy?"[25] In these lines Mont

Blanc, as well as the full wide expanse of nature from earth to the heavens, is addressed as "thou," signaling a kinship of sorts between mind and nature, a relation between them. Commenting on these lines, Eric Wilson argues that they situate the human mind as a part of nature. He says, "If the human mind did not interpret—did not make meaningful and moral—the powers of nature, then these energies would remain insignificant—vacant and barren."[26]

But Shelley's poet remains unsure of his conviction, or we should say his hope about the powers of mind to form nature into meaning. The poet in the poem recognizes that "The wilderness has a mysterious tongue/ Which teaches awful doubt…"[27] In the grip of this doubt Shelley's poet is on the other side of this tension between mind and nature, and on this side he falls into despair. No longer is the sea of ice a "Thou." "Aloof and inaccessible, the icy gulphs strike him as entirely "'other.'" Now these frozen peaks are, as Wilson notes, "threats not only to his identity but also to all human systems of meaning." In the face of this threat, a kind of spirit of revenge appears. "Shelley's poet," Wilson says, "is on the verge of demonizing the icy peaks."[28]

The Spectator Mind was initially born in this spirit of revenge against despair, born as that dream of mind, which, in taking leave of its senses, breaks its bonds with and takes flight from nature. In this sense Shelley's poem is a diagnosis of and therapeutic commentary on that dream. Shelley's poem expresses the darker side of that dream, its forgotten origins: what mind cannot subdue and take the measure of, what it cannot control, it fears and must negate. It is worth citing here the following passage of Wilson, which underscores this tension between mind and nature that Shelley at Mont Blanc and his poet in the poem "Mont Blanc" experience:

> Going to one extreme of self-admiration, the poet severs his mind from the nourishing flows of things and thus undergoes disorientation and despair; pushing to the other extreme by focusing on natural processes devoid of human significance, he feels diminished as a creative agent, afraid of an environment over which he has no control.[29]

Shelley's poem does not resolve this tension. His poet does not exile doubt as a way of silencing anxiety or fear. On the contrary, his poem and the poet in his poem hold this tension of opposites of mind and nature without recourse to splitting it in favor of either the joy of mind to subdue nature or the defeat of mind in the face of nature's icy remoteness. Throughout the poem Shelley's poet "undulates between elation and despair…arrogance and humility."[30] This undulating style is what Wilson calls a negative gnosis, which I have described over the years, most recently in *The Wounded Researcher,* as a metaphoric sensibility.[31] Wilson's description of Shelley's negative gnosis is an apt one for a metaphoric sensibility. Negative gnosis, he writes, is "a sublime yet skeptical sense that no empirical form or psychic intuition reveals the deep cause of existence."[32] Within a Jungian framework I would speak less about the deep cause and more about the deep ground of existence, the deep unconscious of the *unus mundus* world of soul where psyche and matter are one. But this difference aside, I would say that a metaphoric sensibility is the attitude required if one's consciousness is to be responsive to how meaning, undulating between empirical matters of fact and ideas of mind, arises from the unconscious. Susan Rowland makes this point with respect to the style of Jung's writing. She says, "Anything derived merely from rationality risks being profoundly inauthentic unless it also bears witness to the destabilizing influence of the unconscious."[33] The negative gnosis of a metaphoric sensibility is responsive to this de-stabilizing influence of the unconscious. It is a linguistic alchemy, which always dissolves the certitude of "is" in the possibilities of the "is not" and thus holds the tension between the dogmatic arrogance of the fixed mind and the cynical despair of the postmodern mind.

Shelley's poet is both a diagnosis of and therapeutic commentary on the Spectator Mind, which as supremely rational is neither sublime nor skeptical. But his poem, I would argue, is also prophetic, or perhaps I should say, archetypal. Indeed, Shelley's poem is prophetic because it is archetypal. It reaches into the archetypal core of this tension between mind and nature, which, as von Franz has pointed out, is the issue at the heart of alchemy. "The psyche/matter problem," she writes, "has not yet been solved, which is why the basic riddle of alchemy is still not solved."[34]

Prophetic and archetypal, Shelley's poem anticipates the consequences when the Spectator Mind dissolves the tension between mind/psyche and nature/matter into an opposition and aligns itself on the side of mind split off from nature. Prophetic and archetypal, it anticipates the melting ice as the ecological unconscious of the Spectator

Mind. We will find this same prophetic/archetypal vision in Lord Byron's dramatic poem *Manfred*, Mary Shelley's novel *Frankenstein*, and Coleridge's poem *The Rime of the Ancient Mariner*.

To hold this tension between mind and nature is a difficult and constant effort, and its achievement is never complete. Wilson, I believe, addresses this challenge when he says, "Shelley experiences one primary sensation throughout his glacial vision: vertigo, the simultaneous fear and love of falling through empty space or unlocked time."[35] This description captures the two poles of the Spectator Mind's flight from nature at that vanishing point where its despotic vision is turned toward an infinite horizon, a gaze no longer tethered to nature or body. On one hand, there is the narcissistic desire to take hold of that frozen sea of whiteness, to take its measure through that distant vision that knows no bounds. On the other hand, there is that fear of losing one's hold, of falling back into the matrix of that all-embracing *mater natura*, which characterized the pre-linear perspective of the medieval world. The dizziness of Shelley's poet recapitulates this spiritual history of the Polar Regions, which Eric Wilson records so well in his book. The landscapes of the polar ice are and have been both a temptation and a terror. The history of polar exploration, which is at the same time a history of the psyche's relation to these regions, to the *Axis Mundi* of the World-Soul, "is a narrative of the relationships that emerge when the human mind contends with an abyss beyond mental mapping." The Polar Regions are "menacing because they invite and mock man's fantasies of complete order..."[36]

This narrative of temptation and terror, of desire and fear, of invitation and mockery in relation to the Polar Regions, reads like the narrative of the ego in relation to the Self in Jung's psychology. The two narratives mirror each other, especially when the encounter between ego and Self follows the path opened up by Jungian analyst Stanton Marlan in his insightful and powerful book, *The Black Sun: The Alchemy and Art of Darkness*.[37] In that book Marlan re-imagines this encounter through a thorough critique of the emphasis on light not only in Jungian psychology, but also in Western culture. The black sun is a dark light, which is a theme I will consider in the closing section of this paper. It is the *lumen naturae*, the light of nature that overshadows the light of mind, a blackness blacker than black, which, however, shines with its own luminosity. Situated within this image of the black sun, both narratives, the one an account of mind's encounter with the frozen whiteness of the ice of the world, and the other an account of soul's encounter with the darkness of the icy landscapes of soul, converge toward the same themes of invitation and terror. In the image of the back sun we have a symbol of the darkest regions of the Spectator Mind, now mirrored in the event of the melting ice: the dissolution of a world view, of the fixed beliefs of power, control, and dominant mastery over the forces of the natural world, and the collapse of that distant vision, which, in taking the measure of nature, has taken flight from it. There is terror here, the terror of the Spectator Mind that it will be drowned in the rising waters of the melting ice, the terror that its vision of light without darkness will be engulfed by these rising waters, extinguished by a melting created by its own terrible gaze when, looking at the world from afar, it pushed the world toward oblivion at the vanishing point.

But the black sun is, as Marlan notes, a paradox, because its blackness "also shines with a dark luminescence that opens the way to some of the most numinous aspects of psychic life."[38] As paradox, the black sun is not only the possibility of the terror of oblivion, it is also the hope of redemption, and it is that second possibility, held within the first, that gives the black sun in the melting ice its erotic gravity. Its image in the individual psyche, as Marlan so eloquently describes through clinical material as well as through examples from history, literature, and art, and its image in the collective psyche is the temptation to let go, to surrender to the nothing that is everything, to fall into that abyss where soul, waiting as a piece of unfinished business, weighs upon the dream of the Spectator Mind.

Marlan's numerous examples remind us, however, of the danger of this passage from the terror of oblivion to the hope of redemption. The passage requires that the darkness of the black sun not be split off from our images of light, and he reminds us of how Jung saw this split in the figure of Christ. For Jung, Christ represents "'the totality of a divine or heavenly kind, a glorified man…unspotted by sin.'" It is a vision that is dangerously one-sided, a vision that is unbalanced and substitutes perfection for wholeness. Quoting Jung, Marlan adds, "As the Gnostics said,[he] has put aside his shadow, and thus leads a separate existence which manifests itself in the coming of the antichrist.'"[39]

The Spectator Mind is a variation of this Christian motif. As I showed in *Technology as Symptom and Dream* in the chapter entitled "The Abandoned Body and its Shadows," in its flight from nature the Spectator Mind identifies matter with what is dark, corrupt, unruly, and feminine and takes leave of all that in Mind that is light, pure, organized, and masculine. In this variation, the melting ice is the technological version of this split-off darkness; it is the face that the Anti-Christ takes in the technological world, the monster, the creature that Victor Frankenstein created in his flight from the sting and stink of death that haunts the flesh. We will meet Victor and his creature later, where they encounter each other for the last time in the frozen northern ice, but for now I want to underscore the presence of this Christian motif in the technological dream of the Spectator Mind.

Both the Christian narrative and the technological narrative are a kind of imperialism, a forced colonization of the natural world by the light of a mind that knows no darkness. Eric Wilson makes this point when he says, "the spiritual imperialism of the Middle Ages—the Christianization of all space—becomes in the early Modern period a material imperialism—a desire to own and exploit 'unclaimed' lands."[40] In this confluence of a Christian spirituality that splits itself from matter and a technological materialism that takes leave of the flesh, the resurrection takes place at the vanishing point, at that place where the Spectator Mind transcends the body, where it rises above the world, where in a kind of folly it takes leave of its senses. This fantasy of transcendence leaves behind it the melting ice, which is an aspect of the abandoned body of the earth, and forges a dream of an ideal spirituality that in "striving for the heights is sure to clash with the materialistic earth-bound passion of the modern world."[41]

Lord Byron's *Manfred*, which was written in that same magical year of 1816 and only a few months after the famed ghost story sessions that led to Mary Shelley's novel, *Frankenstein; Or the Modern Prometheus*, tells the tale of a magus torn between the dualism of spirit and flesh. Like the Spectator Mind, he was distant from the community of men, and from afar he looked upon the world through the cold, detached, unmoved despotic eye: "though I wore the form,/I had no sympathy with breathing flesh."[42]

Manfred is hounded by guilt, and he seeks the icy peaks in an effort to forget his crime, the death of Astarte, a blood relative whom he loved and with whom he committed the horrible crime left unspoken, but probably incest. In Phoenician mythology Astarte is the goddess of the moon, and in the Greek world she became Aphrodite, the goddess of beauty, sexual fertility, and love. Manfred's crime, therefore, is a violation of the feminine principle in creation, a crime against lunar consciousness whose dark light is the counterpart to solar consciousness, the bright light of the sun, which for the Spectator Mind is the light of reason that knows no shadows, no darkness. His crime is also one against beauty, whose appeals are the foundation for an aesthetic connection to the world, and as well a violation against the bonds of love, those bonds that deeply connect us to each other and weave us into a history. Haunted by guilt, Manfred seeks the icy peaks and frozen waters where he might cool and still the torrent of his passions and there leave behind the limitations of a guilty conscience, the fate of ordinary men.

Manfred makes four attempts to escape his crime, but each effort fails. In the first instance, he "conjures the 'Spirits of Earth and Air'…to convince them to release him from his destiny: perpetual suffering over the tragedy of Astarte." It is forgetfulness that he seeks, which these spirits are unable to grant. In the second instance, Manfred "commands the ice to crush him." When his magic fails to quicken the glaciers' flow, "he decides to leap from the peaks."[43] But at the moment when he leaps, he is restrained by a hunter. Manfred cannot escape his fate either through the willfulness of mind that would rise above matter nor by a suicidal fall into matter in his desire for oblivion. In the third attempt, the Witch of the Alps offers to help, even though she is unable either to return Astarte from death or kill him. But she imposes one condition, which the proud Manfred cannot accept. The arrogant magus to the end, he refuses her demand to obey her will. In the fourth attempt, he calls upon the ruler of earthly fate, Arimanes, who conjures up the specter of Astarte. This image of Astarte, however, does not tell Manfred if he is condemned or pardoned for his crime. He learns only that his earthly suffering will end. Ensconced in his tower, Manfred dies the next day, and while Astarte's presence offers to him a brief vision of eternal beauty that soothes him, he remains at his death the stubborn magus he has been. Not even the spirits that come at the hour of his death to take him to hell can break his will. His death will be his own, and so he asserts that he dies "through the agency of his own will."[44]

From an archetypal viewpoint, Victor Frankenstein is kin to Manfred. They share the same patterns regarding death, guilt, and the role of the feminine in creation, and each in his own fashion is an exemplar of the Spectator Mind. Mary Shelly's *Frankenstein* is structured as a tale within a tale, as an account of the creation of the creature told by Victor Frankenstein to Robert Walton, the captain of a ship that has become ice-bound in the far regions of the Arctic Circle. Victor has been in pursuit of his creation for the purpose of destroying it, but having become ill, he is spotted by Walton and invited to board his ship.

According to Mary Shelley, the novel originated in a vivid waking dream, and in writing the story her dream is translated as the dream of Victor Frankenstein to banish death from life. The creature that Victor creates emerges from the unconscious, and through that creature we are given an image of the shadow of the Spectator Mind. As Victor tells his tale to Walton, it becomes crystal clear that it is the horror of death, the loathsome specter of corruption that lies nestled within human flesh, which drives his dream and his single-minded and obsessive pursuit to create a creature beyond the reach of death. While he initially hesitates if he should attempt to make a being like himself, he does not ever doubt that he can. Here is the willfulness and fixed certitude of the Spectator Mind whose arrogance allows no doubt, and in this, Mary Shelly's Frankenstein is closer in spirit to Byron's Manfred than to the poet in Percy Shelley's "Mont Blanc." Victor and Manfred do not possess that capacity for negative gnosis described above, that ability to undulate between the power of mind to convert nature into a double of itself and the unrelenting quality of fate and necessity that marks our condition as incarnated mind. Manfred and Victor are certain of their ability to dominate and transcend the forces of the natural world, to bend them to their will, including the fate of death. Manfred asserts that he dies from his own free will, and Victor will erase death from the equation of life. And so it is no surprise that Victor says to Walton, "Life and death appeared to me ideal bounds, which I should first break through, and pour a torrent of light into our dark world."[45] The polarity of light and dark is to be sundered by a flood of light that will eclipse darkness. The melting polar ice is this banished darkness that threatens to flood the soul of the Spectator Mind and the coastal cities of the world, the flood of rising waters that threatens to re-draw the earth that the Spectator Mind began to map so long ago.

Victor's motive for his work rests within that spirit of revenge discussed earlier in relation to Shelley's poet. The Spectator Mind, I said, was born in the spirit of revenge against despair, born as that dream of mind, which, in taking leave of its senses, breaks its bonds with and takes flight from nature, and which in this flight anoints itself as superior to nature. For Victor, the despair is rooted specifically in the flesh as *"memento mori,"* and in this context Victor raises the mind that is superior to nature to the status of a creator god. "A new species," he says to Walton, "would bless me as its creator and source; many happy and excellent natures would owe their being to me." Here the Spectator Mind has become the Christian father god in the sky, the paternal god who is all light and goodness, and Victor assures Walton that he is owed the same obedience and admiration. "No father could claim the gratitude of his child so completely as I should deserve theirs."[46]

In the novel Mary Shelley presents this dimension of Victor's inflated image of himself as a creator god through the creature, Victor's double, that he continuously attempts to banish. The creature educates himself by reading Milton's *Paradise Lost.* But, as Joyce Carol Oates says in her commentary on the novel, the creature "reads Milton's great epic as if it were a 'true history' giving the picture of an omnipotent God warring with His creatures." His education is that of the soul, and it reflects the deeper wisdom of the shadow, the wisdom of the cast-off parts of the Spectator Mind. Indeed, throughout the novel the creature is "far wiser and more magnanimous than his creator."[47]

In this regard, the relation between the creature and Victor is very much like the relation between Job and Yahweh as depicted by Jung.[48] Like Job, the creature is the one who calls the creator god into consciousness. He does so through his suffering. His suffering is the vehicle that awakens soul. The creature is the symptomatic voice of the unconscious of the Spectator Mind, calling it to remember what it would forget and deny. That the creature has no name is telling. What is unconscious, what lies in exile, has no name until it is made conscious. In telling his story to Walton, the creature speaks through Victor, and, as Oates asserts, this story "is a parable for our time, an enduring prophecy, a remarkably acute diagnosis of the lethal nature of *denial*; denial of responsibility for one's actions, denial of the shadow-self locked within consciousness,"[49] to which I would add "and frozen in the ice."

Victor's dream of banishing death ends in a nightmare of multiple deaths. Indeed, the death that Victor would banish from life haunts the novel and fills him with the same unrelenting guilt that haunted Byron's Manfred. The creature whom Victor has abandoned first murders William, Victor's younger brother. A peasant girl, Justine Moritz, is falsely accused of the murder and is executed for it. Henry Clerval, Victor's boyhood friend, is also murdered by the creature as is Victor's bride, Elizabeth Lavenza. His father too dies as a result of the shock and grief of these deaths. Finally, Victor himself dies after he has told his tale to Walton. He dies in the frozen Arctic regions, and after his creation has wept over the body of his creator, has felt the deep sting of his solitude, loneliness, and abandonment, he too departs for the farthest regions of the northern ice to die.

But does the creature die? The novel is ambiguous on this point. That he intends to die is clear, since he says he will seek the most northern reaches of the globe and there he will set himself on fire and "consume to ashes this miserable frame, that its remains may afford no light to any curious and unhallowed wretch, who would create such another as I have been."[50] The novel ends, however, not with this definitive act. We know only that in the penultimate line the creature leaps from the ship as he speaks of his intention. In the final line, Mary Shelley gives us the last view of Victor's dream through the eyes of Walton: "He was soon borne away by the waves, and lost in darkness and distance."[51]

We should not miss the ironic twists in the story here. Victor would have flooded the darkness of the world with light, and now his creature will immolate himself to extinguish the light. In addition, Victor's dream, which as exemplar of the dream of the Spectator Mind would have banished that darkness through the distant vision of the despotic eye, now ends in darkness and distance. In these ironic twists, we reach the archetypal depths of the story. The unconscious never dies. It knows neither time nor death. And so this symptomatic personification of the Spectator Mind still lingers there in the frozen Polar Regions, at the farthest boundaries of the world, at the extreme edges of consciousness. The fire of self-immolation is still burning, and it is this fire in the unconscious of the Spectator Mind that is haunting us now in the form of the melting ice, in particular, and the global crisis of climate change, in general. The creature still burns there in the most remote places of the planet, and here in our gardens and within the collective psyche.

Victor Frankenstein and all that he has abandoned lies buried in the frozen ice; and, as the carriers of the Spectator Mind and all that within ourselves that has been abandoned, we lie there with him and beside the creature who did weep at his creator's death. The melting ice is also those tears, feelings locked up and buried deep within that icy cold. Those tears are the tears never shed by the despotic eye.

There is one other aspect of the Frankenstein story that has to be considered. It is the absence of the feminine in the creature's "birth."

Victor's creature is not born of woman. He is a motherless creature, an unnatural being spawned from the mind of man and man alone. Oates says, "he is...a parody of the Word or the Idea made flesh."[52] This parody of the act of creation, which disowns the feminine, is amplified when Victor demolishes the mate that his creature had begged him to produce in order to assuage his loneliness. At first Victor agrees, but, horrified at what he is doing and fearful that together they will produce a race of hideous offspring, he destroys the second creature and dumps the remains into a deep lake. Victor, as exemplar of the Spectator Mind, repeats his initial banishment of the feminine in this act. Dumped into the deep waters of the lake, the feminine is exiled to the unconscious.

The creature of this unnatural genesis is in his form the disowned and disfigured image of the split between the masculine and feminine in creation. In his form he is, I would suggest, an image that anticipates Jung's *Answer to Job* and which personifies what happens when Yahweh forgets Sophia, when the feminine principle is exiled from the work of creation. Moreover, this splitting of the masculine and feminine amplifies the split between light and darkness that animates Victor's dream to flood the darkness of the world with light. The darkness of the world is the darkness of matter, and the darkness of matter is identified with the feminine, while light becomes the symbol of the masculine mind. Victor's creature arises from the abyss formed from the fissure of these splits between matter and mind, darkness and light, the feminine and the masculine, and indeed he continues to rise from the cracks in the polar ice, its fearful noise the howl of that thing we have made and abandoned, which disturbs the sleep of the Spectator Mind even as it continues its dream.

At the other end of the *Axis Mundi*, in the frozen landscapes of the Antarctic Seas, Coleridge's *The Rime of the Ancient Mariner* adds to our psychological understanding of the melting polar ice. It begins as a tale told by the Ancient Mariner to the Wedding Guest, whom the Ancient Mariner stops on his way to that ceremony. In this respect, Coleridge's poem takes the same form as Mary Shelley's novel. The Ancient Mariner, like Victor Frankenstein, addresses his story to a witness; and, as we read both tales, it is we who are being asked to listen. But the Wedding Guest, unlike the sea captain Walton to whom Victor tells his story, carries a specific archetypal charge. He is on his way to a marriage ceremony, a joining of the masculine and the feminine which the Spectator Mind has sundered, and it is that journey—and our journey—that is interrupted by the Ancient Mariner. The interruption suggests that the marriage of the masculine and the feminine cannot take place unconsciously. The Wedding Guest has to pause. The tale of the Ancient Mariner has to be heard. The wedding ceremony, the joining of Queen and King, has to re-member what has been broken.

The Jungian analyst Thomas Elsner has written a most incisive archetypal amplification of Coleridge's *The Rime of the Ancient Mariner*, and it is his extraordinary work that guides my reflections in this essay. In the early part of his work, he situates Coleridge's poem within the same context of the split that has taken place between mind and nature, and which I have elaborated here in terms of the Spectator Mind, and he emphasizes how this split is a crisis of soul and world. Elsner writes, for example, "The Western psyche is split today, perhaps more than it has ever been, so much so that we are in an extreme environmental and psychological crisis." In addition, he shows how the split Western psyche is a variation of the split in the Christian psyche between Christ and Serpent. The Spectator Mind of Western technological consciousness is a creator god, which, like the Christian god, is a god of goodness and light split off from its own darkness. In this respect Elsner's work offers strong support of the view expressed in this essay that beneath the frozen ice lie the dark aspects of the Christian god, which have been exiled by the creator god of the Spectator Mind. The wedding guest on the way to the wedding is, therefore, also on the way to the resurrection of the sacred. Elsner writes,

> Much of Coleridge's terrible suffering, including his opium
> addiction and his horrendous nightmares, can be explained by
> the burden of carrying a *deus abscontidus*, an unknown god, a
> burden which was too much for him, carried at a time which
> was too early.[53]

In this respect, Coleridge's poem, like Shelley's novel, is a prophetic
diagnosis of the extreme religious and environmental crises of our age,
and an early warning of the consequences of their union, when a sense
of the sacred, twisted into religious fundamentalism, is married to the
technological willfulness of the Spectator Mind.

The Ancient Mariner is a personification of the Spectator Mind,
and like Mary Shelley's novel, the poem by Coleridge begins in a dream.
While the dream was not one dreamed by Coleridge but by his
neighbor, Mr. Cruickshank, its image of a ghost ship that sailed toward
the dreamer from out of the setting sun had a profound impact on
Coleridge. Elsner says, "this eerie product of the unconscious got under
the poet's skin…and became the inspiration for a poem." Indeed, Elsner
says, the Rime "was the poem [Coleridge] was born to write."[54] That
Coleridge's poem began with a dream, that Mary Shelley's novel and
Ernest Shackleton's voyages to the poles began with a dream, and that
Helen Thayer's account of her solo voyage to the magnetic north pole
was called *Polar Dream*, suggest that not only have we been dreaming
the ice, but also that the ice has been dreaming itself through us. The
landscapes of frozen ice are places in the geographies of the world and
the soul, and to explore them "outwardly" in journeys to those far places
at the top and bottom of the world is also to explore them "inwardly"
in journeys to the heights and depths of soul.

The Ancient Mariner, like Shelley's poet on Mont Blanc, Byron's
Manfred, and Mary Shelley's Victor Frankenstein, sins against nature.
His specific crime is shooting the albatross, and this act, according to
Elsner, is "…the basic problem of the modern West." It is the basic
problem because the Mariner's arrow is aimed at a bird that is just an
object. For Coleridge, "Objects perceived as objects are soon rendered
fixed and dead," and this vision is for him "Satanic" and heralds the
"fall of man."[55]

The device that the Mariner uses to launch his arrow is the
crossbow, which symbolizes a technological version of the cross. In this
convergence we have again that enfolding of the Christian story with

that of technology. Both tales, as we have seen, depict a kind of imperialism of mind against the natural world, one spiritual and the other materialistic. Both symbolize attitudes of separation and division. Elsner writes, "The symbolism of the cross is a division into opposites which symbolizes separation from nature," and he quotes Jung to the same effect when, with respect to crosses, Jung asks, "Do they not mean a sacrifice of the natural?" Christ, nailed to a tree, triumphs over death with his resurrection. Spirit overcomes matter. The Spectator Mind becomes a creator god.

When the Mariner launches his arrow from the crossbow, he is in effect the personification of a mind not only distant but also divorced from nature. Of course, the arrow is an old instrument, and the ability to distance oneself from nature is, as Erwin Strauss has shown in his classic phenomenological essay, "The Upright Posture,"[56] as old as the ability to stand upright as a subject over against the world as object and say "I." My point, therefore, has not been that only with the development of linear perspective has this ability arisen. On the contrary, my point has been that with that development we have transformed a possibility into a metaphysics, a condition into a method, a way of being into a way of knowing that has transformed distance into separation and has made the world into a double of that "I." In this context, when the Mariner shoots his arrow, he is a personification of the man on the hill depicted in Figure 2. In addition, he is a prophetic image of the increasing distance that the Spectator Mind has placed between itself and the world. The atomic bomb dropped on Hiroshima is psychologically the same instrument as the arrow. Both kill at a distance, which diminishes and even eclipses one's feeling connection to the action. Elsner's description of the Mariner's arrow is an apt portrayal of the despotic eye of the Spectator Mind:

> The Mariner's arrow is the embodiment of Logos, the driving force of power, control, the intellect and will which separates us from nature and breaks our primal bond with the roots of being…It embodies all the virtues of modern progress, the intellect, the sharp, penetrating, clear cutting, and rational willpower. It is the intellectual and egocentric will to power, the impulse to dominate, control, and understand nature.[57]

As the embodiment of Logos, this arrow that flies toward its target is "the modern experience of the devil—a cold, intelligent, efficient rationalism at the root of which is a frozen or retarded feeling function."[58] This frozen feeling function is a primary characteristic of the despotic eye, the eye that is unmoved by what it sees, the eye that fixed in its place never takes its eye off the goal, the eye that never blinks and never sheds a tear. In this respect, the fixed and penetrating gaze of the despotic eye is itself an arrow. "An arrow humming through the air is an image of intent, of aiming deliberately towards a goal, and of the power to hit the target, and achieve one's objective."[59]

In achieving its objective, in slaying the albatross, the Mariner commits the "unpardonable sin…a real sin against the Holy Spirit."[60] As a crime against the Holy Spirit, the murder of the albatross amounts to the destruction of the spirit of nature. The same tension between mind and nature that we saw in Shelley's poet, Byron's Manfred, and Victor's hubris is played out in this violent act. Speaking of the Mariner, Elsner says, "We have ceased to recognize the divinity of nature—and the world is in an ecological crisis."[61] But what he says of the Mariner can be said of the other three personifications of the Spectator Mind we have considered. "We have all of us in the modern West become a crew of trigger-happy Mariners in relation to the spirit in nature." We have all us become trigger-happy cowboys ready to fix our gaze, not blink, and take aim at what is other to ourselves. And as Mariner or cowboy, as the poet dizzy at the abyss or the one ensconced in his tower, or as the creator god in pursuit of his creature in order to destroy him, "we are peculiarly and dangerously oblivious of what we are doing, and of its consequences."[62] The melting ice protests against this vision and its state of denial.

The albatross is the primary symbol of the poem, and Elsner provides an extensive amplification of its potential meanings without reducing the symbol to any fixed category. For the purposes of this essay, it is important to note that as a symbol the albatross is an expression of the transcendent function, which means that it bridges the gap between consciousness and the unconscious. In killing the bird, then, the Mariner destroys the bridge between conscious and unconscious, the bridge between mind and nature. He kills, as Elsner notes, the symbolic attitude. The consequence of such an action is that the wisdom of the unconscious is replaced by the power of the will. This shift is portrayed in the most explicit way. The Mariner looses his arrow, it hits its mark, the albatross dies, and the Mariner says, "I shot the Albatross." As Elsner points out, this is the first time the word "I" appears in the poem. He says, "before the Mariner fires his crossbow, there is only an anonymous 'crew,' a 'we' or 'us' or 'mariners,' who all think and act alike."[63] The Mariner's crime, then, is, on one side, an act of dis-crimination. Through the crime, he differentiates himself from the collective. The "I" of the Mariner is born in the region of the polar ice. On the other side, however, there is the temptation to forget that the "I" who shoots the albatross is a part of nature and not apart from it.

The Mariner fares no better than the other three personifications of the Spectator Mind we have considered. Elsner says this of the Mariner's action:

> In shooting down the bird, the Mariner has killed the unconscious wisdom and Eros by which he might get back home and he has broken his bond with nature. By asserting his power and will over against the living symbol, he has unwittingly started the process of his own destruction.[64]

To solve the problem of the melting ice, the attitudes of the Spectator Mind will have to be dissolved. The melting ice is the way home.

But the Mariner does not find his way home. After he has shot the albatross, the sun rises and blows the fog and mist away. For a time all seems well, but soon the sun, that principle of illumination and consciousness, becomes oppressive. It is the sun at high noon, the time of its maximum brilliance that banishes all shadow from the world, and under its pitiless glare the waters grow still and all movement ceases:

> Day after day, day after day,
> We stuck, nor breath nor motion;
> As idle as a painted ship,
> Upon a painted ocean.[65]

Prophecy is at work in these poetic images. Meditating on these events, Elsner asks, "Looking forward in time, is this not our contemporary predicament?"[66] It is. The despotic eye of the Spectator Mind is consciousness at its brightest illumination. It is a consciousness whose knowledge is beyond the shadow of a doubt, a consciousness that casts no shadows and scrubs the world of its shadows, that kind of vision that Victor Frankenstein embraced when he said he would flood the world with light. In this completely enlightened world the Mariner's ship shrinks to a two-dimensional existence. A painted ship upon a painted ocean, it offers the illusion of depth, just as linear perspective vision, which, in inaugurating the illusion of depth on a two-dimensional plane, reduced the vertical dimensions of the world to a horizontal domain stretching toward an infinite horizon. That glaring noonday sun, brought into being by the Mariner's eye that loosed the arrow from its bow, still shines upon our world, melting the ice. "Our collective sun has got stuck overhead and is never going down anymore. Contemporary Western culture is stuck in an exclusively conscious world."[67]

I can touch upon only one more element in the poem. It is the moment when the Mariner sees the water snakes. Elsner says, "This vision of the water snakes and the flash of golden fire is the redemptive moment in the poem..."[68] The Mariner sees the water snakes in the shadow of the ship and in a dark light that shines from the moon. Filled with love for these creatures that earlier he had cursed, he now blesses them, and when he does, the dead albatross, which the crew had hung around his neck, falls away. Seen now in a different light, in the shadow of the ship cast by the dark light of the moon, all that had been banished into the depths by the penetrating glare of the blazing sun now emerges from below. "A new light is born from the darkness."[69] It is born from the darkness that both the Christian and the Spectator Minds had sundered from their vision. The Mariner's redemption, however, is short-lived. He is, in the end, unable to hold the tension between the light of the sun and the darkness of the moon. He is unable to wed what is above with what is below.

Earlier I said the Mariner does not find his way home, and Coleridge ends his poem in a way that does not augur well for us who are the archetypal descendants of the Ancient Mariner/Spectator Mind. As he finishes his tale, the Mariner and the Wedding Guest hear two different kinds of music. One comes from the bride and her maids singing at the wedding, while the other is the sound of the vesper bell coming from the church. In response to these two invitations, the Mariner says:

> O sweeter than the marriage-feast,
> Tis sweeter far to me,
> To walk together to the kirk
> With a goodly company![70]

The Mariner chooses the church. "Stunned," the Wedding Guest turns away from the Bridegroom's door "forlorn." The journey to the wedding of the masculine and the feminine that was interrupted is not completed. In the last two lines Coleridge says of the Wedding Guest, "A sadder and a wiser man/ He rose the morrow morn."[71] That wisdom is some rough measure of how difficult it was for the Mariner, who, despite his journey, was unable to choose the song of the wedding instead of the conventional vesper of the church. That wisdom is also an index of how difficult it is for the Spectator Mind, so far removed from the world at the vanishing point, to be addressed by the melting polar ice.

We are all of us today polar explorers, just as we have been, as I wrote in *Technology as Symptom and Dream*, all of us astronauts. Both are archetypal personifications of the Spectator Mind, and as the Astronaut leaves the body behind to depart Earth, the Polar Explorer brings the Astronaut back down to earth, to remind him/her not to forget the melting ice. Astronaut and Polar Explorer hold the tension of the opposites between the mind that takes leave of its senses and the body that is drawn to the frozen poles. And just as the lunar footprint is the trace of the one, the carbon footprint is the trace of the other. They intersect, they tell two sides of the same story. Coleridge understood this connection. Fascinated by the moon, he wrote, "Moon has little or no atmosphere. Its ocean is frozen. It is not yet inhabited, but may be in time." Commenting on this passage, Elsner says, "the barren land of ice and snow is a moonscape."[72] Moon and ice: as above, so below!

VIII. Dark Light

In this essay, I have described the genesis of the Spectator Mind and have amplified it through discussions of four literary personifications. Each of these personifications presents a diagnostic and prophetic image of the shadow sides of the Spectator Mind. The melting polar ice is the symptomatic expression of these shadows, an event in the world and an experience of the collective soul, the ecological unconscious of the environmental crisis. There can be no solution to this crisis without some radical change in the fixed attitudes of the Spectator Mind, no solution without some sacrifice of its—our—ways of being in the world, no solution without some alchemical dissolution, an ego-cide of sorts,[73] a symbolic death in place of the countless deaths that it has brought in its wake. For this transformation to take place we will have to develop new rituals, which make room for what has been discarded and ignored, rituals that finally make a place for the inconvenient truth of the unconscious aspect of this crisis. In 1946, Jung said the unconscious "is of absolutely revolutionary significance in that it could radically alter our view of the world."[74]

The melting polar ice is a danger, but it is also an opportunity to radically alter our view of the world. It is a chance to heal the split between mind and nature, a chance to reanimate an aesthetic sensibility that unfreezes the feeling connection that has been lost in the gaze of the despotic eye, a chance to remember the feminine principle in the work of creation, a chance to recover a sense of the sacred within an integrated spirituality that honors the darkness in the light, and a chance to restore the symbolic attitude that bridges the gap between conscious and unconscious, an attitude that is able to witness in the albatross the extraordinary in the ordinary, the miracle in the mundane, the numinous in nature.

But the four literary amplifications of the Spectator Mind do not offer much hope that these changes will or can occur. To cite just one example here, the snakes whose light shines in the shadow of the Mariner's ship and in the darkness of the moon were not integrated into the Mariner's life. For him to do so, for Coleridge to have done so, would have required that the Serpent be given its place on the cross alongside the Christ. Moreover, the pace of technology since Coleridge's day, since the days of Percy and Mary Shelley, since the days of Byron, has exponentially increased. Has technology finally exhausted soul? Is there a place for soul under the gaze of the despotic eye? Is there still a place for depth psychology in this age of technological wizardry where we live at the speed of light, inundated with information from mass media culture and flooded with distractions that invite us to benumb ourselves and renew the Spectator Mind's desire for oblivion?

The temperature is rising—literally on the planet—and psychologically in fevers of fear and dread. And the waters are rising—literally with the melting polar ice—but also psychologically, in dreams that I have been collecting individually, and, collectively, in dark prophesies about the future. Is there still time to approach the melting ice at the poles of the world as a symptom and dream?

I began this essay in the garden and confessed sorrow over the plight of our climate. And now I have a similar feeling, but also different, more intense, and perhaps even more hopeless. I write from this place of near despair, perhaps even as a way to silence it. The pull to go numb, to fall asleep, to be distracted, to grasp at fixed and easy solutions is strong. The collective, archetypal unconscious at the core of the melting ice is an inconvenient truth. But it is truth we cannot afford to ignore. Depth psychology has a special obligation to this truth.

NOTES

1. Robert Romanyshyn, *Technology as Symptom and Dream* (London, New York: Routledge, 1989/2000).

2. Quoted in Robert Romansyhyn, *The Wounded Researcher: Research with Soul in Mind* (New Orleans: Spring Journal Books, 2007), p. 343. The second part of the quotation is from Emanuel Levinas as quoted by Beebe in his book, *Integrity in Depth* (New York: Fromm International Publishing, 1995), p. 33.

3. Verlyn Klinkenborg, "Some doubts upon entering a new carboniferous era," in *International Herald Tribune*, June 25, 2008, p. 9.

4. For a psychological treatment of metaphor, see Robert Romanyshyn, *Mirror and Metaphor: Images and Stories of Psychological Life* (Pittsburgh, Pa: Trivium Publications, 2001).

5. Klinkenborg.

6. *Ibid.*

7. *Ibid.*

8. *Ibid.*

9. For an example of cultural therapeutics, see Robert Romanyshyn, "The Despotic Eye," in *The Changing Reality of Modern Man: Essays in Honor of J. H. van den Berg*, ed. Dreyer Kruger (Cape Town: Juta and Co., 1984), pp. 103-105.

10. Romanyshyn, *Technology*, p. 172.

11. James Hillman and Michael Ventura, *We've Had a Hundred Years of Psychotherapy—and the World's Getting Worse* (San Francisco, CA: Harper, 1992).

12. Romanyshyn, *Technology*, p. 33.

13. *Ibid.*, p. 39.

14. Maurice Merleau-Ponty as quoted in Romanyshyn, "Unconscious as a Lateral Depth," in *Continental Philosophy in America*, ed. Hugh Silverman, John Sallis, Thomas M. Seebohm (Pittsburgh, PA.: Duquesne University Press, 1983), p. 236.

15. Rainer Maria Rilke, *Duino Elegies*, trans. J. B. Leishman and Stephen Spender (New York: W. W. Norton, 1939), p. 75.

16. Romanyshyn, *Technology*, p. 38.

17. *Ibid.*, p. 36.

18. *Ibid.*, p. 38, my italics.

19. *Ibid.*, p. 98.

20. See reference cited in note 9.

21. Quoted in Eric G. Wilson, *The Spiritual History of Ice: Romanticism, Science, and the Imagination* (New York: Palgrave MacMillan, 2003), pp. 141-142.

22. Helen Thayer, *Polar Dream* (Troutdale, OR.: New Sage Press, 2002).

23. Wilson, p. 1.

24. *Ibid.*, p. 131.

25. *Ibid.*, p. 125.

26. *Ibid.*

27. *Ibid.*, p. 123.

28. *Ibid.*, p. 122.

29. *Ibid.*

30. *Ibid.*, p. 126.

31. Romanyshyn, *The Wounded Researcher.*

32. Wilson, p. 112.

33. Susan Rowland, *Jung as a Writer* (New York: Routledge, 2005) p. 23.

34. Marie-Louise von Franz, *Alchemy* (Toronto: Inner City Books, 1980) p. 37.

35. Wilson, p. 128.

36. *Ibid.*, pp. 142-143.

37. Stanton Marlan, *The Black Sun: The Alchemy and Art of Darkness* (College Station, Texas: A&M University Press, 2005).

38. *Ibid.*, p. 5.

39. *Ibid.*, p. 149.

40. Wilson, p. 153.

41. Marlan, p.149.

42. Wilson, p. 134.

43. *Ibid.*, p. 135.

44. *Ibid.*, p. 137.

45. Mary Wollstonecraft Shelley, *Frankenstein: Or, The Modern Prometheus* (Berkeley: University of California Press, 1984), p. 47.

46. *Ibid.*, pp. 47-49.

47. Joyce Carol Oates, "Frankenstein's Fallen Angel," in Shelley, *Frankenstein*, p. 244.

48. C. G. Jung, *The Collected Works of C.G. Jung*, Vol. 11, trans. R. F. C. Hull (Princeton: Princeton University Press, 1952/1958).

49. Oates, p. 252. Author's italics.

50. Shelley, p. 235.

51. *Ibid.*, p. 237.

52. Oates, p. 251.

53. Thomas Elsner, *Coleridge's The Rime of the Ancient Mariner: A Psychological Interpretation*, p. 9. (This unpublished manuscript was submitted to the Research and Training Center for Depth Psychology According to C. G. Jung and Marie-Louise von Franz, Zurich, Switzerland, September, 2005, as his thesis for a Diploma in Analytical Psychology).

54. *Ibid.*, p. 25.

55. *Ibid.*, p. 66.

56. Erwin W. Straus, "The Upright Posture," in *Phenomenological Psychology* (New York: Basic Books, 1966).

57. Elsner, p. 63.

58. *Ibid.*, p. 64.

59. *Ibid.*, p. 63.

60. *Ibid.*, p. 60.

61. *Ibid.*, p. 63.

62. *Ibid.*

63. *Ibid.*, p. 66.

64. *Ibid.*, p. 60.

65. Samuel Taylor Coleridge, *The Rime of the Ancient Mariner* (New York: Dover Publications, 1970), p. 20.

66. Elsner, p. 75.

67. *Ibid.*

68. *Ibid.*, p. 118.

69. *Ibid.*, p. 120.

70. Coleridge, p. 74.

71. *Ibid.*, p. 76.

72. Elsner, p. 50.

73. The term ego-cide is coined by David Rosen to describe a kind of symbolic death that can result in radical transformation. The melting polar ice will require this kind of symbolic death of the Spectator Mind if we are to have any chance of transformative healing. David Rosen, *Transforming Depression: Healing the Soul Through Creativity* (York Beach, Maine: Nicolas-Hays, 2002).

74. Jung, *CW* 8, § 369.

THANATOS IN CYBERSPACE: DEATH, MYTHOLOGY, AND THE INTERNET

MIKITA BROTTMAN

T
he greater and wider the influence of cyberspace in our lives, the more fertile the mythology it both disseminates and acquires. An increasing number of us are coming to rely on the Internet for basic communication, yet most of us have very little knowledge of coding, programming, or the other basics of computer technology. In other words, many of us have a deep emotional investment in a system whose workings we neither understand, nor have much control over; in fact, computer technology can seem random and chaotic, especially when things go wrong. Even those who have a basic knowledge of programming rarely understand all its complex details, and, as a result, often end up appropriating templates based on a programming device, system, or language they don't fully understand. A good example of this is the phenomenon that has come to be known as "cargo cult" or "voodoo" programming—the name given to what happens when large chunks of code are simply copied from one program to the next with no understanding of how (or even if) the coding works. The coding, then, acquires a symbolic, ritual meaning, which, along with metaphors of viruses, vectors, infections, and worms, suggests that, at its deepest level, our conception of cyberspace is governed by magical thinking.

Mikita Brottman has a Ph.D. in English Language and Literature from Oxford University and is a psychoanalyst in private practice. She is the author of a number of books on the pathological aspects of contemporary popular culture, and is currently Chair of the Program in Engaged Humanities at Pacifica Graduate Institute.

In psychoanalytic terms, magical thinking refers to the unconsciously held belief that our own thoughts can influence external events; it emerges from a misperception of self-boundaries. Everyday forms of magical thinking include faith, superstition, taboo, paranoia, belief in the special power of words, and the misperception of symbols for their referents. In this article, I want to consider the particular kind of magical thinking that has developed in relation to cyberspace, and, in particular, how it affects the way we think about death.

"The Transcendence Industries"

Imagine sitting down to check your e-mail and finding a message from your mother, who died six months ago, telling you how much she loved you, and reminding you that her cat is due to visit the vet. If it sounds like a frightening prospect, it doesn't have to be. It may just mean that, before she died, your mother decided to take advantage of a posthumous e-mail service, which, for a reasonable fee, offers you the chance to show your loved ones how much (or how little) you cared by leaving them each an e-mail to be delivered after you pass on.

Posthumous e-mail services are an example of what have been described as the "transcendence industries," enterprises that can be loosely divided into two categories: those that place emphasis on pragmatic issues, and those that cater to emotional fears and needs (though there is, of course, much overlap between the two). The practical services allow you to leave vital posthumous instructions for family and friends concerning such things as funeral arrangements, financial records, estate details, and insurance plans. An example of this kind of enterprise is YouDeparted.com ("Prepare for the unexpected")—the name has recently changed to AssetLock ("Guarantee Your Legacy")—whose website emphasizes that their service "isn't about social networking for the dead or sending scary messages from the grave:"

> It's about organizing your life… Would your family know the
> details if something happened to you? How would they access
> your email and online accounts? Who would know to take care
> of all the things you were responsible for? Taxes? Insurance?
> Where is the will or trust? Where is the key to the safe deposit
> box? What is the combination to your gym locker?

Ironically, although the emphasis is on practical concerns, sites like YouDeparted rarely mention the word "death," preferring such euphemisms as "if something should happen to you" or "when the time comes." An interesting exception is DeathSwitch.com, a computer program invented by a psychiatry professor at Baylor University that lets you ensure that after you die, encrypted details like computer passwords and bank account numbers are automatically transmitted to your pre-selected loved ones. It's difficult to measure the popularity of these "transcendence services," not only because the names of users are kept confidential, but because—for obvious reasons—it's impossible to obtain customer feedback. YouDeparted does offer prospective clients a "User Testimonial" from "Charles, Tokyo, Japan," who comments: "I live abroad and if something had happened to me before I started using YouDeparted, I don't really know how my family would have sorted everything out." Of course, Charles still doesn't know how his family will "sort everything out," if "something happens to him," but— having enrolled in YouDeparted—he presumably feels more confident that "when the time comes," all his papers will be in order.

Other sites offer posthumous services directed at emotional, rather than practical needs. Through such slogans as "you only die once" and "tomorrow may never come," sites like TheLastEmail.com and LetterFromBeyond.com encourage users to prepare e-mails to be sent to family members after they die—or even an old-fashioned letter, "a gift your loved ones will treasure for a lifetime." "After departing," we're told, "a message from the grave can be a great relief to the ones you leave behind."

Most of these sites are built around cheap-looking templates and formulaic imagery of old people looking happy and peaceful. The one exception, PostExpression, has the most clearly articulated vision, which can be summed up by the site's slogan "Death ends a life, not a relationship." In the words of the site's founder, Irish software engineer Mark Wrafter, "PostExpression allows you to communicate with people after you've died"—something everyone needs, according Wrafter. If you leave friends and family behind when you die, PostExpression "gives you the opportunity to communicate final words of encouragement, confession and love." But the service offers other options, too, for those with more complex and ambivalent emotions. "If you have Loved and Lost," urges PostExpression, "Tell that person how you feel about them." Even if "you've been dealt a bad hand in life" and you're probably going to die alone and unloved, you can still communicate with the world on the PostExpression Blog, a place for you to "let the world hear what you have to say," giving you "that final flamboyant finale you so richly deserve." To date, however, no such deserving soul has yet passed on, since the PostExpression blog remains a hollow void.

PostExpression also addresses the intricate netiquette of virtual relationships, since, as Wrafter points out, "many people now have more friends online than off." This service considers the posthumous needs of the techno-savvy, habitués of MySpace, LiveJournal, Flickr, and other community-based sites, as well as online gamers who can spend years building up an in-game personality and maintaining virtual relationships. "People know you, engage with you, expect your presence. Suddenly you are gone. It's inexplicable," says Wrafter. In cases like this, "PostExpression can be used to break the news of your death to members of your online or gaming community, sending them a posthumous message as a group, with a separate message for your best friend, which could include your login details so they can maintain your profile or even take over your avatar, if you see fit." You may be dead, but the game must go on.

One of the best-known networking sites for young people is MySpace.com, which has recently spawned a controversial, unaffiliated offshoot, MyDeathSpace.com, to catalogue the deaths of MySpace members, archive their sites, and link to their profiles. MyDeathSpace was founded and launched in December 2005 by Mike Patterson, a 27-year-old legal clerk from California, who conceived of the site— which brings in no revenue—as a way to mourn the loss of online friends and those who live far away. Not surprisingly, given the average age of MySpace users, the most frequent causes of death on MyDeathSpace are car accidents, unintentional overdoses, and suicide, though there are also some reports of murders and military deaths. Anyone can submit an entry to the site, which apparently receives more than 100,000 hits per day, and currently lists nearly 3000 deaths, mostly of U.S. teenagers (inactive profiles are removed only at the request of a family member).[1]

The tone of these online obituaries varies from reverent to unrestrained, though even the most respectful tend to be erratic in spelling and grammar, often incorporating Instant Message slang and abbreviations as well as logos, buttons, flashing signs, clipart, emoticons, and other net-based gadgetry. Some obituaries are reproduced from local newspapers, but when they are transposed to MyDeathSpace, they appear suddenly surrounded by ads for Texas Hold 'Em and Tanya's Bath and Body Care. Similarly, RIPs and condolences are mixed, often indiscriminately, with private jokes, slang, profanity, advertisements, and links to other members' sites. In the forums, which include chat rooms for suicide survivors and tips for suicide prevention, notices ask users to "please be respectful," and potential contributors are warned, "moderators will remove any obscene or offensive messages."

The practical advantages of a digital memorial page are clear. Losses can be announced online, and obituaries linked to photographs, music, videos, and condolence registers. Those unable to attend the funeral service can watch or listen online, and contribute their own memorial pictures and videos. Nevertheless, MyDeathSpace has its detractors, who see the site as a horrifying vampire's nest deep in the Internet's heart of darkness. Other, more temperate critics accuse the site of catering to morbid curiosity, arguing that its interactive nature subtly panders to young people's denial of death by encouraging them to believe the deceased are still with us, since their sites are still live, and users may continue to post messages there.[2] In an article by Matthew Doyal Proctor[3] in *FALSE* magazine, the site is described as "a virtual graveyard without tombstones or flowers ... where reality blurs into fiction and the living greet the dead." Elsewhere, Proctor describes the site as a "purgatory deep in the shadows of cyberspace," where "souls are trapped forever in their MySpace profiles." Similarly, in a recent essay, scholar Amelia Guemarin describes MyDeathSpace as a "phantom archive" in which, through their profiles, individuals are preserved "in the technology of animation." She writes:

> MySpace users live as their profiles—they represent themselves online through images, sounds, and text—when they die, they "live on and survive" as their profiles. In life, through "a spectacular metaphysic of technology," the body is transferred from person to profile, death only makes this transference more concrete as the body can no longer exist outside of the profile, but will exist forever in the media of MySpace.[4]

Unsurprisingly, there has also been talk of a MyDeathSpace curse, and deceased members are reputed to haunt anyone who tries to remove their profiles—rumors that have circulated as a result of particular well-publicized synchronicities. One of these involved Danielle Toal, 23, who in October 2006 wrote on her MySpace site that a Ouija board had said she would die in her twenties, in a car crash. Four months later, on January 18, 2007, she was killed in a car being driven by 59-year-old Gary Nelson, another MySpace user, whose photo happened to be displayed in Danielle's photo gallery. Another coincidence involved Elizabeth Seholm, 18, a fan of MyDeathSpace and frequent visitor in its chat rooms, who died of a heroin overdose on January 25 2007—a week after Danielle Toal—after being drug-free for six months.[5]

The MyDeathSpace "curse" is perhaps the most conspicuous of its kind, but other networking sites have also attracted rumors of supernatural goings-on. When, in the 12 months between January 2007 and February 2008, 17 young people committed suicide—most of them by hanging—in the small town of Bridgend, in South Wales, part of the blame was directed at the social networking site BeBo, where some of the deceased maintained profiles.[6] On January 27, 2008, the British newspaper *The Independent* reported that police had removed computer equipment from one of the deceased's homes, boasting "Bridgend Deaths: Police Warn of Bebo Suicide Cult" (even though the officer investigating the case denied that "internet suicide links" played any part in their inquiries).[7]

Clearly, incidents like these can easily be explained without evoking the paranormal. Since most social networking sites have thousands of members, it is not statistically improbable that there should be connections between those users who die accidentally. In the case of the Bridgend suicides, there were also familial and social relationships between the deceased, as well as virtual ones. Suicide clusters, especially among young people in a small community, have been reported since ancient times, certainly long before the advent of cyberspace, though social networking sites make an ideal venue for suicide notes. Many people—not only teenagers—find it easier to disclose their feelings online rather than face to face with a family member, therapist, or friend.

Still, when the Internet is somehow involved—however obliquely—in a person's death, the incident is often described as though the computer were somehow complicit, as though it somehow caused the death to happen. It is true, of course, that like any new technology, the Internet facilitates new kinds of crimes.[8] Cases have been reported of murderers, rapists, and child molesters finding their victims online; school shooters have ordered weapons on e-Bay; suicide pacts have been formed in chat rooms, and carried out. Hacker and identity thieves have ruined lives; spree killers have detailed and described their crimes on web forums; disturbed people of all kinds have found kindred spirits in cyberspace. All this is true, but it's also true that the Internet has been an invaluable tool in solving crime. Hard drives, cached files, and e-mails are used increasingly as courtroom evidence; surveillance videos and suspect composites can reach a huge audience when posted online. Beyond this, there are sites devoted to tracking down lost people, locating stolen goods, debunking quacks, and detailing frauds. Clearly, the Internet makes certain kinds of crime possible, but it is also invaluable in preventing and solving other kinds.

CYBERSPACE AND CYBERTIME

When, in his 1962 book *Profiles of the Future*, legendary science fiction author Arthur C. Clarke declared that "any sufficiently advanced technology is indistinguishable from magic,"[9] he was articulating a common superstition about cyberspace, which is often envisaged as a portal through which complex, powerful, and unseen forces can be unleashed—forces that even "experts" can't understand (or control), an electronic shadowland where living people come into contact with the world of the dead.

The anxiety evoked by the idea of posthumous e-mails, "internet suicide pacts," and "live" websites for the dead is just one example of the magical thinking surrounding the Internet, raising the question of why the computer terminal—a chunk of glass and metal—is widely construed to be more dangerous, more frightening, and more powerful than traditional forms of media. After all, the Internet, in its physical manifestation, is nothing more than pixels on a screen, a piece of silicon etched with symbols. Why do we endow it with the mythic power to lure, to corrupt, and to send messages from beyond the grave?

One approach to answering this question involves thinking about what happens to time and space when we're online. The concept of using digital space to represent abstract data is very difficult for many people to grasp. The "space" of cyberspace is basically a consensual illusion with no real-world counterpart, yet we consistently use spatial metaphors to articulate online activities: we go to sites, we enter chat rooms, we explore home pages, and we visit domains. It seems difficult, perhaps even impossible, to think of and talk about this "unreal estate" without using spatial metaphors. References to MyDeathSpace, for example, regularly locate it somewhere "in the depths of Cyberspace," or "on the Internet's margins." Our mythology of the Internet is so tied up with a physical place that cyberspace is believed, often unconsciously, to be a haunting and dream-like dimension that, while in no way separate from the workings of computers, seems to obey its own laws and possess its own reality. Hackers sometimes speak of it as a kind of *bardo*—the term used in *The Tibetan Book of the Dead* to designate the astral plane.[10]

Cyberpsychologists describe how this dimension often becomes a type of "transitional space," an extension of the individual's intrapsychic world. For example, according to John Suler,[11] even people at a developmentally advanced level of object relations may, when using e-mail, have difficulty establishing an accurate sense of the person they're talking to. They may feel, unconsciously, the person is present in the room with them, or somehow "in" the computer. Since we sit and compose e-mails in our own physical space, we tend to think that the e-mail we receive is created in the same way. So if we know the sender of the e-mail is dead, it makes sense to feel, however irrationally, that the message is coming from "beyond the grave."

Something similar is true of Time, which, in cyberspace can seem oddly elastic. From the proliferation of automatic spam and out-of-office replies, we know that our e-mails can be sent automatically—they don't require real human beings to sit and compose them in real time. Yet anyone who uses e-mail on a regular basis has had the experience of receiving a message just as it's written, or very soon thereafter, leading to a palpable feeling of connectedness, of sharing an experience in real time. According to psychologist Michael Fenichel,[12] "many people have a sense of immediacy, constancy, and connectedness" when online, allowing them to feel part of "a different but equally real 'here and now': The Here and Now of Cyberspace."

Fenichel and others have described the potential of the Internet to hypnotize, causing users to feel immersed in the screen, dissociated from their immediate surroundings, even from their body. As Suler puts it, "sitting quietly and staring at the computer monitor can become an altered state of consciousness."[13] Researchers have also been looking into the idea of *telepresence*, which is "the degree to which participants… get the impression of sharing space with the remote site."[14]

Thinkers in the field of depth psychology have generally been wary of technology, regarding it as a binding of the human spirit to the all-consuming logic and rationality of materialist science. Many see the Internet as a trap: a delusion of freedom and progress that wastes our time, draws our energy, and binds us further to the demands of technology. Others, who initially saw radical potential in the Internet's democratizing powers, have since become critical of its wholesale commodification: its porn spam, pop-up ads, and inescapable flood of advertisements. Jungian scholar Robert Romanyshyn has expressed his fears that "our sense of self will become digital, as we float in the empty seas of electronic energy and lose touch with each other even as we are in contact."[15]

Yet there are those who see cyberspace as a locus of profound psychological importance, in which archetypes and images emerge and converge in new, often unexpected ways. Some, such as Mark Stefik[16] in his book *Internet Dreams*, regard cyberspace as a kind of global brain, rather similar to Jung's model of the collective unconscious. Though it has evolved in a very different way from the group spiritual experiences that Jung describes, the Internet, believes Stefik, represents the same collection of mythologies, only in digital form. Computer scientist Ben Goertzel[17] describes the Internet as "a crystallization of the common, collective patterns of the global human mind," and argues that the emergence of the World Wide Web can be seen in terms of the "archetypal Hierarchy of Being."

MASKS AND PERSONAE

It is generally taken for granted that a person's "real self" is revealed only when they appear "in the flesh," as opposed to in the form of text messages and e-mail, for example. The media is full of cautionary myths about online predators and cyberfriends who turn out to be "not who they seem to be," a distinction that assumes the online personality to be a fake veneer of lies smoothing over the "real," flawed, fleshly self.

Why do we make this assumption? It might be worth considering how our online personality says as much about us as our physical body, which, after all, is the result of a random genetic pattern beyond our control, and subject to all kinds of racial, sexual, and cultural prejudices, however unintentional. Indeed, for many people, one of the great advantages of cyberspace relationships is that, online, they can be who they "really are," rather than being judged by their age, gender, race, and other real-world markers of "identity."

As Poster,[18] Turkle,[19] Stone,[20] and others have argued, the online self can be fragmented and multiple. Cyberspace gives us the freedom to obscure and re-create aspects of our identity. It can, in Jungian terms, allow us to explore different manifestations of universal archetypes, to try on masks expressing a wide range of personae, allowing us come to terms with different aspects of our unconscious. Social psychologist Kenneth Gergen[21] remarks that, in cyberspace, individual notions of self can, under the right conditions, vanish into a stage of relatedness. "One ceases to believe in a self independent of the relations in which he or she is embedded… we live in each others' brains as voices, images, words on screens." From a psychoanalytic perspective, of course, it can be extremely liberating to break down the illusion of a coherent, unified, integral self.

In her book *Life on the Screen*, Sherry Turkle[22] makes the case that, like the self that emerges in the analytic encounter, whose slightest shifts can come under the most intense scrutiny, cyberspace encourages users to resist the constructed nature of social reality, allowing different archetypes within the personality to emerge. Online, some have claimed, you can openly confront the most important questions of analytic psychology: who am I? What does it mean to be me?

This is one of the major reasons why the Internet has come to play an important part in therapy. There is obvious potential in using e-therapy to assist the treatment of people with generalized social phobia (GSP), avoidant personality disorder (APD), agoraphobia,[23] and anyone else who suffers from fears of embarrassment, overwhelming anxiety surrounding the missing of social cues, or the inability to risk rejection.[24]

In addition, there may be benefits in actually trying out new behaviors online rather than in the real world.[25] In its purest, most ideal form, online therapy can work the way classical analysis does, in that the patient can experience the analyst as a benign, hovering (albeit electronic) presence. In fact, Suler believes that the altered self-boundaries promulgated by cyberspace can encourage a regression to primary process thinking:

> The distinction between inner-me and outer-other is not as clear. ... Boundaries between self and other representations become more diffuse, and thinking becomes more subjective and emotion-centered. Within the transitional space of online communication, the psyches of self and other feel like they might be overlapping. We allow the hidden self to surface because we no longer experience it as a purely inner self...[26]

Perhaps the most significant feature of online therapy is its potential for disinhibition. Disinhibition among computer users has proved to be a difficult term to define[27] and can encompass behaviors ranging from being impolite[28] to the use of capital letters and exclamation marks[29] and expressions of personal feelings towards another person by means of e-mail.[30] In this context, however, the most applicable use of the term is in relation to what Suler, in reference to online therapy, terms "the disinhibition effect:"

> The disinhibition effect is not the only factor that determines how much people open up or act out in cyberspace. ... People with histrionic styles tend to be very open and emotional. Compulsive people are more restrained. The online disinhibition effect will interact with these personality variables, in some cases resulting in a small deviation from the person's baseline (offline) behavior, while in other cases causing dramatic changes.[31]

The Internet has a well-known capacity to distort object relations, and this distortion can be liberating, partly because it allows relationships to become very intense very quickly. Cyberspace can feel like an isolated, remote, and unfamiliar world with its own rules, rather like the sanatorium in Thomas Mann's *The Magic Mountain*. We relate very differently to a disembodied party than we do to a flesh-and-blood human being, which explains the proliferation of cyberspace relationships, and the common difficulty of transferring those relationships into "real life." As Suler[32] puts it, "transference reactions tend to be magnified by the ambiguity of text communication. The mind-merging that results sometimes may even cause developmentally advanced people to dip into periods of self-object transferences." In other words, elements of our correspondent's identity may be distorted by our own needs and feelings, especially in the case of someone we've never met "in the flesh." Add these complex transference reactions to the guilt, grief, and anxiety surrounding the death of a loved one, and we can start to understand the mystification and superstition surrounding the idea of posthumous e-mails, and user profiles for the recently dead.

CYBERSPACE, MYTHOLOGY, AND THE UNCONSCIOUS

Cyberspace is not only now an integral part of our daily life, it's also the primary means by which contemporary mythology is spread. In an earlier article on the subject of sex and the Internet,[33] I discuss the similarities between people's fear of cyberspace and their anxieties about the unconscious in its popularized form: a bottomless pit of incestuous mayhem. In this article, I suggest that these two metaphorical structures—the Internet and the unconscious—share important similarities. Unlike other manifestations of popular culture (television or movies, for example), which are often considered by the psychoanalytically inclined to reveal the unconscious of a nation, a culture, or a generation, what appears on our computer screen is summoned up by the individual in response to particular   prompts. Just as repressed sexual urges tend to find their own outlet in erotic dreams and nocturnal emissions, I argue that those whose sexuality is repressed in the service of a higher ideal are precisely those most gripped by the fear of being "seduced" by "torrents of filth" unleashed by the Internet.

Another superstition about the unconscious centers on its scary tendency to betray its owner by slips of the tongue. Similarly, according to those who fear it, the easiest way for the Internet to seduce the innocent is by "misinterpreting" a word or phrase normally considered inoffensive, and suddenly releasing a "flood of filth" on to the screen. Warnings about the "dark side of the net" often take the form of anecdotes describing vulnerable people being led astray by a innocently misplaced word, phrase, or typo, as though the internet, with its filthy and lascivious mind, has the dirty habit of finding sexual connotations and double entendres in the most innocent of expressions. In this, it resembles the "ghostly voice" of the hypnotist's dummy, or the parrot that—in the old convention of the dirty joke—"accidentally" reveals the secrets of its owner, usually hinting at lascivious desires, or a sordid past.

According to computer expert John Ives,[34] "The social changes which have followed the Internet explosion, themselves quite abrupt, have led to stories which suggest near-apocalyptic scenarios in which innocent users find themselves at the mercy of forces beyond their control." Ives explains how people's fear of the Internet's power to disrupt community stability and organization is typified by anxieties about computer viruses that are capable of physically eating their way through your hard drive, or making your computer screen literally explode. In fact, however, what we call "technology" is fundamentally no more than an extension of the relationship between human beings, and to think of it in any other way is to engender the kind of mystification, passivity, and scapegoating typical of most media panics. When enough time has passed, however, these mists will clear, and we'll learn to see cyberspace for what it really is: a simple metaphor, a projection of our current fears and fantasies. Truth be told, only the digital nature of the medium separates MyDeathSpace from obituary pages in newspapers, most of which also include advertisements, and also permit readers to send in their own tributes, poems, photographs, and memorials. Yet nobody thinks of ordinary newspaper obituaries as "trapping souls in purgatory," even when—as is increasingly the case today—they're accessed on the web. True, the online personality, in the form of e-mails or avatar, has no physical body , which makes its absence through death less of a transition, but there's nothing essentially new or mysterious about the fact that a site can still be visited and "added to," qualities which also apply, don't forget, to actual gravesites, as well as electronic ones. The truth is, posthumous e-mails do not come from "beyond the grave," any more than a book published by an author who's no longer alive, or—for that matter—a Last Will and Testament.

SITES REFERENCED

www.Flickr.com
www.DeathSwitch.com
www.LetterFromBeyond.com
www.livejournal.com
www.MySpace.com
www.MyDeathSpace.com
www.TheLastEmail.com
www.Postexpression.com
www.YouDeparted.com (now www.AssetLock.com)

NOTES

1. See Gina Damron, "Young Friendships are Alive After Death in Internet Postings,"*Detroit Free Press*, October 23 2007, http:// www.freep.com/apps/pbcs.dll/article?AID=2007710230369, accessed Feb 28, 2008; see also Dan Glaister, "Website logs deaths of MySpace Users," *The Guardian*, August 21 2007, http://www.guardian.co.uk/ technology/2007/aug/21/news.myspace, accessed Feb 28, 2008.

2. See Shia Levitt, "Web Site Serves as Memorial and Warning," NPR, December 18, 2007, http://www.npr.org/templates/story/ story.php?storyId=17354815, accessed Feb 28, 2008.

3. Matthew Doyal Proctor, "The AfterLife Waits: MyDeathSpace.com," *FALSE Magazine* 1.1, 2008, http:// falsemagazine.org/content/afterlife_awaits.php, accessed March 21, 2008.

4. Amelia Guimaren, "MyDeathSpace and the Revival/ Imortalization of Early Cinematic Architecture," Society for Cinema Studies Convention, March 8 2008, archived at: http:// www.conceptlab.com/amelia/2008march6-guimarin-scms.html, accessed March 11, 2008.

5. Paige Ferrari, "Is the Web's Most Ghoulish Site Cursed?", *Radar Online*, February 2007: http://radaronline.com/features/2007/02/ fatal_attraction_1.php, accessed Feb 28, 2008.

6. See Nick Britten and Richard Savill, "Police Fear Internet Cult Inspires Teen Suicides," *Daily Telegraph*, London, January 23, 2008,

http://www.telegraph.co.uk/news/uknews/1576338/Police-fear-internet-cult-inspires-teen-suicides.html, accessed May 16, 2008.

7. Jack Sargeant, "Suicide Club," *Fortean Times* 236, June 2008, 32-33.

8. For an account of these and other crimes with a connection to the Internet, see "Technology's New Breed of Crime," *Investigation Discovery*, http://investigation.discovery.com/investigation/internet-cases/internet-cases.html, accessed May 17, 2008.

9. Arthur C. Clarke, *Profiles of the Future: An Inquiry into the Limits of the Possible* (New York: Phoenix Books, 1962), p. 14.

10. For further discussion of this subject, see Erik Davis, *TechGnosis: Myth, Magic and Mysticism in the Age of Information* (Maine: Five Star Press, 2004).

11. John Suler, "Presence," *The Psychology of Cyberspace*, Hypertext book, 1996, http://www-usr.rider.edu/~suler/psycyber/presence.html, accessed March 21, 2008.

12. Michael Fenichel, "The Here and Now of Cyberspace," 2008, http://www.fenichel.com/herenow.shtml, accessed March 21, 2008.

13. Suler, "Presence."

14. L. Muhlbaoh, M. Bocker, & A. Proussog, "Telepresence in videocommunications: A study of stereoscopy and individual eye contact. Special Issue: Telecommunications," *Human Factors*, 37: 1995, 290-305.

15. Robert Romanyshyn, "On Technology as Symptom and Dream," an interview with Dolores Brien, *The Jung Page*, June 5 2005, http://www.cgjungpage.org/index.php?option=com_content&task=view&id=683&Itemid=40 accessed May 16, 2008.

16. Mark Stefik, *Internet Dreams: Archetypes, Myths and Metaphors* (Cambridge, MA: M.I.T. Press, 1996).

17. Ben Goertzel, "World Wide Brain: Self-Organizing Internet Intelligence as the Actualization of the Collective Unconscious," in Jayne Gackenbach, ed., *Psychology and the Internet: Intrapersonal, Interpersonal, and Transpersonal Implications* (San Diego, Academic Press, 1998), p. 297.

18. Mark Poster, *The Second Media Age* (Oxford: Polity-Blackwell, 1995).

19. Sherry Turkle, *Life on the Screen: Identity in the Age of the Internet,* (New York: Simon & Schuster, 2007).

20. S. Stone, "Will the real body please stand up? Boundary Stories about Virtual Cultures," in M. Benedikt, ed., *Cyberspace: First Steps* (Cambridge, MA: MIT Press, 1991).

21. Kenneth Gergen, *The Saturated Self: Dilemmas of Identity in Contemporary Life* (New York: Basic Books, 1991), p. 17.

22. Turkle, "Life on the Screen."

23. S. A. King & S. T. Poulos, "Using the Internet to treat generalized social phobia and avoidant personality disorder," *Cyberpsychology and Behavior,* 1, 1998, 29-36.

24. S. A. King & D. Moreggi, "Internet Therapy and Self-Help Groups—The Pros and Cons," in Gackenbach, *Psychology and the Internet,* pp. 77-106.

25. K. Glantz, N. I. Durlach, R. C. Barnett, & W. A. Aviles, "Virtual Reality (VR) for Psychotherapy: From the physical to the social environment," *Psychotherapy* 33: 464-473.

26. John Suler, "The Online Disinhibition Effect," *CyberPsychology and Behavior,* 7, 2004, 321-326.

27 M. Lea, T. O'Shea, P. Fung, & R. Spears,"Computer-mediated communication, de-individuation and group decision making," *International Journal of Man-Machine Studies,* 39, 1991, 283-301.

28 Sara Kiesler, D. Zubrow, A. M. Moses, & V. Geller, "Affect in Computer-mediated communication: An experiment in synchronous terminal-to-terminal discussion," *Human Computer Interaction* 1, 1985, 77-104.

29. Lee Sproull & Sara Kiesler, "Reducing social context cues: Electronic mail in organizational communication," *Management Science,* 32, 1986, 1492-1512.

30. See Kiesler *et al.*

31. Suler, "The Online Disinhibition Effect."

32 *Ibid.*

33. Mikita Brottman, "Is the Internet a Portal to Hell? Inner Space, Superstition and Cybersex," *Bad Subjects* 74 (2005), http://bad.eserver.org/issues/2006/74/brottman.html, accessed April 18, 2008.

34. John Ives, "Computer Virus Hoaxes: Urban Legends for the Digital Age," *Bad Subjects* 37 (1998). http://bad.eserver.org/issues/1998/37/ives.html, accessed May 15, 2008.

Encountering the Symbolic Aspects of the Smartphone

Henry Gros

The smartphone is a powerful technological artifact that has the potential to enhance some human faculties while leaving others underdeveloped or even diminished. Various psychological phenomena may be associated with its use, from cognitive pleasure, to regression, narcissism, and addiction. A closer look at its symbolic aspects and how they relate to mythological themes may give us a clearer sense of our true relation to this marvel of modern technology.

The smartphone has the densest concentration of functions of any device ever invented. Primarily, it is a mobile phone. However, it also has the capability of connecting to the Internet: it has a screen, a keypad, and a mouse, and offers the possibility of sending and receiving e-mails as well as buying and selling goods and services. In addition, it has a built-in video camera, which makes it possible to see the person you are talking to. On top of all of this, it has a GPS (Global Positioning System) receiver, so one can find one's way around unfamiliar areas,

Henry Gros received his training as a Jungian analyst at the C. G. Jung-Institute Zürich in 2006 and currently maintains a private analytic practice in Zürich and Geneva. Prior to that, he earned a Ph.D. in Engineering from the Eidgenössische Technische Hochschule Zürich (Swiss Federal Institute of Technology Zürich), following which he worked as an engineer, and later as a manager in an environment technology company. Since 1994 he has served as an independent strategy and team-management consultant and coach for individuals and business.

and one never has to worry about getting lost. In short, the smartphone concentrates in one single object almost all the latest features offered by telecommunications and information technology.

As a tool, it enhances certain human cognitive and sensory functions. By its intimate involvement in our inner life and our mental activities, it takes on the role of our "personal assistant," facilitating and stimulating—but also sometimes dictating—our thoughts, expressions, and communication abilities. Because of its intrusiveness into our inner lives, it has the power to seduce us into developing fantasies that can lead to regressive, dissociative, or addictive behaviors. It is in contemplating this power that I first asked myself how our relation to such artifacts might be described in terms of the classical Jungian scheme of transference and counter-transference between two individuals.[1] It seemed to me that it might be represented by the diagram shown in Fig. 1.

Artifacts are not living entities, and as such they have neither the consciousness nor the unconscious that we do. In the relationship between human being and artifact, it is only the human subject who is sentient, so the projections go in only one direction (as shown in the diagram), and this can result in the subject's identifying with the artifact. How do we experience this identification? A person who uses a given tool repeatedly begins to perceive that tool as an extension of his or her arm, and the tool becomes incorporated into the user's body-image. Such a projection onto the tool may well manifest itself in corresponding

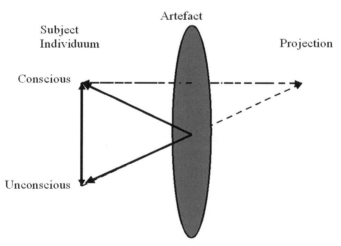

Fig. 1: Projection and Transference in Relation to Artifacts

physiological phenomena. Alain Berthoz,[2] a neurophysiologist who specializes in perception, has shown that repeated tool use can alter brain physiology, a change that can be observed using brain imaging techniques. Experiments done on monkeys (who were trained to use a certain tool) measured the intensity of activity, during tool use, in the visual-tactile neurons in those regions of the brain that are related to the monkey's manipulation of its hand. It was found that there was an expansion of the visual receptive field in this area of the brain when the monkeys were engaged in using a tool, as opposed to when they were not (Fig. 2).[3]

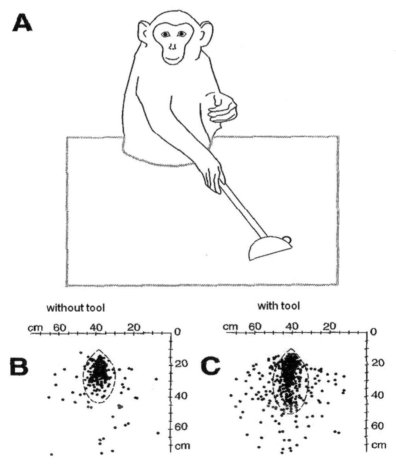

Fig. 2: The Effect of Body Extension on the Neurophysiology of the Brain

On a cognitive-psychological level, we may relate this finding to the following observation by Jean Piaget:

> If a stick is placed within reach of an ape but in any position, it is seen as an indifferent object; placed parallel with his arm, it will promptly be perceived as a possible extension of the hand. Thus the stick, until then neutral, will receive a meaning from the fact of its incorporation in the complex structure. The field will then be "restructured" and … it is these sudden restructurings that are characteristic of the act of intelligence.[4]

The artifact may thus also become a stimulus for setting in motion certain mental processes, especially that of arriving at a sudden insight (so-called "Aha! moments"). Recall the pleasure we experience during creative activity when our creative output matches what we imagined in our mind. One of our brain's most important tasks is making projections, and the neurobiologist would say that the brain loves it when it gets the process right. When our projections square with reality, in other words, when we "get it right," the brain produces dopamine, which induces feelings of pleasure. This process may be the source of the addictive power of artifacts such as the smartphone, with its multiplicity of functions and all the related excitement they engender.

C. G. Jung was well aware of the power that such technological artifacts (as "ersatz objects") can have over humans in the form of obsessions or demons in the unconscious. He saw in the power of technology a modern analogue of the power that magical objects once held.[5] He also suggested that the almost religious devotion that some scientists bring to the object of their research may well spring from a more or less conscious experience (on the part of the scientist) of the object's numinosity. And in one of his letters he bewailed the fact that

> … in the unconscious of modern human beings, the animals, dragons … were replaced by trains, engines, bicycles, planes and other artifacts. … And how much nature and the animals lost of their numinosity![6]

But there have been others as well who have been intrigued by the effect of artifacts on the human psyche. The psychoanalyst Harold Searles has spent a lifetime exploring, from the psychoanalytic point of view, the relation of humans to the non-human environment, both in psychopathology and in "normal" development. He notes that we all "have unconscious memory traces of infantile experiences in which we were surrounded by a chaotically uncontrollable nonhuman environment that was sensed as being a part of us ...."[7] For many of his patients, identification with machines served a "defensive function."[8] Such individuals are subject to internal impulses as a result of concretization and projection. For them, the non-human element is a kind of buffer onto which they can project certain aspects of themselves until they are strong enough to integrate these aspects into their identity.

The Medial Artifact as Virtual Object between Individuals

But what happens when the artifact is a medial tool, as is the case with the smartphone, a tool that enables us to communicate with other people at a distance, to access social and medial data on the Internet, to be a member of various online communities? In this case, the artifact becomes a virtual object between one person and another, both literally and psychologically. This comes through rather dramatically in a Swisscom advertisement for a smartphone, in which the medial gadget is interposed directly between two women (Fig. 3). This configuration suggests that when we are dealing with medial artifacts such as the smartphone, the diagram shown in Fig. 1 needs to be modified to include the other person.

Fig. 3: Swisscom Advertisement

A modifed version of Fig. 1 is presented in Fig. 4. Here, the diagam contains not one individual but two: "subject" and "object." From the diagram, we can see how the projected "virtual" object is not simple any more (as in the earlier diagram), but becomes more complex in that it now contains elements of the subject, the artifact, *and* the object, all heavily loaded with the projections of the subject, and, to some extent, of the object as well. When we speak of "virtual" objects here, we have in mind something similar to the sort of virtual images that are produced by lenses and mirrors. It is worth noting that in video communication, both kinds of virtual images are present: the subject's camera serves as a sort of mirror, the object's camera as a sort of powerful telescopic lens. The virtuality of such images is brought home to us rather vividly when we communicate through devices such as videophones or webcams on the Internet, especially if the person we are talking to is someone with whom we have already had face-to-face contact and whom we know well. That person comes across as flat, two-dimensional, lacking in depth, strangely alien. A similar effect is experienced in reverse when we meet face to face, for the first time,

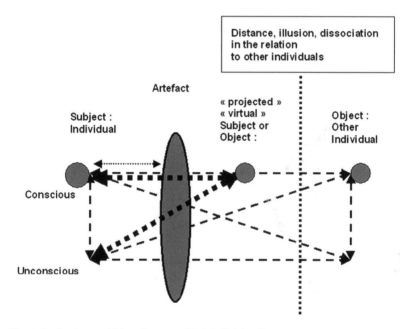

Fig. 4: Projection and Transference with Medial Artifacts

someone we initially made contact with only through medial devices. We are immediately struck by the artificiality of our mental image of that person and the extent to which that mental image is constructed from the contents of our unconscious. Just how narcissistic the process can be may be seen in the self-constructed *mise en scène* we place ourselves in under such circumstances, and the amount of self-mirroring that is required when we have to broadcasting ourselves in this manner. This self-promotion is often accompanied by a corresponding regression and a feeling of omnipotence: everything is possible; with a single touch of the screen I can reach out and touch the whole world.

The psychological aspects of our relation to and experience with such medial artifacts have attracted the attention of a wide range of psychological institutions, researchers, and thinkers around the world. In France, the research team headed by Sylvain Missonnier[9] has published several articles and books on the topic, addressing a range of issues, from the anxiety-diminishing value of the mobile phone to the virtual and partial object relations that might be achieved through it. The team has also examined matters such as disconnecting from the virtual game and healing through virtual images. In Germany, Claus Braun[10] has explored the sort of relations that might be possible through the Internet. He has analyzed the conditions that are necessary for a transformative relationship—and even possibly a therapeutic relationship—to develop in cyberspace. In view of the "as if" quality of cyberspace and its narcissistic overtones, he is highly critical of "cyber" relationships. He believes that a triangulation between the subject, the virtual object, and the real object is necessary for a satisfactory relationship to emerge and develop.

In the U.S.A., the psychoanalyst and professor Michael Civin has devoted his time to understanding the varying effects that Internet use has on his patients. In his book *Male, Female, e-mail,*[11] he documents how virtual communication may lead individuals to deep regression, but he also notes that in many cases the regression has been a transitional phase on the way to personal development. Civin makes reference to Winnicott[12] in describing how the virtual object can become a transitional object that enables the individual to engage in progressive reality-testing, moving from the world of illusion, in which the virtual object "obeys" him or her implicitly, out into the reality of the other individual. Civin suggests that, as in dreams and the unconscious, virtual space is symmetrical, that is, there is no distinction between good and evil, real and unreal—as opposed to the real world, which is asymmetrical, and where such differences do exist and have significant consequences. Thus, when adolescents play online games night and day, or when adults become addicted to online trading, gambling, or pornography, they may well be entering a dream-like state of pure symmetry. These states, however, often appear to be transitional phases, induced by some trauma or a difficult but necessary change. The virtual world, where everything seems possible, is a sheltered world, a world within which the relation to other individuals and to the real world may gradually, through reality-testing experiences, be safely re-established. Civin thus describes a "third dimension," in which the virtual dimension and the real dimension may enter into a relation. But this third dimension requires *psychological work* to effect a *transformative relationship.*

Both Jung and Searles wrote about the power of the non-human object and hinted at the importance of getting in touch with its unconscious aspects. This may be done by looking at the symbolic aspects of the virtual object.

THE HERMETIC QUALITIES OF THE SMARTPHONE

What happens when the two modes of psychological functioning—the symmetrical and asymmetrical—are brought together is similar to what happens in therapy when the client is moved by a powerful symbol that is associated with a situation, a relationship, or an object in his or her life. Experiencing the numinosity inherent in the symbolic representation of an object allows us to become conscious of that object's unconscious attributes. We can thus experience and become increasingly aware of the formerly unconscious emotional quality of the object, and thus more attuned to other related dimensions of the psychological complex being accessed in the process. In the case of the smartphone (and the virtual world with which it is connected), given the fascination it produces in us, we can conclude that there are strong archetypal images underpinning our relationship to it. Our task, then, would be to identify the archetypal and symbolic resonances of the smart phone.

For me, the most obvious archetypal resonance is the association to Hermes, the messenger of the gods. I will attempt to expand on this idea by examining the various qualities attributed to Hermes. Quoting Michael Vannoy Adams, we will not follow "what Giegerich calls 'truly mythic experience' but, like Jung, … [the] *psychic experience of myth*" (his italics).[13] Thus, the present paper does not seek to delve into the divine aspect of technology, as developed by such authors as:

- Wolfgang Giegerich,[14] who, quoting James Hillman, writes: "… [T]oday the 'only one God left that is truly universal, omnipresent, omnipotent, observed faithfully in thought and action, joining all humankind in daily acts of devotion' is 'The Economy' …, or as I would put it, Money."[15]
- Jacques Ellul, who, writing in a similar vein about the almost religious zeal with which we pursue technological perfection (our new definition of "the absolute"), notes: "The technical phenomenon is the main preoccupation of our time; in every field men seek to find the most efficient method."[16]

I will look at the archetypal elements to be found in Hermes in the spirit of Giegerich's answer to Hillman when he writes that the true place for images of the ancient gods is "the private, personal, subjective sphere of the modern individual."[17] We would, also, do well to remember that "Jung says that the psyche is intrinsically mythopoeic. The psyche … spontaneously projects myths—or produces modern dreams, fantasies, and experiences similar to ancient myths."[18]

The qualities, desires, fantasies, and possibilities that people today project onto the smartphone and its virtual world arise from quite basic human needs and longings, which are in fact not so far removed from the hopes and dreams of people long ago. Back then, they projected their yearnings onto gods, such as Hermes; today we project similar yearnings onto technological gadgetry, the new "gods." Being able to communicate at a distance, to engage in trade and/or seduction, to relate to and transform the all-pervasive twilight dimension of the symmetrical—these are what our distant ancestors yearned for, no less than we do today, whether consciously or not, and these are what we project onto our gods, whether they be Hermes or smartphones.

In Greek mythology, Hermes was said to be the originator of many human skills, including fire making, lyre making, the production of various handicrafts, cattle raising, and olive cultivation. He was a civilizing god, reputedly the inventor of the alphabet, the musical scale, and astronomy. But he was also duplicitous, exhibiting more shadow-like qualities. Homer writes of him: "Born with the dawning, ... in the evening he stole the cattle of far-shooting Apollo ..."; and later, Homer has him to say to Apollo: "... I will swear a great oath by my father's head and vow that neither am I guilty myself, neither have I seen any other who stole your cows—whatever cows may be; for I know of them only by hearsay."[19] Hermes is thus one of the most human of the gods. One could almost say that he lived to the fullest extent many of the processes that neurobiologists are now gradually discovering in our brains: the neural connections that bring together cognition, emotion, projection, and action. Hermes and neurobiology both tell us that we are more *Homo faber* than *Homo sapiens*.

In view of Hermes' duplicity, Jung maintained that the presence of Hermes (or Mercurius) hovers over the process of individuation and therapy,[20] especially in the form of the trickster figure, ever ready to play, to frustrate, to drive crazy, and to bring individuals to regression and *nigredo*, the dark, black phase in the alchemical process. On the other side, his function as mediator between human beings, between subject and object, allows him to preside over transitional phases, to provide an opportunity for deeper relations between conscious and unconscious. This is Hermes as psychopomp, about which more will be said later.

Like Hermes, the smartphone is ambiguous. It may be an omnipotent "ersatz object"; it may disturb the relationship between people and promote regression. But it is also a transitional object, and as such it may also develop the relational capacity of the subject towards his or her object(s), and thus possibly towards himself or herself on the way to individuation. In understanding the archetypal parallels between smartphones and Hermes, it may be well worth setting out the similarities between the way people in antiquity related to Hermes and the way we relate to the smartphone and its virtual world today.

The 2nd-century C.E. Greek writer Pausanias provides the following description of a Hermes shrine in southern Greece:

> The marketplace of Pharae is of wide extent ... and in the middle of it is an image of Hermes, made of stone, ... of square shape, and of no great size ... It is called Hermes of the Market, and by it is established an oracle. ... [T]he inquirer of the god ... puts on the altar on the right of the image a local coin, called a "copper," and asks in the ear of the god the particular question he wishes to

put to him. After that, he stops his ears and leaves the marketplace. On coming outside he takes his hands from his ears, and whatever utterance he hears he considers oracular.[21]

I find in this description a remarkable parallel to what people do today when they ask questions of our modern-day "oracle," Google, and to the endless fascination that this activity exerts on many of us, as the oracles did on the ancient Greeks. Instead of whispering in the god's ear, we type our question into the seach box and click on a simulated button. Google even offers us the ancient oracular element of luck: it has an "I'm feeling lucky" button (Fig. 5). Choosing this option takes the searcher straight to the first search result (or answer), bypassing the search results page, with all its hundreds of thousands of possible "answers." If you are lucky, the first result will be just the answer you are looking for. Interestingly, its position in first place on the list is the result of the sum of all conscious and unconscious clicks made collectively by everyone who has ever consulted Google.

Hermes was also the god who laid out roads. His name is thought to have been derived from the word "*herma*," meaning "stone heap." Originally a pile of stones used as a boundary marker, the *herma* (or herm) later became a square or rectangular pillar of stone, terracotta, or bronze.

Fig. 5: "I'm feeling lucky" (Google)

Fig. 6: An Example of a Herm

The pillar was topped with a representation of Hermes' head; the base was adorned with an erect phallus (Fig. 6).[22] The herms were placed by the side of roads, at the entrances of houses, and at crossroads. We can imagine how for travelers in those times these pillars invited a projection of the protection and spatial orientation afforded them by Hermes. To find these herms along the journey, never too far away, must have been tremendously reassuring, and it no doubt provided a sense of security while negotiating the road network of those times.

Conceptually and psychologically, today's smartphones with their GPS capabilities are not so far removed from the ancient herms of Hermes. What do *we* project onto our smartphones when they tell us which way to turn at the next intersection or where we are when we find ourselves lost in an unfamiliar place? Essentially, the smartphone is a "pocket-herm": it keeps us linked to the great network of highways and backroads; it takes us by the hand and tells us where the boundaries are, where to turn, where to stop. It has an "authority" that is so all-encompassing that we cannot afford to ignore it. We have no choice but to put our trust in it. Clearly, the unconscious fantasies, expectations, and hopes that we project onto our smartphones are not so different from the ones the ancient Greeks projected onto their herms.

Hermes has yet another aspect that connects him to modern medial technology: he is the god of materialism—of self-advancement, of progress, of commerce and worldly success. In the Homeric Hymns we read that Hermes was not content to remain cooped up in the dark cave where he and his mother Maia were living in seclusion. He says to his mother:

> Better to live in fellowship with the deathless gods continually,
> rich, wealthy, and enjoying stories of grain, than to sit always in
> a gloomy cave: and, as regards honour, I too will enter upon the

rite that Apollo has. If my father will not give it to me, I will seek—and I am able—to be a prince of robbers.[23]

We can understand the attraction the ancient Greeks felt towards such a god, a god who understood their longing to live a more prosperous life—surely a very natural drive in the unconscious. And when they sacrificed to Hermes, god of merchants and thieves, and aksed him to prosper their businesses and forgive their minor swindles, they were not so different from the online traders of today, who follow their eBay results or the latest quotes from Wall Street on their Blackberries, and hope that the sacrifice of buying a better smartphone will give them an edge—a faster connection, a better insider tip. To win when others are losing brings us very close to the Hermes orientation to life.

To the alchemists, Hermes was also the mediator. He brought opposites together: sun and moon, male and female, people in conflict. Like Hermes, smartphones too bring people and opposites together. Consider, for example, the advertisement of a mobile phone service provider shown in Fig. 7. Note how the image suggests not only the perfect match between male and female, that is, the *coniunctio*, but also the *unio mystica*, the new "*philosophorum*," symbolized in the *Rosarium* by the figure of

Fig. 7: Orange Mobile Phone Company Advertisement

the hermaphrodite (Fig. 8), the symbol of wholeness, which, according to Jung, was the ultimate goal of the alchemists in their work with the spirit Mercurius (Hermes).[24] On a mundane level, we can see here a parallel to Hermes in his role as *proegestes*, the leader of the bridal procession at ancient Greek weddings, in which the bride rode in a chariot from her house to the house of the groom[25]; it was Hermes' duty to ensure the safe passage of the female from her state of singleness to her state of oneness with the male. On a more subtle level,

PHILOSOPHORVM.

Fig. 8: The Hermaphrodite from the *Rosarium*

it is the desire for wholeness that somehow draws humans on in their quest for the "significant other," but with varying degrees of success. The Mercurius of the alchemists is bright and compelling, but at the same time disturbing and destabilizing.[26] He may disrupt existing relations in order to create new ones. This calls to mind all the relationships that have been formed, broken, and re-formed through the new medial technology, through text messaging, instant messaging, online chatting, and e-mailing—and the deception, lying, and trickery that invariably go along with such communication at a distance. We may recall here our earlier discussion of the idea of transitional phases proposed by Civin.

A consideration of the darker, wilder aspects of Hermes leads us inevitably to his major role, that of psycopomp, guide of the soul into the kingdom of death. The ancient Greeks believed that Hermes was sent by Zeus to lead the souls of the dead into the kingdom of Hades, the underworld. This role highlights his ability to be in both the upper and the lower worlds, and to pass easily from one world to the other—from life to death, from consciousness to the unconscious. This ability also makes him the presider over sleep and dreams, which were often not sharply distinguished from death in ancient times. It is not so surprising, then, to find smartphones associated with death in today's world. In Ghana, there is a custom by which a dead person is buried in a coffin that is shaped like (or in some way represents) an important object in that person's life, an object he wishes to use again in the afterlife. As might be expected, one can choose for oneself a coffin shaped like a mobile phone or some other medial artifact (Fig. 9).[27] Can there be any doubt that the contemporary psychopomp is the smartphone? One can only imagine the trust that people have in such devices to choose to be guided by them into the afterlife. Or is it anxiety at being cut from life and a strong desire to have a foot in both worlds? If it is the latter, then what better symbol is there for such connectivity than the smartphone, the ultimate means of staying connected in our times? Note how in the case of the Ghana coffins the attributes of Hermes (as the god who has power over and contact with both worlds) are projected onto the smartphone.

Turning to contemporary dreams in which smartphones appear, we could say that their appearance is simply a matter of what Jung described as "*canis panem somniat, piscator pisces* (the dog dreams of bread, the fisherman of fish)."[28] But if we look deeper, we might also find some of the unique qualities of Hermes evoked in these dreams.

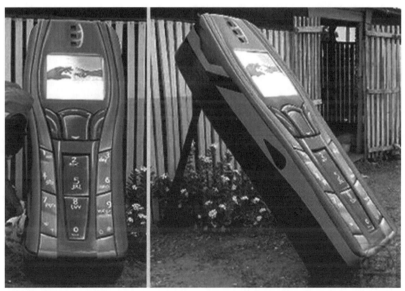

Fig. 9: Coffin in Ghana

In dreams that have been described to me, or that I have had myself, I have noticed that medial devices often serve a linking function, that is, they guide the dreamer to some more fundamental goal or object: a parent, a close relation, a strong symbolic image. Thus, the smartphone image in the dream leads the soul in its dream-journey to deeper levels of the unconscious. In one dream, a mobile phone manifested quite clearly a transformative quality:

> *My mobile phone is linked to an abnormal emitter; it becomes all green with small red dots, like a toad. A female colleague is walking by; I tell her about it when she reaches my office. At that very moment, my mobile phone turns black and smooth, then reverts back to its original form.*

In this dream we see manifested basic archetypal properties similar to ones found in animals in fairy tales, where they symbolize basic drives, but also mutation, transformation, adaptation, and individuation. We are immediately reminded of Hermes' shapeshifting antics and his mercurial quality: he is difficult to pin down, frustrating—but ultimately an agent of metamorphosis on the journey of transformation.

To conclude, being aware of archetypal forces and their manifestations will enable us to recognize and deal with their presence and fascinative power in such modern gadgets as the smartphone. Like the young forester in the fairy tale "The Spirit in the Bottle," referred to by Jung in his essay "The Spirit Mercurius,"[29] we may be able to say to the spirit of the smartphone, "Show me how you re-enter in the smartphone, if you are so powerful." Even if, as Jung says, this is an "alchemically incorrect" approach—since allowing oneself to be seduced into opening the container is not the way of the alchemist—in everyday life, it just may be our destiny to go into the *nigredo* of opening the "Pandora's Box" (another object designed by Hermes) that the smartphone is rapidly becoming. Likewise, the ability to close the box when necessary may also be something we need to develop in the real world. Perhaps, a secondary objective of this paper has been to set up a connection between merely observing our relationship to (and through) our artifacts and enriching these relationships with the insights of mythological wisdom. Like the ape learning to use a tool in the experiment described above, we too may experience an "Aha! moment" with out smartphones when that connection clicks into place. Becoming aware that our smartphones and other medial gadgets have certain qualities similar to those of Hermes may thus lead us to uncover the still-unconscious aspects of ourselves and inspire us to cultivate relationships and engage in dialogue with others at a real, deeper level.

NOTES

1. C. G. Jung, *The Collected Works of C. G. Jung*, trans. R. F. C. Hull, vol. 16 (Princeton, NJ: Princeton University Press), § 422, 457, 525. (Hereafter referred to as *CW* followed by volume and paragraph number.)

2. Alain Berthoz, *Emotion and Reason: The Cognitive Neuroscience of Decision Making*, trans. Giselle Weiss (Oxford, UK: Oxford University Press, 2006).

3. Berthoz, citing Atsushi Iriki, Michio Tanaka, and Yoshiaki Iwamura, "Coding of Modified Body Schema during Tool Use by Macaque Postcentral Neurones," *Neuroreport 7*, no. 14 (1996): 2325-2330.

4. Jean Piaget, *The Psychology of Intelligence*, trans. Malcolm Piercy and D. E. Berlyne (London: Routledge Classics, 2001 [1950]), p. 66.

5. Jung, *CW* 8, § 139.

6. C. G. Jung, *Briefe: Vol. 3 (1956-1961)*, ed. Aniela Jaffé (Olten and Freiburg im Breisgau: Walter-Verlag, 1973), p. 389, my translation.

7. Harold Searles, *The Nonhuman Environment: In Normal Development and in Schizophrenia* (Madison, CT: International Universities Press, 1960), p. 39.

8. *Ibid.*, p. 73.

9. See the online special feature on their work: "Le virtuel, les nouvelles technologies de l'information et de la communication (NTIC) et la santé mentale," le Carnet/PSY, 2004, http://www.carnetpsy.com/Archives/Dossiers/Items/SpecialVirtuel/p17.htm.

10. Claus Braun, "Das virtuelle Selbst und virtuelle Andere—Was finden wir in Cyberspace? Psychotherapie-relevante Dimensionen der Kommunikation in Inernet," lecture given at the C. G. Jung-Institut Munich, 2007. Available online at: http://www.jung-institut-muenchen.de/download/vortraege/Virtuelles_Selbst_1007e_.pdf.

11. Michael A. Civin, *Male, Female, e-mail: The Struggle for Relatedness in a Paranoid Society* (New York: Other Press, 2000).

12. D. W. Winnicott, *Playing and Reality* (London: Tavistock Publications, 1971).

13. Michael Vannoy Adams, "Does Myth (Still) Have A Function in Jungian Studies? Modernity, Metaphor, and Psycho-Mythology," paper deliverd at "Psyche and Imagination," Conference of the International Association for Jungian Studies, London, 2006, para. 14. Available online at: http://www.jungnewyork.com/myth_function.shtml.

14. See, for example, Wolfgang Giegerich, *Technology and the Soul: From the Nuclear Bomb to the World Wide Web, Collected English Papers, Vol. II* (New Orleans, LA: Spring Journal Books, 2007).

15. Wolfgang Giegerich, *Soul-Violence, Collected English Papers, Vol. III* (New Orleans, LA: Spring Journal Books, 2008), p. 323.

16. Jacques Ellul, *The Technological Society*, trans. John Wilkinson (New York: Vintage Books, 1964), p. 21. Originally published in French as *La Technique ou l'enjeu du siècle* (1954).

17. Wolfgang Giegerich, "Once More the Reality/Irreality Issue: A Reply to Hillman's Reply," in *Soul-Violence*, p. 321.

18. Adams, para. 16.

19. "Homeric Hymn IV: To Hermes," ll. 1-29; 260-277, in *Hesiod, The Homeric Hymns, and Homerica*, ed. and trans. Hugh G. Evelyn-White, rev. ed. (London: Heinemann, 1936).

20. See Rafael Lopez-Pedraza, *Hermes and His Childern* (Dallas, TX: Spring Publications, 1977), pp. 27-28, 66-67.

21. Pausanias, *Description of Greece*, trans. W. H. S. Jones and H. A. Omerod, vol. 3 (Cambridge, MA: Harvard University Press, 1918), 7.22.2.

22. Lopez-Pedraza, pp. 14-15. Image in Fig. 6 adapted from Plate I, p. 16.

23. "Homeric Hymn IV: To Hermes," ll. 162-181.

24. Jung, *CW* 16, § 386, 422, 457, 525, 536, 537. The image in Fig. 8 is taken from p. 307.

25. John H. Oakley and Rebecca H. Sinos, *The Wedding in Ancient Athens* (Madison, WI: The University of Wisconsin Press, 1993), p. 29.

26. See the discussion on the hermaphrodite in Lopez-Pedraza, pp. 39ff.

27. There is even a website where one can browse through an online catalog, select the kind of coffin one would like to be buried in, and

have it custom-made to one's specifications. The information provided here is taken from the descriptive passages on this website, as are the images of the Nokia coffin shown in Fig. 9; on the website, the blurb under the Nokia coffin image reads: "Keep your line to heaven open—go to the afterlife in a Nokia." The URL for the site is: http://www.eshopafrica.com/acatalog/Ga_Coffins.html.

28. Jung, *CW* 13, § 251.

29. *Ibid.*, § 247-303. See also Giegerich's discussion of Jung's interpretation of this fairy tale in Wolfgang Giegerich, "Closure and Setting Free, or The Bottled Spirit of Alchemy and Psychology," *Spring 74: Alchemy* (Spring, 2006): 31-62.

Soul Speed

MARIA DE JESÚS NORIEGA

Today "speed" is synonymous with "high speed." Industrialization planted this seed for speed, for a lifestyle characterized by fastness. Over the past one hundred and fifty years, we have been habituated to live a hectic life, applauding and expecting rapidness even in acts where slowness may be more appropriate. There now appears to be no choice regarding velocity. High speed is a modern god that demands to be worshipped, encouraging a profound gusto for accelerating everything. The supremacy of haste is associated with triumph and progress, while slowness is disdained with its archaic and annoying undertones.

High speed is also affirmed through its affinity with contemporary culture, sometimes as a means to an end, at other times just for the pleasure of it. Associated with the extraordinary and with a lack of limits, high speed encourages an aggrandized human, floating and flying beyond the merely human. The cult of rapidness has permeated all corners of life, promoting a self-generating need and appeal for acceleration. Perhaps it's time to consider the archetypal fantasies that fuel this proclivity.

Maria de Jesús Noriega is a clinical psychologist who has worked in private practice as a psychotherapist in Mexico City for the past 20 years. She has a Ph.D. in Depth Psychology from Pacifica Graduate Institute. This article draws from material contained in her doctoral dissertation "Timelessness."

Australian culture critic Elizabeth Farrelly remarked: "Probably the will-to-speed was always with us; only the means is new."[1] Fastness extends from the invention of the wheel to the creation of sophisticated machines. Today, cyberspace and the new technologies are the driving forces propelling our attraction to every fast-track manifestation, fostering and pushing it to extremes. Impatience now appears whenever a few extra seconds are needed—while navigating in cyberspace or driving on the freeways. This intolerance is often cloaked by a socially-sanctioned eagerness to make time more profitable, and filling time with fastness is a close companion to the idea that waiting is a waste of time. As long as fastness and our technological culture have an infatuated relationship with one another, we are unable to see any hidden agendas. The luminous aspect of high speed is amplified, and unconscious elements go unacknowledged. Fastness and technology nurture each other, encouraging images of omnipotence and transgression of limits as if they can satisfy every imaginable desire.

Lee Worth Bailey, the author of *The Enchantments of Technology* (2005), suggests that technology is, among many things, a provider of diverse enchantments that represent both conscious and unconscious desires. "Enchantment is a fascinating spell that takes over consciousness, a state of feeling that immerses the soul in dreamy reverie or fearful anxiety."[2] Bailey differentiates between trance and enchantment: "Trances narrow the scope of consciousness, reducing one's scope of awareness,"[3] while "enchantments introduce certain meanings into cultural life that take on a serious, rational tone but have a deep undercurrent of emotional and imaginative power."[4] In a sense, technology's enchantment with high speed remains underground, yet its spell accompanies every technological move and mode, becoming its main fuel.

Michael Staples, in a 1999 article in *Spring Journal*, points out that there are two contrasting senses of technology; one is "a way of seeing the world, and the second, the local manifestations derived from this way of seeing the world."[5] Exalting fastness through technology has changed both senses, with the consequence that "new technologies cannot be discussed using traditional language."[6] New terms for the measurement of time address the race toward quickness; think of the wide-spread utterance of "nanosecond"—one thousand millionths of second. Although created to describe processes at a nuclear level, the term is now used in colloquial conversations, a novel way of expressing the importance of tiny pieces of time.

The term "speed" itself is a noun, and as such can be qualified by any number of different adjectives. Speed can oscillate between the extremes of fast and slow and the vast intermediate states in between. The recent identification and limitation of "speed" to mean "high speed" only glorifies high speed and eliminates other slower speeds as adverse or inadequate. With high speed dominant, an imbalance is created, transforming our ways of doing and being in the world. As Robert Romanyshyn has stated:

> Technology is not just a series of events which occurs over there on the side of the world. It is, on the contrary, the enactment of the human imagination in the world. In building a technological world we create ourselves, and through the events which comprise this world we enact and live out our experiences of awe and wonder, our fantasies of service and of control, our images of exploration and destruction, our dreams of hope and nightmares of despair.[7]

THE HARE AND THE TORTOISE

One of the most famous of Aesop's Fables, "The Hare and the Tortoise" addresses the opposite poles of speed. As you will recall, this fable recounts how one fine day a tortoise, tired of everyone laughing at her slowness, decided to make a bet with the hare, telling her that she is certain she can beat her in a race. The hare takes on the challenge and the entire animal kingdom gathers together to watch the contest. The hare, confident in her speed and agility, allows the tortoise to get a head start, mocking her slowness and awkwardness. In the meantime, the tortoise proceeds slowly, but without stopping. When the hare runs past the tortoise, she stops at the side of the road to rest while the tortoise continues slowly on. This episode, where the hare passes the tortoise, takes place several times, until the hare, feeling quite sure that she can win the race, lies down under a tree and falls asleep. The tortoise continues on her way until she crosses the finish line. When the hare wakes up, she runs as fast as she possibly can, but it is too late—the tortoise has won the race.

The hare and the tortoise have very different physiques and this effects the speed at which each can move. The hare is "fast and agile,"[8] while the tortoise is slow, slowness being associated with "endurance, longevity, safety,...water." The tortoise "carries his house on his back." In various mythologies "[the tortoise is] a creator god or world support."[9] We tend to associate the hare with youth and the tortoise with maturity because quickness is an ability that is developed during childhood, reaching its peak at adolescence, while slowness becomes a faithful companion in old age. "One of the worst mistakes is to be hasty. If in old age one still wants to go fast, then naturally, because one has slowed down physiologically, one will forget to perform even the most obvious tasks."[10] In *The Force of Character*, James Hillman emphasizes that slowness is an indispensable part of the adventure of becoming old. He compares the rhythms of various animals: "Once we learned from the fox and the hawk; now the walrus, the tortoise and the moose in a dark bog are our mentors. The adventure of slowness."[11] Animals' natural rhythms reflect different ways of living. They show us that there are options to choose from and develop, each with its own virtues, flaws, and consequences. "Animals wake up the imagination."[12]

This fable emphasizes how different movement possibilities, different speeds of moving, are closely related to the instincts. Although at first it seems that Aesop was trying to show that there is no better or worse speed, only its appropriateness as determined by the physical characteristics of each animal, ultimately he appears to emphasize the virtues of slowness by having the tortoise win the race. Aesop also recognizes that different value judgments are made about fastness and slowness.

Fables such as this one take us down conscious and unconscious roads. A popular interpretation of the moral of this fable is that pride and arrogance, as exhibited by the quick hare, are bad, while constancy and perseverance, as seen in the slow tortoise, are praiseworthy. The fable presents polarities like pride-humility and constancy-inconstancy. At the same time, it plays with the value judgments that are culturally ascribed to fast and slow. Pierre Sansot writes: "Slow beings did not have a good reputation. It was said that they were dimwits and they were assumed to be clumsy, even if they performed difficult tasks."[13] The reputation of the tortoise seems to become more positive once he wins the race and his slowness is associated with the trait of constancy. It could be argued that slowness alone is insufficient, but must be joined with constancy to be highly valued.

The word slow is also used as an adverb in certain specific contexts, including, such as "slow acting" and "slow moving," and in the expression to "go slow." As an adjective or an adverb, the function of "slow" is to act as a qualifier for a noun or a verb. The word slowness is a noun, and our culture has diminished the breadth of its meaning by either pathologizing it or, in a compensatory movement, reifying it.

There are several sayings that are associated with "The Hare and the Tortoise:" "It is better to have a pace that endures than a toil that tires;"[14] "slow and sure is better than fast and uncertain;"[15] and, of course, "slow and steady wins the race." Rapidity extols the achievement of goals, while slowness praises the process. Perhaps Aesop, through this fable, not only uses contrast to help us better reflect upon the characteristics of slowness and speed but also encourages us to recognize that we have a choice in determining which speed is appropriate for what purpose and the damage that may be caused by honoring one level of speed to the exclusion of others.

In *Hare Brain Tortoise Mind* psychologist Guy Claxton explores how speed often has been a focus in research about the mind, starting with studies of what he calls "d mode" where the "d'" stands for deliberation. He analyzes three processing speeds of the mind. The first one is the fastest, "faster than thought,"[16] and corresponds to our instincts. The second one is "thought itself: the sort of intelligence which does involve figuring matters out, weighing up the pros and cons, constructing arguments and solving problems."[17] The third one is a process that is slower: "It is often less purposeful and clear-cut, more playful, leisurely and dreamy."[18] With many examples of these three types of thinking, Claxton underscores the relationship of slowness with the unconscious and how culture has favored the kind of intelligence that is highly related to quickness, i.e., quick thinking. However, he observes that "thinking slowly is a vital part of the cognitive armamentarium. We need the tortoise mind just as much as we need the hare brain."[19] Thus we see how unconscious processes may be undervalued and dismissed through their association with slowness.

THE ORIGINS AND LURE OF HIGH-SPEED

The origins of our yearning for speed are located in the Industrial Revolution, which began in England around 1789. This movement changed the face of many aspects of life, but especially the way humans relate to speed. During the Industrial Revolution, the word "civilization," the state of human social development and organization that is considered most advanced, was coined. This "most advanced" state exalted swiftness, as more and more new machines were created, each faster than those preceding it. These machines became icons of progress and prosperity. And, many of these inventions were powered by steam, an "airy" fuel. Fastness shares with steam its airy consistence, and the principle of fastness at all costs was established and re-enforced during this period. It became an implacable taskmaster, dominating not only the machines themselves but also the people who operated them. The high speed ethos became most visible in mass production, and with it, the reinforcement and exaltation of man-technology power.

The psychological monotheism of the Industrial Revolution marked an era where humanity, based upon the assumed superiority of science and the value placed upon efficiency, stopped tolerating a variety of speeds so that it could worship high speed exclusively. "As modernity developed, godlike powers were slowly transferred from the heavens to the mortal egos of industrial humans."[20] This high speed monotheism is related to a style of life that affirms its affinity with a hectic culture. For Paul Virilio, the French philosopher of technology, the industrial revolution was really a *dromocratic* revolution.[21] Virilio, in his seminal book *Speed and Politics,* coined the term "dromology," the science of speed, from the ancient Greek word meaning "to race." "Dromos" in Greek refers to the avenue or passage generally located between rows of columns or statues that people ran through on their way into an ancient Greek temple or tomb. A running avenue evokes a place to challenge conventional rhythms, to trespass limits. Virilio explains that although we live with the belief that fastness is the same as progress, fastness is also a way of dealing with time: it often disguises the anxiety we experience from not knowing what to do with our time. In other words, fastness creates the illusion of controlling time so that it doesn't seem to disappear, like sand through our fingers.

Fastness also gives the illusion of power through efficiency. As Hillman notes:

> Two insanely dangerous consequences result from raising efficiency to the level of an independent principle. First, it favors short-term thinking—no looking ahead, down the line—and it produces insensitive feeling—no looking around at the life values being lived so efficiently. Second, means become ends; that is, doing something becomes the full justification of doing regardless of what you do.[22]

Efficiency overrides the decision of choosing the *appropriate* speed for the circumstances and what rhythm is better for a particular endeavor. The *New Oxford Dictionary of English* defines "efficient" as achieving maximum productivity with minimum wasted effort or expense. If we compare an artisan creating a work of art to someone engaging in a Google search, we can see the different ways we deal with speed and time as well as how they effect our relationship to psyche. With the artist, there is mixture between fastness, slowness, and efficiency in the creative process without losing a connection to psyche. On the other hand, the Google searcher is focused upon getting the information he wants as soon as possible. The search itself is of not value, only what is next, namely the result. The artist stays in the present moment, whereas the Google searcher lives in the future. The sense of the present or future is important for this topic, but so is the difference between quantitative or qualitative time. Fastness seems governed by quantitative time and slowness by qualitative time.

"The New Accelerator" by H. G. Wells

"The New Accelerator," a short story written by H. G. Wells in 1901,[23] offers some insight into the effects of living a "high speed" life. From a depth point of view, the story provides an archetypal amplification of the effects of the speed extremes of fastness and slowness in inner and outer landscapes.

The New Accelerator is a liquid substance created by Professor Gibberne, a chemist and physiologist who is an expert on drugs and the nervous system and believes that this substance will "revolutionize human life." The New Accelerator compound gives the person who takes it "The power to think twice as fast, move twice as quickly, do twice as much work in a given time as you could otherwise do."[24] But while the accelerator speeds up one's entire being, there is a counterbalancing effect in terms of how the person experiences the world around him. After the narrator of the story and Professor Gibberne take the New Accelerator and go out into the world, they experience the strangest of sensations: the rhythm of the world does not agree with what they experience internally. They are fast, very fast, and the world is slow, very slow. The opposites counterbalanced. "We had lived half an hour while the band had played, perhaps, two bars. But the effect it had upon us was that the whole world had stopped for our convenient inspection."[25] This clash of rhythms is a constant theme in the short story. While an individual is operating at high speed, the world is following its own rhythm, but in the eyes of the accelerated ones, the world appears to be very slow.

Informal conversations with people that spend a considerable amount of time each day navigating in cyberspace reveal that when they disconnect from the internet, they feel like their whole world has slowed down in a tremendous and drastic way. They often experience this as some sort of conspiracy against high speed in the non-technological realm, when in fact they are unconsciously possessed by the fantasy and need for the fastness offered by technology.

The narrator of Wells's short story seems to extol what we would call the Type A personality, which is characterized by ambition, impatience, and competitiveness, and is also thought to be susceptible to stress and heart disease. Their precept in life is that it is best to live life so fast that it would seem you are living twice instead of once:

> I have always been given to paradoxes about space and time,
> and it seemed to me that Gibberne was really preparing no less
> than the absolute acceleration of life.[26]

At the same time, one of the consequences of swallowing the accelerator is that it also accelerates the process of aging. You live faster, but the years also accumulate faster; in other words, you have to choose, there are risks, but it is implied that it is worth living faster with more heroic challenges rather than living a slow life.

Yet the story ends with the announcement of a new potion created by the professor called The Retarder that "used alone it should enable the patient to spread a few seconds over many hours of ordinary time, and so to maintain an apathetic inaction, a glacier-like absence of alacrity amidst the most animated or irritated surroundings."[27] This quotation provides a vivid description of slowness and the value judgments ascribed to it: slowness is associated with indifference ("apathetic inaction"), and coldness (it's "glacier-like"), but also with constancy (refusing to move in the midst of stimulating circumstances). I think it is symbolic that the story ends up with this meditation on slowness, and opens up a scenario where fastness and slowness appear together. This suggests that Wells was conscious of the importance of slowness and the unknown realms that it opens, and that this story foretells the huge ignominy of slowness and the prominence of fastness in contemporary culture.

BEYOND HUMAN PULSE

Recently, I had an experience that illustrates high speed in relation with new technologies. My doctor asked me to get a CAT scan. The date of the exam arrived, and everything seemed to be going fine. Ready and lying down on a special table in front of the CAT scan machine, a very young doctor said that I had to hold my breath to begin the exam. I was lying down, looking up at a huge donut-shaped apparatus with a hole at the center. The table on which I was resting was running smoothly in a forward-backward direction through the hole. On the inside of the donut I could see and also hear many big and tiny steel balls revolving together at a very high speed. The doctor asked me to hold my breath so that my breath could be synchronized with the computer speed of the CAT Scan machine. Although I tried again and again, I could not hold my breath long enough for this synchronization to happen. Another doctor, also very young, then came in. He said that I did not understand that I was being exposed to one of the most marvelous devices of modern medical technology ever created and that my body was not meeting up with the expectations of this fantastic machine. When the procedure was finished, a third, older doctor explained to me that his colleagues were too young to understand that the machine is at the service of the body, not the opposite. Maybe the young doctors were contaminated by what Umberto Eco signals when he writes about the difference between technology and science: "Technology gives you everything instantly;

science proceeds slowly."[28] In any event, the young doctors couldn't see beyond their fastness-technological addiction.

When I left the clinic, I was disillusioned because I had not been able to meet the faster, outer demands imposed by the doctors and the CAT Scan machine itself. This sophisticated technology and my body were not in sync, they had different cadences. I also felt punished for being a baby boomer and old. Perhaps if I were younger, I would have understood how sophisticated technological machines work and been able to establish a communion between the technology and myself. At an unconscious level, a fast-slow complex possessed me, which can also be seen in relation to the puer-senex archetype.

Hillman, in *Senex and Puer*,[29] analyzes the puer-senex configuration. Puer is fast, primordially perfect, follows a vertical direction, and adores new adventures, while senex is slow, perfected through time, horizontal in direction, and adores habit, tradition, and memory. "The puer embraces youth, beginning, wanderings, inspiration invention and flight. He dislikes attachments and plodding, measured development."[30] The puer's relationship with speed is one of high velocity, while senex's relationship with speed is one of reflection and moderation.

"The senex is the old man, solitary and systematic, an upholder of tradition and history."[31] The puer has wings; he elevates and flies, so he hates to stay on the ground, while senex needs to be grounded to flourish. In his introduction to Hillman's volume, Glen Slater underscores puer-senex pairing as a fundament of archetypal psychology, reflecting its pervasive presence in the life of the psyche. The speed issue is another reiteration of this pair manifesting in technology and cyberspace, weighted toward the puer side of things. But as López-Pedraza warns:

> We should never lose sight of the fact that, if these extreme velocities of the puer's consciousness are an essential part of his nature, the more rapid his consciousness is, the slower the elements of the senex inhabiting his unconscious will be.[32]

SPEEDY GONZÁLEZ

Speedy González is a popular cartoon created in the 1950's that illustrates the effects of high speed through animation technology.

Speedy is a clever, funny, agile, and lighthearted Mexican mouse that has the ability to run extremely fast. He is frequently racing against Sylvester the cat, his main enemy, as he tries to defend his mouse community from Sylvester and his tricks. While Speedy's fastness makes him a hero, his crew of mice is characterized by slowness and sluggishness. The slowest of these is named Slowpoke, Speedy's opposite. Speedy's and Slowpoke's adventures portray the effects of fastness and slowness and the value judgments associated with each that we discussed earlier: high speed is seen as desirable and slowing down is disparaged.

A repeated image in these cartoons shows how fastness operates, especially on the body. When Speedy runs, a huge cloud of dust forms, impeding our vision of him. We deduce that he is behind the dust cloud, but we can't really see him. I think this image is a metaphor for the obliteration that occurs with fastness and also shows us the ungrounded nature of it. Fastness evokes flying, ungrounded actions where the main focus is on reaching the goal as soon as possible. A sense of firm ground is lost in this process. Speedy is a manifestation of the unleashed puer archetype, emulating flying by running so fast. His intense desire to run as fast as possible has the effect of considerable body lightness. He is "light on his feet." Meanwhile, the slow beings in the cartoon, like Slowpoke, are negative manifestations of the senex archetype, worn-out, sluggish, foolish, and non-productive.

When there is no time to stay for long in one place, when we rush from one place to the next, lightness prevails. We stay on the surface, moving as fast as we can. This prevents us from going down into the depths of things. As Alessandro Baricco wrote:

> The idea that understanding and knowing means to penetrate to the bottom of what we are studying, until reaching its essence, is a beautiful idea that is dying; it is being substituted by the instinctive conviction that the essence of things is not a goal, but a trajectory.[33]

In order to journey to the depths, it is imperative to follow gravity, either by staying put on the ground, or going under it, but always affirming our human condition as earthly beings. This need for speed impedes our ability to get to the bottom of things. We stay on the surface, ungrounded. Our cartoon character Speedy prefers fastness and does not value the whole range of body rhythms just as our culture does today. This results in the illusion that fastness has substance and that depth is something that can be found at the surface.

MAKE HASTE SLOWLY

My father frequently repeated the proverb, "Dress me slowly because I am in a hurry," especially when he was confronted with an event that evoked the arrival of a New World that demanded adaptation to a fast-track life. This proverb incites freshness and confusion by rescuing slowness as a companion of soul without excluding haste. I asked myself how was it be possible that someone's acting slowly also could be connected with rapidity? Intuitively, I knew that this saying contained within it a rare kind of wisdom and a foretelling.

At the end of the 1950s, the world was being subtly initiated into the cult of speed, and baby boomers were born. On the day the first supermarket opened a few blocks from where I lived, I experienced how fastness was taking over the way we shop. In the blink of an eye, instead of buying groceries by closely and carefully interacting face-to-face with different food vendors, speed now ruled with the aid of two fast machines—the shopping cart and the cash register machine.

Baby boomers were special witnesses of high-speed beginnings, with a name that even suggests the adoration of fastness. The Baby Boom is defined as the temporary marked increase in the birth rate following the Second World War. The word "boom" refers to the experience of a period of great prosperity or rapid economic growth. Baby boomers grew up with a deep knowledge of the importance of high speed. They developed a strong sensitivity to it that sometimes took the form of enthusiasm and, at other times, defiance.

When researching the proverb "Dress me slowly . . .," I found that its origin is obscure and controversial. Experts cannot agree upon on the identity of its author. This proverb has been attributed to Emperor Augustus, to Charles III, and to Ferdinand VI. But popular belief indicates that Napoleon Bonaparte was the first to say it. In his *National Episodes*, Benito Pérez Galdós recounts that when Napoleon escaped from Elba and returned to France, in an encounter between Ferdinand VII and Napoleon, his valet was so nervous that he couldn't manage to dress Napoleon for his cabinet meeting. Thus Napoleon said, "Dress me slowly, because I'm in a hurry."

This saying situates an activity as mundane and close to daily living as getting dressed as an opportunity to reevaluate the value of slow actions. The proverb is expressed in an *enantiosis*, a contradiction that is a figure of speech by which what is to be understood affirmatively is stated negatively, and the contrary—affirmation by contraries. The conjunction in one single phrase of fastness and slowness produces an element that questions whether fastness is good and slowness bad, or if one is a condition of the other. Another interpretation of this proverb is that in addition to presenting slowness and fastness together, it reconciles and conditions speed to the will of slowness. Calm and tranquility are what appear to predetermine action. Haste, instead of diminishing problems, tends to thwart the best of intentions.

Another version of the same proverb is "More haste, less speed," or "Make haste slowly"—*festina lente*. It was proverbial in ancient Greek that too much haste meant tasks were performed badly and not on time. This saying passed into English, the earliest known record of it being in the Douce manuscript (c 1359). "The more haste, the worse speed," was a common form of the saying from the fourteenth to the early twentieth century.[34]

RECOVERING SLOWNESS

The *New Oxford Dictionary of English* defines "slow" as an adjective meaning moving or operating or designed to do so, only at a low speed, not quick or fast—taking a long time to perform a specified action, not prompt to understand, think or learn, uneventful and rather dull.

With the focus on fast production and performance, slowness has been pathologized and given different negative labels. For example, in education, if a child is diagnosed as a slow learner, it implies that learning has to be fast, that is it somehow wrong to learn slowly. However, there are certain skills that require slowness in order to master them.

Diverse movements are now being born to recover and value slowness. Carl Honoré, in his book *In Praise of Slowness,* shows how slowness is now gaining more and more acceptance. The starting point for his book on this topic comes from his experience with children's books containing fairy tales intended to be read quickly. Discovering the tragic fact that even his contact with his daughter was governed by high speed, Honoré mixes personal experiences from his profession as an investigative journalist to recount the origins and the development of the different world movements aimed at respecting and adding value to slowness as a lifestyle. He writes: "A genuinely slow world implies nothing less than a lifestyle revolution."[35] The subjects explored by Honoré cover diverse areas: the slow food movement, the need to balance work rhythms with free time, the value placed to the cultivation of slowness in human relationships, the diseases and ailments produced by the breakdown in the natural rhythms of the body, and finally the free time and the boredom associated with slowness.

Fastness, technology, and cyberspace constitute powerful tools for reaching goals and succeeding. Together they awaken a sense of progress and productivity in the world. But they need to be counterbalanced with slowness. Puer fastness invites senex slowness. Technology has not found depth located on the surface and is beginning to be forced to hold the opposites fastness and slowness together. If we could hold the fast-slow tension in technology, we could envision the psyche and also the technological psyche in its full puer-senex manifestation. Maybe through consciously uniting process and goal, qualitative and quantitative time, flying and grounding, hesitation and action, technology may fulfill *festina lente* and the senex-puer union under the premise "technologize me slowly, because I am in a hurry."

Rafael López Pedraza states that collective consciousness, by putting so much pressure on being successful, has repressed failure, which has a gravitational pull, necessary to the psyche. As for the Puer Aeternus he says that "acceleration [is] the dominant feature of . . . expression, a feature which is closely bound up with irreflection."[36] He also states, as Jung, that reflection is one of the five instincts humans possess— the others being hunger, sexuality, doing things, and creativity. "Reflection is actually hermeneutic, the art of phenomenological interpretation, as easy as it is difficult. It seems to be the simplest thing in the world and at the same time the most complex."[37] Reflection needs time, a slow pace, but today's world seems to be missing the expression of this instinct. What technology and cyberspace are yet to reflect is the totality of the psyche and not just the ego functioning to the rhythm of the times.

NOTES

1. Elizabeth Farrelly, *Blubberland: The Dangers of Happiness* (Sydney, Australia: University of New South Wales Press, 2008), p. 130.

2. Lee Worth Bailey, *The Enchantments of Technology* (Chicago: University of Illinois Press, 2005), p. 1.

3. *Ibid.*, p. 2.

4. *Ibid.*, p. 3.

5. Michael Staples, "Technology and Non-Efficient Practices," *Lost Souls-Spring 65* (1999): 143-149.

6. *Ibid.*, pp. 143-149.

7. Robert D. Romanyshyn, *Technology as Symptom and Dream* (New York: Routledge, 1989), p. 10.

8. Juan Eduardo Cirlot, *Diccionario de Simbolos [Dictionary of Symbols]* (Madrid: Siruela, 2004), p. 451.

9. Gertrude Jobes, *Dictionary of Mythology Folklore and Symbols* (New York: Scarecrow Press, 1962), p. 1610.

10. Marie-Louise von Franz, *Archetypal Patterns in Fairy Tales* (Toronto: Inner City Books, 1997), p. 170.

11. James Hillman, *The Force of Character and the Lasting Life* (New York: Random House, 1999), p. 43.

12. James Hillman, *Dream Animals* (San Francisco: Chronicle Books, 1997), p. 2.

13. Pierre Sansot, *Del Buen Uso de la Lentitud [Concerning the good use of slowness]* (Barcelona: Tusquets, 2001), p. 11.

14. Delfin Carbonell, *Diccionario Panhispánico de Refranes [Panhispanic Dictionary of Proverbs]* (Barcelona: Herder, 2002), p. 368.

15. *Ibid.*, p. 368.

16. Guy Claxton, *Hare Brain Tortoise Mind: How Intelligence Increases When You Think Less* (New York: Harper Perennial, 2000), p. 1.

17. *Ibid.*, p. 2.

18. *Ibid.*, p. 3.

19. *Ibid.*, p. 2.

20. Bailey, *Enchantments,* p. 221.

21. Paul Virilio, *Speed and Politics* (Los Angeles, 2006), p. 69.

22. James Hillman, *Kinds of Power: A Guide to its Intelligent Uses* (New York, 1995), p. 39.

23. Herbert George Wells, "The New Accelerator," in U.K. Le Guin (ed.), *Selected Stories of H.G. Wells* (Modern Library Classics) (New York: Modern Library 2004), pp. 80-93.

24. *Ibid.*, p. 82.

25. *Ibid.*, p. 91.

26. *Ibid.*, p. 83.

27. *Ibid.*, p. 92.

28. Umberto Eco, *Turning Back the Clock: Hot Wars and Media Populism* (Orlando, 2007), p. 105.

29. James Hillman, *Senex and Puer: An Aspect of the Historical and Psychological Present* (Dallas: Spring Publications, 1979).

30. Glen Slater, "Archetypal Fundamentalism in the Twenty-first Century," in *Psychology at the Threshold*, ed. Dennis Patrick Slattery & Lionel Corbett (Carpinteria, CA: Pacifica Graduate Institute Publications, 2001), p. 205.

31. *Ibid.*, p. 205.

32. Rafael López Pedraza, *Cultural Anxiety* (Einsiedeln, Switzerland: Daimon Verlag, 1990), p. 88.

33. Alessandro Baricco. Los barbaros: Ensayo sobre la Mutación [The Barbarians: Essay on mutation] (Barcelona: Editorial Anagrama, 2006), p. 110.

34. Linda Flavell & Roger Flavell, *Dictionary of Proverbs and Their Origins* (London, 1993), p. 221.

35. Carl Honoré, *In Praise of Slowness: How a Worldwide Movement is Challenging the Cult of Speed* (New York, 2004), p. 17.

36. Lopez Pedraza, *Cultural Anxiety*, p. 85.

37. *Ibid.*, p. 85-86.

PART III:
LOST AND FOUND

TRICKSTER AND THE DELINQUENCY OF *LOST*

TERRIE WADDELL

> No narrative category, or construct is ever fully watertight. Each
> one leaks, some more than others.
>
> —William Hynes[1]

C hris Carter's television classic, *The X-Files* (1993-2002), tickled
and coaxed us along with the possibility that the "truth" was
out there. The series pitted the authoritarian baby boomer
fatherhood against its more identity-challenged generation-x progeny,
who, despite their rebellious angst, looked to these establishment figures
for *the* answers to their uncertainties. While the American Broadcasting
Company's more delinquent sci-fi-cum-action series *Lost* (2004-) still
encourages us to imagine some form of resolution, it's all tongue in
cheek. Stripped of its prerogative to offer or withhold truths, the

Terrie Waddell, Ph.D., is a senior lecturer in Media Studies and convener of Gender, Sexuality, and Diversity Studies at La Trobe University (Australia). Her previous books include: *Mis/takes: Archetype, Myth and Identity in Screen Fiction* (Routledge, 2006); (co-editor) *Lounge Critic: The Couch Theorist's Companion* (ACMI, 2004), produced in conjunction with The Australian Centre for the Moving Image and the Australian Film Commission; and (editor) *Cultural Expressions of Evil and Wickedness: Wrath, Sex, Crime* (Rodopi, 2003). She is currently completing her second book on film, television, and analytical psychology for Routledge, *Wild/lives: Trickster, Place and Liminality on Screen*.

fatherhood finally gets its comeuppance. Literal patricide is par for the course in the series, and even the more sympathetically played dads are exposed as emotionally and/or socially incompetent. The voice of the father, in all its cultural symbolism, is muted, debased, and as a consequence unable to provide any sureties. The key to *Lost,* then, is that the truth isn't really out there at all. What we're forced to deal with are a multiplicity of possibilities, all dependent on our unique relationship to the convoluted screen material before us. The ongoing ambiguity of characterization, thematic development, and blatant screen/literary allusions is infused with the unmistakable odor of trickster. In riding the confusion we're guided by this energy and led to interpret *Lost* beyond any authoritative source. Metaphorically speaking, daddy gets the kiss off.

We might say that *Lost,* with all its textual borrowings, internet marketing strategies, and fan input, echoes the bigger picture of multi-platform media culture where no one is ultimately in charge, answers are merely further questions in disguise, and audiences have become so participatory that the division between viewer and producer is often blurred. Reality begins to kick in when meanings are made in the cracks between audience and text, inner and outer, sense and nonsense. Crevices and ambiguities are, after all, the comfort zone of trickster. The following study of *Lost's* play with audiences, meaning, and the cross-fertilization of other cultural influences is framed through this motif.

Anthropological discourse on global, multidimensional, and ultimately unfixed trickster figures tends to avoid categorical definitions. William Hynes, though, has tiptoed through six common features useful to this discussion: ambiguity and polyvalence; deception and trick-playing; shape-shifting; manipulating situations; mimicking the gods and couriering their messages; and fixing or transforming in ways that are both lewd and sacred.[2] Although Hynes takes a sceptical stance against trickster as archetype in his co-editorship of *Mythological Trickster Figures: Contours, Contexts, and Criticism* by claiming to be "less interested in origins than in cultural manifestations" and pointedly distinguishes his collected authors from those "who see the trickster as so universal a figure that all trickster figures speak with essentially the same voice," he nevertheless treads an archetypal paath.[3] As Jung repeatedley claimed, archetypes are ultimately irrepresentable but have been visualized differently over time and across cultures. Their presence in myth, art, fantasy, and behavior has the potential to impact on a soiciological and psychological level.[4] The archetype therefore functions way beyond "figures that speak with essentially the same voice." One might even say they function in a similar way to the energy of both the media and trickster—all three related by the lack of any definitive meaning. Luke Hockley efficiently sums up the situation when he argues that, "Much like an archetype, a film, or any sophisticated media product, evades any attempt to pin it down. Meanings are in a state of contestation, shifting and changing."[5] Although there are no blindingly obvious trickster figures dominating *Lost*, what I want to argue is that the archetypal trickster *energy* pulsing through this contemporary myth not only guides our attitudes to uncertainty, meaning-making, and empowerment, it also echoes our rewarding and frustrating relationship with the current media landscape.

Inspired by Robert Zemeckis' film *Cast Away* (2000), ABC's president Lloyd Braun pitched a television version to producer Aaron Spelling. Braun and head of drama Thom Sherman then secured J. J. Abrams, credited with *Felicity* (1998-2002) and *Alias* (2001-2006), as the lead creative and directorial force behind the *Lost* pilot.[6] Along with Bryan Burk and Damon Lindelof, Abrams continued to executive produce and write the series that since 2004 has built its audience from web interactivity, repeat episode plays for local viewers, DVDs, and a variety of related paraphernalia.[7] Nine specials promising to tie up convoluted storylines aired in the first four years to give us faith, but I'm still confused. It seemed that the writers were so keen to pump out the pilot that any vision of how an ensuing series might unfold was secondary to the practicalities of casting, scripting, and production. Thrown into action by ABC's take-up of a first season, bewilderment itself became, and continues to be, *Lost's* dominant theme.

The primary storyline is built around a core group of passengers who miraculously survived the mid-air rupture of their fictional Sydney-Los Angeles bound Oceanic Airline flight 815. Washed up on an uncharted Pacific island (shot on Oahu, Hawaii), 1,000 miles off-course and remarkably intact, the fourteen main cast survivors, along with a floating population of peripheral victims (acting extras), begin to discover that the island has both secrets and agency. The series plays with time, flashing back to the characters' past lives in the first three seasons and their futures in the fourth (currently airing at the time of writing this article). Like Stanislaw Lem's 1970 classic sci-fi novel *Solaris*, where the ocean of a mysterious planet manipulates the unconscious of orbiting research scientists, *Lost's* island initially appears to play on the dreams, fears, and conscience of its inhabitants. It also has a redemptive role of healing, conjuring images of dead relatives and bestowing second sight.

While the series maintains its thematic focus on imperfect fathering, death/renewal, and neotribalism, each of the four seasons provide a new challenge for the survivors. Broadly speaking, the first season of twenty-four episodes (including the pilot) concentrates on the passengers' survival, exploration of their new home, and discovery of the island's magical qualities. The characters are confronted by what seems like a huge smoke-swirling force that tramples palm trees, roars on arrival, and violently snatches the odd secondary character, pummeling them against large objects or sucking them into the earth. To amp up the bestial overtones, a survivor faction scouting the tropical island is charged by a polar bear that we're encouraged to think of as the supernatural embodiment of a comic book image belonging to "Walt" (Malcolm David Kelley), *Lost's* psychically gifted survivor child.[8] John Locke (Terry O'Quinn), a paraplegic on boarding the flight, finds that he's able to walk again; the unlucky numbers once plaguing the "comic relief" survivor Hurley (Jorge Garcia) magically reappear on the island; and the miraculously intact eight-month-something pregnant Claire (Emilie de Raven) delivers what is hinted to be a "special" child. The fact that Claire is the only surviving Australian passenger we ever see from this Sydney-LA flight is even more curious. The second season (twenty-three episodes) plays on the discovery, past occupants, and significance of an elaborate system of deserted underground bomb-shelter-like hatches. The third (twenty-two episodes) focuses on the power plays of the survivors, a pre-existing island community ("the others" or "hostiles"), and a second group of Oceanic 815 survivors. The struggles of these various factions continue in the fourth fourteen-episode season, where we're introduced to a new group of mercenary intruders from the offshore freighter "Kahana," and given some insight into the futures of those who manage to escape the island.

As well as the characters' lives oscillating from the present to either their problematic histories before the crash or their precarious futures after rescue, *Lost* relies on its ability to not only cross-reference other television programs, but film, literature, and philosophical movements to help us grapple with the convoluted story/character twists. The series merely emphasizes the notion that all texts are leaky, and as John Frow argues, not "structures of presence but traces and tracings of otherness," formed out of "cultural and ideological norms; out of the conventions of genre; out of styles and idioms embedded in the language; out of connotations and collective sets; out of clichés, formulae, or proverbs; and out of other texts."[9] Overtly self-conscious pop-culture plays, trendy in the 90s but virtually obligatory this century, owe much to the trickster dynamic. When looked at through its mythological projections, this energy takes the form of a notorious transgressor, beyond containment, always on the move or make, and existing outside classifications: "No borders are sacrosanct," says Hynes, "be they religious, cultural, linguistic, epistemological, or metaphysical."[10]

Throughout *Lost* we're asked to channel trickster by traversing time, culture, and artistic mediums. There is the screen and literary castaway genre hinted at either fleetingly or blatantly: *Gillian's Island* (1964), the *Survivor* franchise (TV-2000-), *The Flight of the Phoenix* (1965), *Lifeboat* (1944), *Castaway*, Swift's *Gulliver's Travels* (1726), Golding's *Lord of the Flies* (1954), Wells' *The Island of Doctor Moreau* (1896), Shakespeare's *The Tempest* (1623), Defoe's *Robinson Crusoe* (1719), Wyss' *The Swiss Family Robinson* (1892), even shades of Barrie's *The Admirable Crichton* (1902). Then there are the more inspired allusions to Orwell's *1984* (1949) and *Animal Farm* (1945), *The X-Files*, *Groundhog Day* (1993), Steinbeck's *Of Mice and Men* (1937), Karinthy's story "Chains" in *Everything is Different* (1929), Guare's play *Six Degrees of Separation* (1990), Locke's *An Essay Concerning Human Understanding* (1689) and *Two Treatises of Government* (1689), Hume's *Treatise of Human Nature* (1739), Lorenz's *The Essence of Chaos* (1995), and very possibly Jung's

seminal writing on synchronicity.[11] Indirect references are also made
to the Bermuda triangle mystery, advances in fertility/reproductive
technologies, and the (Jim Jones) Jonestown massacre in Guyana (1978).
Lost's fourth season even includes the actor Jeremy Davies, one of the
small ensemble cast from Soderbergh's 2002 film version of Lem's *Solaris*.
On it goes—this is, of course, only a brief taste of *Lost's* cultural reach.

Although the concept of intertextuality is popularly thought to
focus on the relationship between interweaving texts, it incorporates
the dynamics and implications of how texts are received and created.
When these factors are taken into consideration, as Michael Worton
and Judith Still argue, it's extremely difficult to imagine any work as
fixed, or any imposed meaning as authoritative:

> The theory of intertextuality insists that a text … cannot exist as
> a hermetic or self-sufficient whole, and so does not function as a
> closed system. This is for two reasons. Firstly, the writer is a
> reader of texts … before s/he is a creator of texts, and therefore
> the work of art is inevitably shot through with references,
> quotations and influences of every kind.[12]

Because writers/creators are initially readers/viewers, infusing their
work with inspirational images, sounds, ideas, and plots, their products
are multimodal, and in turn, as Gunther Kress,[13] Ulrike Meinhof,
and Theo Van Leeuwen[14] explain, read multimodally. That is, meaning
is not just dependent on an awareness of influential cross-references,
their histories, styles, and how they contribute to narratives and images,
but on the multiple ways these variously manipulated influences are
perceived, experienced, and discussed by the reader/viewer. Similarly
for Hockley,

> What matters is the negotiation that takes place between the
> screen and the viewer; it is in the imaginal and liminal space, the
> void between viewer and screen, that the new and living image
> comes into being which holds the meaning and reality of the
> situation.[15]

By taking the language of pop culture, presumably second nature
to *Lost's* demographic, the series speaks beyond the screen to the
experiences and tastes of its viewers. The play of in-jokes and references
builds a sense of camaraderie between the program and those watching
it. Interviewed on the *Lost* DVD special feature "Mysteries, Theories

and Conspiracies" (2006),[16] executive producer Cuse admits that "people put more time into the theories of the show than we actually put into plotting the show." In the companion special "Secrets From the Hatch" (2006)[17] he also acknowledges being responsive to fans' expectations and disappointments when planning season two. This reciprocal playfulness suggests that *Lost* isn't as concerned with definitive answers provided by an authoritative source, as much as coaxing out each viewer's unique relationship to the screen material, allowing them to formulate, however fantastic, their own narrative trajectories. Here's what creator J. J. Abrams says about the way fans share his enthusiasm for the series:

> We did this thing thinking this would be a cool show that we would love. It became this thing that surprisingly a number of people embraced and had a following and the coolest thing is to see that people are not just thinking about it [*Lost*], but are really smart about it and coming to these very interesting and very complex conclusions about what may or may not be happening there ... it allows people to engage and creatively start to hypothesize.[18]

This teasing relationship of inner and outer, the open play of images and language presented onscreen for those watching to interpret and manipulate, is certainly not unique. *Lost*, though, seems to distinguish itself in the sheer volume of cross-referencing and the flexible relationship it claims to have with its fan base. It's intertextuality on show—energetic and commercially savvy.

Fans continually swap thoughts, fantasies, likes, dislikes about television programs of all genres through, for example, variously located internet message boards, fan events, YouTube offerings, and fan fiction (often divided into relationship-based "shipper" stories and "slash," same-sex characters' fantasies). *Lost's* offical website capitalizes on these cyber modes of communication. It offers information about the series —episode recaps, actor/character biographies, brief production details/ credits, photographs and full-length episodes after their airdate for local viewers, as well as video games, the "official" *Lost* magazine, downloads, and "revelations" about each episode. As well as basic guidelines for each season, we're also provided with weekly podcasts where Cuse and Lindelof discuss the current episode and respond to fan queries. While these emails often attempt to solicit explanations to nitty gritty plot or character quirks, point out mistakes, or ask for revelations about *Lost's* many secrets, Cuse and Lindelof skirt around disclosing any "spoilers" to protect the mystery of the series and its global syndication. Of course maintaining an air of mystery also keeps audiences guessing, projecting, and participating in the viewer/text relationship. The most distinguishing features of *Lost's* official website, though, are the "Lost Theories" and "Lost Video Theories" pages where fans share their insights.

This kind of oscillation between the series and the various ways it can be interpreted, as well as the complementary and conflicting nature of all the interlinked references within it, is reflected in qualities attached to trickster: confusion, contradiction, ambiguity, disorder, anarchy, cunning, humor, and shape-shifting. Robert Pelton's discussion of the West African tricksters, Ananse, Eshu, Legba, and Ogo-Yurugu, touches on the implications of these complex swings by arguing that meaning is made via the traversing of boundaries:

> They transform the meaningless into the meaningful, not by becoming saviors, but by remaining ambiguous, facing both ways on every boundary. Indeed they are transformers just because their passage beyond these boundaries continually provokes intercourse between what is outside man [sic] and what is inside him.[19]

This is comparable to the premise of intertextuality. Producers and readers not only respond to texts through other texts already in circulation, but they must also necessarily draw on inner feelings, perceptions, desires, and experiences to foster this engagement. Coupled with this reading/producing mobius strip-like cycle, trickster's sense of the anarchic helps us to understand the necessity of structure and disorder as complementary forces that govern life.[20] Or to be more relevant to *Lost* and the bigger picture it offers, the structure and disorder that govern media and cyber communication: "As in his [trickster's] contradiction of the contradictor," says Pelton, "he negates negation and thereby gives birth to a dialectic whose aim is not synthesis, but a never-ending juggling of thesis and antithesis."[21] Through this process we are able to come to a keener understanding of ourselves as well as the permutations, limitations, infinite possibilities, and impact of the material before us. This juggling extends to ideas of closure and open-endedness. While some may expect resolution in *Lost* and look for its boundaries, there's arguably a great deal of pleasure in the chase *and* the lack of an controlling voice: "it's a lot like life," says Cuse, "you march forward, you get answers to certain issues and certain questions in your life, but new ones always arise and I think that's what we always try to do on the show."[22]

WRESTING CONTROL

Within the over-riding confusion, intertextuality, and anarchic nature of the series, there's nevertheless an attempt to rationalize on the creators' part—explain away the eco-magicality of the first season with each of the seasons that follow. Bit by bit the illogical becomes dislodged. As this happens, the island loses its power. It no longer has the lead character status of *Solaris*, able to govern the thoughts and guide the behaviors of its inhabitants. While the television special, *The Genesis of Lost* (2005) intimates that Abrams initially thought of the island as a mysterious force/character unto itself, it develops less and less agency as *Lost* becomes more and more governed by the tropes of the action/conspiracy genre. In its first season, the series promised all the intrigue and boundlessness of a rumbling unconscious, but in trying to rein in this unsettling force, the logic just became increasingly complex. But in trying to rein in this unsettling force, the logic just becomes more convoluted. The way that *Lost* has unraveled is comparable to a story spun by an unskilled liar, unable to retain enough of the original event to make the expanded, fabricated, and self-serving version credible. More lies have to be told, and the unfolding tale becomes so complex and riddled with justification that the narrator either gets tangled in it, or those to whom it is directed lose interest. In using the liar analogy, I'm not saying that the creators have been deceptive, just that in straying from the thrill of the inexplicable, they've become too enraptured in their own more controlling fantasies. The trickster element has not been subdued though—quite the opposite.

For Mac Linscott Ricketts trickster "is the symbol of the self-transcending mind of humankind and of the human quest for knowledge and power that knowledge brings."[23] He controversially argues that as the embodiment of human ingenuity, trickster pits itself against the supremacy of gods and shamans. This opposition, according to Ricketts, is rooted in trickster's refusal to acknowledge a higher authority than itself: "using his one weapon, his devious brain, he attacks and defeats the supernaturals, none of whom are his friend."[24] This disrespect for the gods is apparent in the various acts of thieving attributed to the figure: the Greek Hermes' rustling of Apollo's cattle, for example,[25] or the adventures of the South Pacific's Maui who casts the earth below the sky, lassoes the sun, and steals fire from the gods.[26] "This condition of being more than human and less than divine, of being intermediate between heaven and earth," argues Laura Makarius in relation to the African tricksters Manabozo and Legba, "makes the trickster a mediator—an intercessor ...".[27] In their aspect as culture heroes, trickster figures are often initially descended from, and cared for by, the gods, who they deceive for the benefit of humanity. It's possible to see this kind of heathen behavior in *Lost*. Why should any of the clashing islanders submit to a sense of environmental awe, religiosity, or superstition in preference to their own human power struggles? In placing the focus squarely on the characters' wit, strength, and will to survive by manipulating the island's "gifts" to their own advantage, *Lost* contributes to the canon of trickster mythologies.

One of the ways of wresting control back from the strange behavior of the island was to introduce guns, dazzle us with past and present technology, and progressively amplify the neotribalism as various survivor factions developed (the two groups of flight 815 survivors; the already existing others/hostiles; a community of fertility scientists; the crew of the rescue freight ship "Kahana," another group of scientists trapped on the island sixteen years before the survivors arrived; and the "Dharma Initiative," a defunct 1970s research group behind the underground system of hatches and sociological experiments they were designed for). Rather than the island choosing or beckoning the survivors via flight 815's mysterious splitting over the shoreline, we discover that an electromagnetic pulse emitted from one of the underground hatches via human error was to blame. The magical uncharted nature of the island, that no one initially seems able to escape from, is justified through a character called Ben (Michael Emerson), the ruthless leader of the others/hostiles who thwarts any opportunity of rescue by exploiting the variety of computer, defense, and medical technologies at his disposal. He also has the ability to "move" the island,[28] a possible allusion to the island of Laputa in *Gulliver's Travels,* able to float or fly through the manipulation of a magnetic loadstone.[29] The magical polar bear is explained as a surviving escapee from experimental cages set up by the Dharma Initiative, and the roaring gigantic smoke monster is hinted to be a high-tech security system that protects the island[30] and manipulates human memories.[31] Even the character Desmond's clairvoyance and time travel, presumably gifted to him by the island, is justified as the upshot of his exposure to high levels of electromagnetism within the bowels of an underground hatch and/or the depths of the island.[32] Many mysteries remain, but the drive to arrive at logical explanations by introducing ideologically clashing "tribes," their various political or scientific agendas, and their manipulative power plays, has, in the current climate of environmental erosion, an underlying message. "We" control the land/gods—it/they don't control us.

The use of guns in *Lost* is startling for its uncritical and wildly enthusiastic adoption of the USA's second amendment— "the right to bear arms." From a marshal's pistol that appears in the second pilot episode,[33] the survivors come into possession of a case of hunting knives,[34] a briefcase of guns,[35] and eventually a cache of armory.[36] A military tone creeps into the dialogue from the pilot episode onwards, and the display and use of weaponry is a constant throughout the series. One tribe usually attacks another through exhibitions of gunmanship. Power is decided on who owns guns and who is able to load and shoot the most efficiently. Whenever a new tribe meets an alien group/person on the island, the encounter, like 1950s sci-fi invasion films, is met with xenophobic hostility. Guns are drawn and attack is often thought to be the best form of defense or greeting. It's worth noting that the phallic displays often associated with trickster figures, as Karl Kerényi suggests,[37] are signs of transgressive boundary breaking. He writes of Hermes, for example, as "represented either by the phallus alone, set up as a 'Kellenic image,' or by the ithyphallic herm, the erect phallus and pillar bearing the god's head."[38] As I've mentioned elsewhere, the exaggerated phallic/penile proportions of tricker images like the New Guinean "Iba Tiri," West Africa's "Eshu" and "Aanse," the Winnebago's "Wakdjunkaga," and even the film *Sex and Zen's* (1992) "Mei Yeung-Sheng" are celebrated examples of transgression, potency,

and the power of unruliness.[39] Like these erect tricksters, the bulk of
Lost's male and female characters are also permanently pistol-pumped,
insubordinate, and ready for action. While this excessive preoccupation
with weaponry lapses into a Mars/Ares show of machismo, it's also
undercut with the procreative death/rebirth aspects intrinsic to most
tricksters. The only way to progress, survive, protect, and rescue is
through penile/gun display.

In keeping with trickster's inclination to call attention to
ambiguity and the farcical nature of the human condition, the
frequency with which guns are predictably drawn, bit-part players
killed off in a shower of bullets, areas of land captured and secured
then lost again in a seemingly endless cycle of violence, becomes
increasingly ridiculous. Despite all this "Operation Iraqi Freedom"-
like conflict and bravado, more is *lost* than gained (pun intended).
Indeed, the very idea of control on the island is problematic. When
power is wrested from one group or person to another, it doesn't remain
in their hands very long but oscillates back and forth, desired rather
than attained. And although the acquisition of weapons (let's include
the smoke monster here, presuming it's synthetic) carries the illusion
of power in the series, at odd moments we do return to the enigmatic
nature of the island. It no longer has the ability to terrify its human
inhabitants (that's been replaced by tribal conflict), but it still has the
power to haunt, surprise, and subdue. So although it seems that the
island's various occupants have wrested control from the environment,
the trickster energy guiding this showy usurpation reminds us that
authority and power are ephemeral. Who is in charge of the island
becomes analogous to who is in charge of the seeping *Lost* text itself.

DISCOURSE AND STORY

While the nature or substance of trickster cannot be ultimately
defined, it's possible (as mentioned earlier) to identify the figure and
its cultural/psychological importance through a few recurring
characteristics. In her article "Inhabiting the space between discourse
and story in trickster narratives," Anne Doueihi questions the validity
of any definitive meaning in ancient trickster stories, read as they often
are through the discourse of the colonizing West. She does, however,
argue that the margins separating *discourse* (the ways in which narratives

or theories are discursively discussed) and *story* (narratives that precede such exposition) in all the fables create an "undecidable coexistence" of these two aspects of mythmaking: "for what is the story," she says, "but a trick played by the discourse of the trickster?"[40] According to Doueihi, this notion of trickster riding the space between narrative events and the presentation of these sequences, in effect embracing both, allows us to understand just how inappropriate it is to apply any culturally specific, ideological, or political discourses to these bizarre stories and in so doing claim to have discovered their meaning/agenda. In taking this approach, we stand apart from trickster—render it "Other." Rather, trickster tales reveal "the way our minds function to construct an apparently solid but ultimately illusory reality out of what is on another level a play of signs."[41] Not only does the teasing language in these tales allow for conventional meanings to be made, but also "meaning that is extraordinary, unconventional, and sacred."[42]

> A 'signified' —a local unit functioning in a specific field where it makes meaning possible—turns out to be only a 'signifier' and functions as a signifier. … On the other hand, the story loses its solidity and breaks down into an open-ended play of signifiers. Language becomes a semiotic activity. In this game played with and through signifiers, meaning is made possible by the space opened between signifiers. It is in the reversals and discontinuities in language, in the narrative, that meaning is produced—not one meaning, but the possibility of meaningfulness.[43]

Although she bases her discussion around the specific linguistic patterning of ancient trickster myths, as is obvious in the above citation, her general thesis might also be applied to contemporary visual imagery. The rupture of conventional narrative structure, the refusal to provide a unified meaning, and the bizarre boundary breaking dis-plays of the figure/s in these stories, opens up a multiplicity of interpretations and exposes the inadequacy of oral, written, and visual language to, in itself, provide any absolute sense of reality. The sacred nature and power of Doueihi's trickster, who she sees as playing between discourse and story, lays not in its ability to endow meaning, to provide us with any clear and definitive *sense*, but to make "meaning possible."[44] Might we, in a leap, claim *Lost* as an ancestor of these trickster tales?

It's reasonable to conclude that neither the creators nor the audience can provide any unified understanding of the series and so rein it in. To do so, in fact, becomes impossible if we return to the earlier discussion of intertextuality. We might think of all involved in the experience of *Lost* as being guided by trickster energy and so able to tap ino multiple meanings. Like trickster itself, the text doesn't impose or even offer a sense of judgment as to how we should nogotiate its twist and turns, just that in order to find meaning we have to travel through the uncertainty. While the executive producers push our "need for resolution" buttons with various interviews, television specials, and boys-own podcast banter, the series only ever feigns closure. We're still kept guessing, interpreting, theorizing, and dangling through all this extra-texual chat. Although the characters' systematic father killings operate as metaphors for shaking off the authoritarian voice that inhibits freedom, their post-patricidal adventures also warn us that negotiating the liberated yet liminal beyond can be even trickier. Still, it's bracing to get lost in possibilities, speak to texts as they speak to us, and allow ourselves to be led through this process by trickster whose "constant chatterings and antics," as Hynes notes, "remind us that life is endlessly narrative, prolific and open-ended."[45]

For a further examination of *Lost* in relation to trickster and liminality, refer to Terrie Waddell's forthcoming book, *Wild/lives: Trickster, Place and Liminality on Screen*. The author gratefully acknowledges the permission of Routledge to borrow from this work.

NOTES

1.William Hynes, "Inconclusive Conclusions: Tricksters—Metaplayers and Revealers," in *Mythical Trickster Figures: Contours, Contexts, and Criticisms*, eds. William J. Hynes and William C. Doty (Tuscaloosa and London: The University of Alabama Press, 1997), p. 212.

2. William Hynes, "Mapping the Characteristics of Mythic Tricksters: A Heuristic Guide," in *Mythical Trickster Figures*, pp. 34-43.

3. Hynes and Doty, *Mythical Trickster Figures*, p. 2.

4. C. G. Jung, *Collected Works of C. G. Jung*, Volume 8, eds. H. Read, M. Fordham and G. Adler, trans. R. F. C. Hull (London and New York: Routledge/Princeton, N. J.: Princeton University Press, 1969). (All future references to Jung's Collected Works will use the abbreviation "*CW.*")

5. Luke Hockley, *Frames of Mind: A Post-Jungian Look at Cinema, Television and Technology* (Chicago: Intellect Books, 2007), p. 15.

6. Michael Rosser, "This Man has Lost the Plot," *Television Business International*, 8 (2006): 1. "The Genesis of Lost," in *Lost: The Complete First Season*, DVD disc 7 (Buena Vista Home Entertainment Inc. and Touchstone Television, USA, 2005).

7. *Lost*, ABC. http://abc.go.com/primetime/lost. (accessed June 27, 2008).

8. Season 1, episode 14.

9. John Frow, "Intertextuality and Ontology," in *Intertexuality: Theories and Practices*, eds. Michael Worton and Judith Still (Manchester and New York: Manchester University Press, 1990), p. 45.

10. Hynes, "Mapping the Characteristics of Mythic Tricksters: A Heuristic Guide," p. 34.

11. C. G. Jung, *CW* 8.

12. Worton and Still, *Intertexuality: Theories and Practices*, p. 1.

13. Gunther Kress, "Text as the Punctuation of Semiosis: Pulling at Some of the Threads," in *Intertextuality and the Media: From Genre to Everyday Life*, eds. Ulrike H. Meinhof and Jonathan Smith (Manchester and New York: Manchester University Press, 2000), p. 135.

14. Ulrike Meinhof and Theo Van Leeuwuwen, "Viewers' Worlds: Image, Music, Text and the Rock 'n' Roll Years," in *Intertextuality and the Media*, pp. 61-62.

15. Hockley, p. 124.

16. "Mysteries, Theories and Conspiracies," in *Lost: The Complete Second Season*, DVD Special Features disc (Buena Vista Home Entertainment and Touchstone Television, USA, 2006).

17. "Secrets From the Hatch," in *Lost: The Complete Second Season*, DVD Special Features disc.

18. "Mysteries, Theories and Conspiracies."

19. R. D. Pelton, *The Trickster in West Africa: A Study of Mythic Irony and Sacred Delight* (Berkeley: University of California Press, 1980), p. 234.

20. Paul Radin, *The Trickster: A Study in American Indian Mythology* (Great Britain: Kegan Paul, 1956), p. 185.

21. Pelton, p. 37.

22. *Lost: The Answers* (Met/Hodder, USA, 2007).

23. Mac Linscott Ricketts, "The Shaman and the Trickster," in *Mythical Trickster Figures*, p. 87.

24. *Ibid.*, p. 104.

25. Homer, *The Homeric Hymns*, trans A. N. Athanassakis (Maryland: The John Hopkins University Press: Baltimore, 1976).

26. Laura Makarius, "The Myth of the Trickster: The Necessary Breaker of Taboos," in *Mythical Trickster Figures*, p. 77.

27. *Ibid.*, p. 84.

28. Season 4, episode 13.

29. Jonathan Swift, *Gulliver's Travels* (London: Pan Books, 1726/1977), p. 168.

30. Season 1, episode 23 and season 4, episode 9.

31. Season 3, episode 24.

32. Season 4, episode 5.

33. Season 1, episode 2.

34. Season 1, episode 4.

35. Season 1, episode 12.

36. Season 2, episode 2.

37. K. Kerényi, "The Trickster in Relation to Greek Mythology," in *The Trickster*, p. 182.

38. *Ibid.*

39. Terrie Waddell, *Mis/takes: Archetype Myth and Identity in Screen Fiction* (London: Routledge, 2006), p. 37.

40. Anne Doueihi, "Inhabiting the Space Between Discourse and Story in Trickster Narratives," in *Mythical Trickster Figures*, p. 197.

41. *Ibid.*, p. 198.

42. *Ibid.*

43. *Ibid.* p. 199.

44. *Ibid.*, p. 201.

45. Hynes, "Inconclusive Conclusions: Tricksters—Metaplayers and Revealers," p. 212.

THE LIVES OF OTHERS AND THE INDIVIDUATION OF HGW XX/7

JAMES PALMER

> Anthropologists have suggested that the cultural function of
> tricksters is to destabilize the social order. Tricksters are in-
> house revolutionaries . . . They are, after all, according to Jung,
> symbols of the unconscious self.
> — Andrew Samuels

Ostensibly a Cold War thriller set in communist East Germany
(the German Democratic Republic, hereinafter referred to as
"GDR"), *The Lives of Others* is a stunning examination of solitude,
psychological transformation, and Jungian individuation. German
writer/director Florian Henckel von Donnersmarck offers an incisive
character study of Stasi agent Gerd Wiesler (Ulrich Mühe) as Gerd
spies on an East German playwright, and the playwright's actress
girlfriend and dissident friends. The film marks Gerd's slow change
from a cold, calculating Stasi agent to a more psychologically integrated

James Palmer, Ph.D., is Professor of Film Studies and a President's Teaching Scholar at the University of Colorado at Boulder. He has published numerous articles on Jung and film, including an essay in Spring's *Cinema and Psyche* issue (vol. 73, 2005). Currently the Director of the Conference on World Affairs, he also teaches several interdisciplinary courses, including Jung, Film, and Literature.

man.[1] There are parallels here with films such as Coppola's *The Conversation* (1974), in which Gene Hackman plays a paranoid wiretapper and Tony Scott's *Enemy of the State* (1998), another high-tech conspiracy film starring Hackman and Will Smith. These films surely illustrate the nefarious uses of technology. In the world of realpolitik, many of the most pernicious abuses of technology are practiced by totalitarian regimes such as the GDR. In the post-9/11 world, we are no strangers to the moral quandaries and governmental violations surrounding warrantless wiretaps, ruthless interrogations, and torture. Paradoxically, however, the act of surveillance in *The Lives of Others* helps to transfigure a soul, a hardened but ultimately receptive soul. In a context of political tyranny and artistic repression, Jung's concept of individuation provides the means to explore the many complexities of *The Lives of Others*—the trickster archetype, the crossing of physical and psychological borders, the creative arts, liminal spaces, and active imagination.

The year is 1984, and the Orwellian significance of the date is reinforced by the legend that opens the film.[2] The Stasi, the East German secret police, is described as a "force of 100,000 employees and 200,000 informers [that] safeguards the Dictatorship of the Proletariat. Its declared goal: 'To know everything.'" Big Brother is everywhere and little brothers infest the populace. As historian Tony Judt describes the scope of the state security bureaucracy, "Husbands spied on wives, professors reported on students, priests informed on their parishioners. There were files on 6 million residents of former East Germany, one in three of the population."[3] Only five years later, in 1989, the Berlin Wall will fall. Great writers and dissidents such as Czech President Vaclav Havel will eventually reflect on the communist drive to "know everything:"

> The fall of communism can be regarded as a sign that modern thought—based on the premise that the world is objectively knowable, and that the knowledge so obtained can be absolutely generalized—has come to a final crisis. This era has created the first global, or planetary, technical civilization, but it has reached the limit of its potential, the point beyond which the abyss begins. I think the end of communism is a serious warning to all mankind. It is a signal that the era of arrogant, absolutist reason is drawing to a close, and that it is high time to draw conclusions from that fact.[4]

In *The Lives of Others* von Donnersmarck portrays the turbulent period leading to the sudden collapse of the East German regime as he focuses on the personal transformation and redemption of his central character, Gerd Wiesler. In linking two entirely dissimilar men— Weisler and playwright Georg Dreyman (Sebastian Koch)—von Donnersmark depicts their complementary roles in bringing down the Wall and ending "the era of arrogant, absolutist reason." The principal representatives of the GDR are Gerd's immediate superior, Anton Grubitz (Ulrich Tukur), an ambitious and unprincipled Communist Party hack, and Minister Bruno Hempf (Thomas Thieme), a brutal and predatory senior bureaucrat, whose sexual exploitation of Dreyman's actress and lover, Christa-Maria Sieland (Martina Gedeck), leads to her death. From their school days together, Grubitz has depended on Gerd's shrewd and superior intelligence, but Grubitz has climbed the Party hierarchy, and continues to use, manipulate, and suspiciously monitor Gerd, even as he assigns Gerd the task of spying on Georg (Stasi code name "Lazlo") and Christa.

Early in the film, Minister Hempf's cynical view of human nature is revealed in his critique of Georg's plays and worldview. Both Gerd and Grubitz watch as Hempf tells Georg, "But that's what we all love about your plays. Your love for mankind, your belief that people can change. Dreyman, no matter how often you say it in your plays, people do not change!"[5] Gerd's development throughout the film not only contradicts such cynicism, but it fundamentally undermines the manipulative Hempf, the ambitious status seeker Grubitz, and, by implication, the entire GDR society. Hempf's words could hardly offer a clearer challenge to Jung's concept of individuation—the ability to change, grow, separate from the collective, and integrate material from the unconscious.

Individuation, as a drive for integration and wholeness, brings to consciousness shadow material, persona limitations, and identifications with the collective; awareness of the anima and animus, as well as other archetypes and polarities, arise from the unconscious. The ambivalent Wiesler is surely caught between Grubitz, who embodies Gerd's darker, negative shadow, and Georg, who carries many of the positive traits (creativity, sensitivity to the arts) that Gerd has also repressed and stuffed into his shadow. Gerd also struggles to break his identity with the collective as he vacillates in his loyalty to the GDR and Stasi duties.

I am indebted to Murray Stein's detailed articulation of the individuation process in his book *The Principle of Individuation: Toward the Development of Human Consciousness*. Using alchemical terms *separatio* and *coniunctio* to help define the two major movements in the individuation process, Stein writes:

> This analytic separation includes dismembering both the identities one has forged with figures and contents that have their primary basis in reality outside the psyche (i.e., other people and objects) and those that are grounded first and foremost in the psyche itself. … This movement of disidentification brings about the creation of a more lucid consciousness, a clean mirror. The second movement, which comes into play simultaneously, requires paying careful and continuous attention to the emergence of archetypal images of the collective unconscious as these appear in dreams, active imagination, and synchronistic events. This movement involves taking up this new material into the patterns of conscious functioning and everyday life.[6]

Much of Gerd's psychological and ethical struggles in the film revolve around dismembering his persona as a loyal Stasi agent and dealing with "new material" that emerges from the monitoring of his creative targets, playwright Georg and actress Christa. If the drive or impulse to individuate comes from within, it is triggered in Gerd's case by his paradoxically distant and intimate relationships with these two artists. Both Georg and Christa recognize him as a "good man," and his relationship to them highlights his need to integrate animus and anima material. His growing sensitivity to words and music (the Brecht poem, his own "creative" reports, the *Sonata for a Good Man*, and his final purchase of Georg's novel), as well as his interest and insight into acting and authenticity, marked by his encounters with Christa, all reflect his struggle with and integration of unconscious archetypal material.

The opening scene stresses an Orwellian world of grey settings and nameless, uniformed officers and prisoners with assigned numbers. Throughout much of the film, Gerd wears either a grey uniform or his tight-fitting grey jacket, both emblematic of an ideological straitjacket. Before the interrogation of prisoner 227, Gerd starts the recording machine, and the prisoner sits down, nicely placed between Gerd and the Big Brother picture of GDR head of state, Chairman Eric Honecker, on the wall. Gerd's Stasi persona is on full display—an efficient, relentless interrogator, a defender of "our humanistic system," who takes offense at the denials and perceived arrogance of the prisoner whose friend has fled to the West. This recorded interrogation is then crosscut with Gerd now teaching a class of young, aspiring Stasi agents. Using this recorded interrogation, he lectures in detail on taking odor samples from the prisoner for the dogs who might later need to track this man. He praises the effectiveness of non-stop interrogations. When one of his students objects to the inhumane use of sleep deprivation, Gerd marks the student's name for later reprisal. Gerd continues his lecture by noting how suspect it is that the prisoner's statement is repeated word for word, whereas innocents reformulate their statements. In a cut back to the interrogation room, Gerd threatens the prisoner's family and succeeds in breaking the prisoner, who then informs on a friend. In short, Stasi agent Gerd Wiesler is a brilliant, psychologically manipulative, and ruthless apparatchik for the GDR.

Buried in this frighteningly effective and efficient lesson is the seed for Gerd's transformation. The prisoner's rehearsed statement alerts Gerd to how practiced this non-confession is; the prisoner's repeated account of his activities with the friend who fled to the West contains this innocent line: "We went to his place and listened to music until late." Although this sentence is hardly an admission of the prisoner's subversive activity, listening to music will later prove to be the crucial transformative experience that shatters Gerd's unfeeling persona.

Considerable time is spent crosscutting between Georg and Christa in their flat and Gerd in the attic directly above them, his headquarters for monitoring their lives. These two settings are drastically different— one the intimate space where Georg makes love to Christa, writes his plays, and meets with his friends and the other space empty except for electronic equipment. After the agents bug Georg's flat, Gerd alone climbs the stairs to view the attic. When he first surveys the attic, the initial full shot of the wooden studs and rafters of this long room is reminiscent of the ominous, terrifying rooms of German painter Anselm Kiefer. Gerd's spying surely links these two settings; as he records, he must also listen, and what he hears slowly begins to transform him. The outer ear of recording, of knowing everything, becomes the inner ear of listening, of comprehending things "feelingly," as Shakespeare's Gloucester expresses it. Because of the barren attic setting, sound— whether music, dialogue, or even silence—is sometimes privileged over the image. Such moments, sometimes falsely accused of being un-cinematic, convey the powerful interiority of a character. It is worth recalling Robert Bresson's comment, "When a sound can replace an image, cut the image or neutralize it. The ear goes more towards the within, the eye towards the outer."[7] How Gerd experiences the lives and intimacy of Georg and Christa profoundly affects him. What he hears as a wiretapper enters his mind and activates his imagination, and the attic setting now becomes both physical and psychic liminal space.

Although one might impose Joseph Campbell's hero/quest structure onto Gerd, the Stasi agent's individuation is more aptly linked to the trickster archetype, a more primitive embodiment of the culture hero. Closely associated with the god Hermes, the characteristics of the trickster aptly describe much of Gerd's activities and his individuation. Hermes is associated with liminal space and is referred to as the god of borders and boundaries, a fluid and shifting edge-man at the margins. As trickster and magician, he is the crosser and transgressor of borders, known both as a thief and a psychopomp or soul guide. Hermes is the messenger god, a god associated with humor, transformative energy, and creativity. As an outsider and iconoclast, he is the breaker of both taboos and the group *participation mystique* in favor of individuation. Though far from exhaustive, the above list of Hermes/trickster traits will help amplify the trajectory of Gerd's transformation.[8]

Different as Gerd is from Georg, the former develops similar interests with the playwright. Even their names echo one another, and throughout the film they are linked to people, objects, and actions. A different but caring relationship with Christa links the two men; so does music, Brecht, boundary crossing, writing, subversive actions, and the hidden typewriter. As Georg writes at his desk, a cut to Gerd shows him also concentrating on writing. Gerd is actually drawing in chalk on the attic floor the blueprint of Georg and Christa's flat below. Oddly, the surveillance attic, through this diagram, incorporates the flat, and as Gerd stands amidst his diagram, he slowly steps across a chalked threshold into a space labeled CMS (Christa's initials). This unusual overhead shot emphasizes Gerd's engagement, however abstract, with the anima and specifically with Christa. The brief moment seems ritualistic and presages his yearning for intimacy and his physical intrusions into the flat. This is the act of the trickster/thief and his magical mastering of liminal space, and as such is a precursor to Gerd's lone break-ins of Georg's flat, where each break-in marks the theft of a significant object—first, the Brecht book of poems (a gift to Georg from his blacklisted friend and director Jerska) and later the incriminating typewriter.

Inside the chalk diagram, Gerd is the potential trickster affected by his entry into Christa's space. By direct contrast, this symbolic, psychological moment is crosscut with Minister Hempf's intimidation and sexual assault on Christa in the backseat of his black limo. When Gerd sees the car dropping off Christa in front of Georg's flat, Gerd says aloud, "Time for some bitter truths." He buzzes the flat, interrupts Georg's writing, and forces the writer to witness Christa exiting Minister Hempf's car. Gerd's motivation here is unclear. Is he forcing the naive and, he thinks, smug Georg to face a harsh and hurtful reality? Is Gerd, lacking any intimacy in his own life, jealously sowing distrust between Georg and Christa? Is he exposing Hempf's sordid and vicious behavior? Perhaps all of these motivations are at work. Only at the end of the film do we see parallel actions here. Just as Georg stands unseen inside the shadowy doorway as Christa enters and climbs the stairs to their flat, so Gerd later stands in these same shadows holding the typewriter he has retrieved from the apartment as Georg returns home.

The film is replete with Gerd's comments, actions, and reactions that mark his progress from Stasi agent to subversive counter-revolutionary. Obvious indicators of change in Gerd include the following scenes: first, lunching with Grubitz, Gerd refuses to sit where the bosses sit and tells Grubitz, in a comment laced with droll humor and irony, "Socialism must start somewhere." At this same lunch, Gerd questions Grubitz's overt ambition and careerism ("Is that why we joined?"), and Gerd carefully observes Grubitz, the informer and party apparatchik, demand the name of the young worker who tells a joke about Chairman Honecker. When he invades Georg's apartment, Gerd touches the couple's unmade bed in a poignant gesture that points to his own isolation and lack of intimacy. This absence and need for personal intimacy is further underlined by his brief, desperate, and empty encounter with the business-like prostitute whom he begs to "stay awhile" and also by the poem that he reads from the Brecht book stolen from Georg's flat.[9] When a neighbor boy in Gerd's elevator unwittingly reveals his father's dissident view of the Stasi, Gerd consciously passes up the chance to inform on the boy's family. This act of omission foreshadows his even more subversive refusal to alert the Heinrich Heine Street crossing guards (note the irony invoked by using the name of the great German poet and writer) about Georg's illegal activities. Though offended by the arrogance of Georg and his friends, Gerd rationalizes his own failure to inform the border guards with a quick acknowledgment to his inchoate and changing loyalties to Georg by saying to himself, "Just this once, my friend."

Dynamic character transformation drives this film. Known only to us and finally to Georg, Gerd's moral and psychological quest has transfigured an apparatchik for the collective into "a good man." The subtleties of Gerd's transformation and individuation are explored in four particular scenes that all relate to Gerd's new and complicated response to the arts—to music, to acting, and to writing. The four scenes include Gerd's overhearing Georg playing the *Sonata for a Good Man*, Gerd's synchronistic meeting and conversation about acting with Christa in a neighborhood bar, Gerd's reaction to Grubitz's chilling account of techniques for imprisoning artists and destroying their creativity, and finally, Gerd's disconcerting interrogation of Christa. To look closely at these scenes is to witness an integration of feeling and art and to see the trickster at work—in short, it is to chart Gerd's complex metamorphosis and individuation.

As a playwright, Georg is especially close to his former director, the now "blacklisted" Jerska. When Georg learns of Jerska's suicide, this man of words cannot speak. Putting down the phone, he is joined by Christa as he moves to the piano to play the music that Jerska had given him as a birthday gift, the *Sonata for a Good Man*. Intercut with Georg's playing is a shot of Gerd, headphones on, listening to the music. A slow, intricate, and elegant camera movement seamlessly links these men. Both the dirge-like music and the continuous tracking shot unite Georg and Gerd in their two very different settings. A shrewd, observant man, Gerd is generally stoic, his face characteristically free of overtly readable expressions; here, however, the ennobling, slightly low-angle tracking shot gradually reveals his tears, and the music and camera movement capture the restrained, but shared sense of mourning. Gerd now experiences for the first time the animating power of a *Sonata for a Good Man*. A passage from Oliver Sacks's *Musicophilia* provides an ideal gloss on this scene:

> Music, uniquely among the arts, is both completely abstract and profoundly emotional. It has no power to represent anything particular or external, but it has a unique power to express inner states and feelings. Music can pierce the heart directly; it needs no mediation. One does not have to know anything about Dido and Aeneas to be moved by her lament for him; anyone who has ever lost someone knows what Dido is expressing. And there is, finally, a deep and mysterious paradox here, for while such music makes one experience pain and grief more intensely, it brings solace and consolation at the same time.[10]

After he finishes playing, Georg adds two grace notes by telling Christa of Lenin's comment that listening to Beethoven's *Appassionata* so diverts him that it endangers the revolution. Even more pointedly, Georg says, "Can anyone who has heard this music, I mean truly heard it, really be a bad person?" This last comment seems to confirm how the music affects Gerd. The sonata form, according to Anthony Storr, resonates with the process of individuation because

> creativity usually consists of forming new links between formerly disparate entities, the union between opposites described by Jung. ... Sonata form in music usually consists of an exposition stating two distinct themes, the first and second subjects, which are then juxtaposed and combined in various ways in the development section. Our delight in this kind of music is related to the skill with which the composer creates a new unity out of themes which at first appeared quite separate.[11]

Finally, the structure of the film and the scenes that bracket this musical epiphany work in concert with the sonata, for Gerd is shown reading the lyrical poem from the Brecht book immediately before the sonata scene. As if to reinforce Georg's emphasis on the ethical impact of such music, the scene that follows the sonata depicts Gerd and the boy in the elevator where the Stasi agent forgoes the opportunity to inform on the boy's father.

In a scene both painful and disturbing to Gerd, he overhears the mutual recriminations of Georg and Christa. Knowing how sexually compromised and intimidated Christa is, Georg urges her to stay in the flat and not submit to Minister Hempf's sexual exploitations and to his threat to end her acting career. Both pleading and persuading, Georg tells her, "You are a great artist. I know that and your audience knows it, too." Christa in turn accuses Georg of political accommodations and compromises, telling him, "You get in bed with them, too." Christa's accusation here is both a rationalization and a projection. Georg may be circumspect, even naïve, in regard to the GDR, but he is surely no political toady. Early in the film, he confronts Minister Hempf about the government's unfair treatment of Jerska, arguing that the blacklisted director should be allowed to practice his craft. Listening to the couple's quarrel sends a distraught Gerd into the night to drink in a neighborhood bar. Fearing Christa has gone to meet Hempf, Gerd is stunned to see her enter the bar, and he initiates a most unlikely conversation. Their exchange is quoted below, with my commentary in italics:

C-M: Do we know each other?

Gerd: You don't know me, but I know you. Many people love you for who you are. [*One senses here that Gerd, in speaking for Christa's audience, is also speaking for Georg and for himself. Gerd is also able to speak with uncharacteristic feeling and intimacy because of what he knows and has experienced through monitoring the couple's life, including the recent fight about Minister Hempf.*]

C-M: Actors are never "who they are."

Gerd: You are. I've seen you on stage. You were more who you are than you are now.

C-M: So you know what I'm like.

Gerd: I'm your audience. [*This ironic, ambiguous line not only echoes Georg's "your audience" in his argument in the apartment, but Gerd is Christa's audience in two distinct ways—first, and obviously, as one who has seen her perform on stage in Georg's "Faces of Love," but also as her "audience," her listener, in his role as wiretapper.*]

C-M: I have to go.

Gerd: Where to?

C-M: I'm meeting an old classmate. I . . .

Gerd: You see. Just now you weren't being yourself.

C-M: No?

Gerd: No. [*Like Georg, Gerd is not fooled by her lies. Indeed, he acts as a touchstone of authenticity for Christa, catching her out in her dissembling, and distinguishing that from her true artistry, her acting on stage. Gerd is more than audience here, as he becomes Christa's director, critic, and therapist. Throughout this exchange, Gerd insists that she be who she is and that she act out of that sense of integrity and out of a commitment to her art. Important as this exchange is for Christa, it reveals Gerd's growth, his new level of care, sensitivity, and awareness about theater, about acting, and about relationships.*]

C-M: So you know her well, this Christa-Marie Sieland. What do you think…

Would she hurt someone who loves her above all else? Would she sell herself for art?

Gerd: For art? You already have art. That'd be a bad deal. [*Christa speaks of herself in the third person, as though she is trying to sort out her own insecurities to find the courage to act on her convictions. The prospect of betraying her lover to save her art becomes a reality under Gerd's later interrogation, an interrogation where Gerd seemingly argues in favor of the same "bad deal" he condemns here.*]

This conversation ends when Gerd tells Christa, "You are a great artist." Whether consciously or unconsciously, Gerd has repeated the exact words Georg used in the previous scene. In response, Christa ends their conversation by declaring to Gerd, "And you are a good man"—the very appellation Georg later uses in the title of his novel to valorize Gerd. As if to confirm this judgment, Gerd's influence on Christa causes her to skip her assignation with Hempf and return to the flat and to Georg.

Gerd's understanding, his identification with both Christa and Georg as artists, is crucial to his individuation, but his change is halting and often inconsistent. By having Gerd vacillate in his loyalties, the film generates suspense and keeps the viewer off balance. To be sure, Gerd shows a growing distrust and disgust with Grubitz and Hempf, with their pettiness, their hypocrisy, their ambition, and their abuse of power. Nevertheless, one of the first things Gerd tells the students in his class is "The enemies of our state are arrogant. Remember that."

Gerd is no fool, and he is clearly angered by the growing confidence, indeed arrogance, of Georg and his subversive friends, who, because of Gerd's actions or inaction, remain protected and undetected. Listening in on the men discussing the suicide article to be smuggled to the West, Gerd is startled by the popped champagne cork, a sound that seems to release his resentment, which is further exacerbated by a co-conspirator's toast to Georg: "To you. To letting all of Germany see the true face of the GDR."

An incensed Gerd writes a report to expose their scheme and carries the report to Grubitz. Before he can say a word or give the report to Grubitz, Gerd must listen to his arrogant superior describe Dreyman as a Type 4 artist, one who can be easily broken given the right kind of detention. Dreyman can't be alone and needs friends, could be detained and broken by ten months of complete isolation and good treatment, which would leave nothing for the prisoner to write about later. With the camera focused on the silent but observant Gerd, Grubitz continues his diatribe: "Know what the best part is? Most Type 4s we've processed in this way never write anything again or paint anything, or whatever artists do. And that without any use of force. Just like that. Kind of like a present. What brings you here? Developments with Dreyman?" Instead of turning in his damning report, the appalled Gerd, repulsed by Grubitz's smug maliciousness and relish in destroying artistic creativity, proposes to reduce the size of the surveillance operation. Has Gerd, one might speculate, come to value and even identify with the artist's creativity?

What exactly has motivated Gerd's change of heart here? No longer just a Stasi spy, Gerd now becomes a collaborator and, in an odd way, a kind of co-author with Georg. Anthony Storr argues for the strong connection between creativity and individuation:

> The path of individuation and the changes of attitude which take place can be closely matched with accounts of the creative process given by men and women of genius. First, the mental state during which new ideas arise or inspiration occurs is exactly that which Jung recommended to his patients and which he called "active imagination." Although, occasionally, the germ of a new composition or hypothesis occurs in a dream, by far the greater number of new ideas occur during a state of reverie, intermediate between waking and sleeping.[12]

At different times Gerd, earphones on, is seen nodding or half asleep, occupying that liminal space between the conscious and unconscious. His reports are born out of this psychic, threshold space. The attic itself becomes a temenos, a sacred space and laboratory containing not only the chalk drawing of "Lazlo's" flat, but an alchemical process where Gerd's ego and persona are dissolved, where the Stasi apparatchik, through conscious decisions, instinct, and intuition, turns to soul-making. How odd that all that eavesdropping equipment and dark isolation should provide the alchemy for Gerd's transformation, his receptivity to the unconscious. Storr does point out that "the creative process and the process of individuation are both phenomena taking place largely in solitude."[13] Gerd's creativity and individuation are both possible because of his isolation. Marginalized and alienated, he has the solitude to act creatively, to engage in active imagination.

As a cover story, the playwright and his co-conspirators claim to be writing a stage play celebrating the GDR's 40th Anniversary. Gerd and Georg switch roles with Gerd becoming a kind of faux dramatist with his false reports becoming ever more "creative." As playwright Georg writes his exposé on the censored GDR suicide statistics that are provided through his voice-over, Gerd types "5:00 pm. 'Lazlo' reads the first act of his anniversary play to Hauser and Wallner." In another report, he writes, "4:00 pm. The group is exhausted from so much writing." Georg, reading Gerd's reports near the end of the film, comes upon this passage, this flight of revolutionary fantasy: "We expect further information on the play, a plot summary, etc. Contents of the first act: Lenin is in constant danger. Despite increasing external pressure, he sticks to his revolutionary plans. Lenin is exhausted." One is tempted to substitute Gerd's name for Lenin's here, as Gerd might rightly be viewed as the exhausted subversive. In any case, Georg notes that each report is signed and dated by HGW XX/7. In defiance of Grubitz's sadistic delight in destroying artists' creativity, Gerd mirrors Georg's playwriting skills by creating scenes about a play that doesn't exist. It seems only appropriate that Gerd, the creator of false reports, should end up with the incriminating typewriter, which he rescues almost like buried treasure, or to turn Grubitz's own words against him, the typewriter becomes "kind of like a present."

As Georg and Gerd become more committed to their subversive activities, Christa becomes more vulnerable to the Stasi. She is "caught" and brought in for interrogation in a delivery truck marked "*frischfisch*" (fresh fish). Whether this detail is the result of von Donnersmarck's dark humor or a historically accurate depiction of the Stasi's modus operandi is unclear to me. Ultimately, there is nothing amusing about the threatening pressure Christa feels to collaborate. She proves weak and informs on Georg, identifying him to Grubitz as the writer of the suicide article in *Speigel*, but she initially withholds the crucial information about the hidden typewriter. When the first raid on the flat produces nothing, Grubitz becomes suspicious of Gerd and forces him to interrogate Christa. With Grubitz observing through a mirrored window, Gerd seemingly reverts to his old persona as a ruthless and efficient interrogator. What characterizes this scene, making it especially tense and disturbing, is our own uncertainty about Gerd's motives. Gerd, not unlike Christa, seems to be caving in to pressure by demonstrating to Grubitz that the wiretapper is "still on the right side."

In contrast to the bar scene, Gerd appears instrumental in forcing Christa to betray Georg and her own sense of self. What are we to make of Gerd's calculated and effective interrogation of Christa? This disturbing scene seems to call into question Gerd's integrity, his individuation, his designation by Christa herself as "a good man." Is there nothing that can allay our general discomfort and ambivalence toward Gerd and his tactics here? Because we cannot yet know how the trickster will deal with the typewriter, his actions would seem to indict him. Understanding Gerd's manner and motivations in "turning" Christa is crucial to his identity as both a trickster and a changed man. In retrospect, Gerd can be seen as playing a complicated and dangerous game, juggling multiple motives and negotiating liminal space; the interrogation room where he once exercised absolute control is now a dangerous proving ground for him.

Careful attention to Gerd's performance here reveals levels of communication and even caring that could easily go unnoticed. To get the secret information from Christa, Gerd must reassure her that turning informant will save her career, not destroy her. He must also try to convince Grubitz of his loyalty and still buy time to execute his plan. By contrast, the interrogation scene that begins the film portrays a one-dimensional Gerd, effective in breaking prisoner 227, but a man unaware of and unschooled in human complexities. As Christa's interrogator, Gerd is dressed for the first and only time in a suit coat and tie, apparel more befitting a courtship than a hostile questioning. Because Gerd now has two audiences, Grubitz and Christa, his demeanor is a complex mix of conventional Stasi tactics and threats and an oddly gentle, almost pleading courtship of Christa.

Throughout this seemingly ruthless interrogation, Gerd is sending signals and instructing Christa to inform, to save her acting career, and to play at dissembling. Gerd has himself become a consummate actor, dissembling and deceiving Grubitz, while coaxing information from Christa. Gerd tells Christa, "Save yourself, at least. You have no idea how many people are in jail here for senseless heroics. *Don't forget your audience* [italics added]." The reference to her audience is surely meant to recall (for us, the film audience, as well as for Christa) everything that Gerd has said to Christa in the bar scene. That we are to understand this line as code is reinforced by a cut to Grubitz, who repeats the line, and offers his own puzzled response to Gerd's words: "'Don't forget your audience.' He has some funny ideas." Finally, unlike the linking of authenticity and acting that characterized the conversation in the bar, Gerd here equates Christa's ability to act with her skill in dissembling. Acting and authenticity, as any trickster knows, are not always aligned. Reassuring Christa that he will not allow the raid on the flat to ruin her stage career or expose her to Georg as the informer, he tells her, "I'll let you go immediately and we'll strike only after you're back with him. You'll manage to feign surprise, I'm sure. And tonight. You'll be back on stage. In your element. In front of your audience."

Asking more than demanding, Gerd says, "Tell me where the documents are." As the couple gaze at each other, Gerd almost imperceptibly nods his head twice, gestures that call on her to trust him, to acknowledge his genuine concern for her. Whether she succumbs to the pressure and threats to her acting career or responds to Gerd's more subtle signals, coaxing and cajoling, Christa now reveals the secret location of the typewriter. The hiding place is literally liminal space, the doorsill between the living room and the hallway. She tells Gerd, "You can remove it." In retrospect, her line is most ironic, for Gerd as trickster/thief does indeed remove the typewriter, but not, as she might assume, in the presence of his fellow Stasi agents. Gerd's plan to save Christa's career, to protect her from exposure as an informer, tragically fails. His reassurances, never fully understood by Christa, cannot mask the fact that she has betrayed Georg and herself, thereby sealing her fate. Christa, never knowing of Gerd's plan or its success, panics during the raid; fearing her own exposure and shame, she rushes from the flat to her death.

Gerd, too, pays a hellish price and suffers for his actions and his individuation by witnessing Christa's death and enduring Grubitz's suspicions and recriminations. Gerd is no designated or recognized hero; from the outside, he seems little changed, except that he is further ostracized and demoted within the Party. Grubitz rightly suspects him of betraying the state, and consigns him to a bureaucratic hell: "You'll end up in some cellar, steam-opening letters until you retire. That means 20 years." It is in just such a cellar four-and-a-half years later that Gerd learns from a young co-worker—another victim of Grubitz's reprisals as the one who previously told a subversive joke about Chairman Honecker—that the Wall has come down. On hearing the news, Gerd is the first to leave the cellar; a Hermes-like psychopomp, he leads his fellow workers out of this Kafkaesque hell. Without acknowledgment or reward, Gerd remains at this point a faceless man whose hard-won integrity is recognized only by us. As James Hollis writes,

> Individuation is not self-absorption, narcissism or self-interest. On the contrary, individuation is a humbling task to serve what our deepest nature asks of us. For some it will be a path which brings public recognition, for others suffering and public calumny, for others still, private epiphanies never seen by anyone else.[14]

Director von Donnersmarck takes considerable risks in drawing out his ending with a timeline of events separated by years; indeed, death and redemption converge in the multiple endings of this film— Christa's death, the fall of the Berlin Wall, Georg's search for answers and for the identity of HGW XX/7, and, not least, the confirmation of Gerd Wiesler's individuation. The third of these endings is initiated when Georg learns that his status as a trusted East German playwright was completely illusory. Former Minister Hempf informs the confused Georg that he was under constant surveillance, a revelation that sends the playwright searching through stacks of files and secret reports on his activities. Georg, puzzled as to why he was not exposed and arrested, recognizes the red typewriter ribbon smudges he finds on Gerd's final report. This epiphany confirms for him who took the typewriter from its hiding place, and the ink also resembles bloodstains, a reminder perhaps of Christa's death and the human cost of ending the GDR's repressive regime. Cued by the discovery of the red ink, Georg asks a bureaucrat, "Who is HGW XX/7?" A security card identifies HGW XX/7 as Gerd Wiesler. Georg can then answer his own question by tracking down this man. Our Hermes-like trickster is now reduced to the role of postman delivering mail, and Georg, watching him, hesitates and then declines to confront and thank him. Von Donnersmarck should be praised for his restraint in never allowing the two men to meet. Such a strategy privileges viewers by allowing them to secretly acknowledge the unspoken respect and shared concern the men have for one another. Only we can understand how Georg, through his art and his political resistance, has influenced Gerd, just as we can attest that Gerd, through his actions, his integrity, indeed his individuation, has saved the writer.

Georg does acknowledge Gerd with his novel, *Sonata for a Good Man*, and its dedication to HGW XX/7. Few words are spoken in the final minutes of the film, though we recognize the importance of the music, judiciously used throughout the film, and the motif that accompanies Gerd's discovery of the dedication.[15] Buying the book, Gerd declines to have Georg's novel gift-wrapped. "No, it's for me," he says and with this last line he acknowledges and confirms his own psychological transformation.

The novel *Sonata for a Good Man* suggests that what is exchanged though unspoken between Georg and Gerd finds form and expression in both music and words—anima and animus. Music speaks for the soul, words for the indomitable spirit of humanity—the syzygy of anima and animus. Music, plays, articles, poems, and novels all point to the power of the creative imagination. Everything that the spying was designed to accomplish—to control and compromise Georg, to quash resistance, to suppress the flow of information to the West, and to advance the careers of the Stasi command—has failed.

The ultimate triumph of the creative spirit over totalitarian repression is far from cost free because suicide plays no small role in the film. For Georg, Jerska's suicide is traumatic, though a powerful motivation for his exposé on suicide rates in *Der Spiegel*. Christa, believing that Georg is about to be arrested and that she is about to be exposed as his betrayer, runs from the apartment and in what looks as much like an act of suicide as an accident, steps in front of an oncoming truck. This first of four endings is horrific, but the events and revelations to follow mark the costly, hard-earned redemption of both Georg and Gerd.

Borders and boundaries have indeed been breached in this film. Jerska and the boundary between life and death are recalled in the title of Georg's article, "One Who Made It to the Other Side." The Berlin Wall is down, the boundary between East and West Germany is erased, and thanks to the psychodynamics of the film, there is no fixed, impermeable border between the conscious and the unconscious.

Perhaps we should close where we started with the words of writer, playwright, and political dissident Vaclav Havel, whose commentary on the collapse of communism has a humanistic and even Jungian resonance to it; the passage might stand as a tribute to Gerd Wiesler and a fitting coda for *The Lives of Others*:

> Communism was not defeated by military force, but by life, by the human spirit, by conscience, by the resistance of Being and man to manipulation. It was defeated by a revolt of color, authenticity, history in all its variety, and human individuality against imprisonment within a uniform ideology.[16]

NOTES

1. *The Lives of Others* won dozens of international awards for von Donnersmarck's direction and original screenplay, for the acting (particularly Ulrich Mühe as Gerd Wiesler), and for best foreign film. It won the 2006 Academy Award for Best Foreign Language Film.

2. Christopher Hitchens, in *Why Orwell Matters,* offers the following comment: "To describe a state of affairs as 'Orwellian' is to imply crushing tyranny and conformism. To describe a piece of writing as 'Orwellian' is to recognize that human resistance to these terrors is unquenchable." (p. 5) The first meaning is clearly operative above, but *The Lives of Others* can justifiably be considered a powerful "Orwellian" work that also depicts the unquenchable human resistance to the terrors of oppression.

3. Tony Judt, *Postwar: A History of Europe Since 1945* (New York: Penquin Books, 2005), p. 698. Judt's statistics provide a chilling context for the controversial back-story to the film. When Ulrich Mühe died of stomach cancer in July, 2007, the Associated Press wire story, Thursday,

July 26, 2007, offered the following comment: "The role [of Gerd Wiesler] had particular resonance for Muele [sic], who was under surveillance by the Stasi when he was a star of East German theater. He later discovered that his then-wife, German actress Jenny Groellmann [*sic*], was registered as an informant for the Stasi during their years of marriage. Groellman [*sic*], who died last year of cancer, had denied she was an informant."

4. Vaclav Havel, *The Art of the Impossible* (New York: Alfred A. Knopf, 1997), pp. 89-90.

5. All quotations are subtitles taken directly from the film.

6. Murray Stein, *The Principle of Individuation: Toward the Development of Human Consciousness* (Wilmette, IL: Chiron Publications, 2006), p. 5.

7. Robert Bresson, *Notes on Cinematography* (New York: Urizen Books, 1975), p. 28.

8. There is an extensive body of work on the Trickster archetype. In addition to Stein's *The Principle of Individuation* and his earlier work, *In Midlife: A Jungian Perspective* (Spring Publications, 1983), readers might want to consult Lewis Hyde's *Trickster Makes This World: Mischief, Myth, and Art* (New York: Farrar, Straus, and Giroux, 1998), as well as two books focusing on women and the trickster archetype, Deldon Anne McNeely, *Mercury Rising: Women, Evil and the Trickster Gods* (Spring Publications, 1996) and *The Female Trickster: The Mask That Reveals* (Routledge, 2007). My use of Hermes and the trickster in this essay generally celebrates the archetype's positive aspects. Two fascinating articles that explore the negative side of Hermes inflation are Bernie Neville, "The Charm of Hermes: Hillman, Lyotard, and the Postmodern Condition," *Journal of Analytical Psychology* 37 (1992): 337-353 and James Hillman's response, "A Note on Hermes Inflation," *Spring* 65 (1999): 7-14.

9. The quotation from a Brecht poem is heard in voice-over with accompanying music:

"One day in blue-moon September./Silent under a plum tree,/I held her, my silent pale love/in my arms like a fair and lovely dream./Above us in the summer skies/was a cloud that caught my eye./It was white and so high up,/ and when I looked up,/it was no longer there."

This verse, so evocative of intimacy, quietude, the beauties of nature, and the transitory, clearly moves the lonely Gerd in his sterile urban isolation.

10. Oliver Sacks, *Musicophilia: Tales of Music and the Brain* (New York: Alfred A. Knopf, Inc., 2007), pp. 300-301.

11. Anthony Storr, *Solitude: A Return to the Self* (New York: Ballantine Books, 1988), p. 199.

12. *Ibid.*, p. 198.

13. *Ibid.*, pp. 199-200.

14. James Hollis, *Creating a Life: Finding Your Individual Path* (Toronto: Inner City Books, 2001), p. 135.

15. Gabriel Yared is the composer of dozens of film scores, including several of the late Anthony Minghella's works—*The English Patient* (1996), *The Talented Mr. Ripley* (1999), and *Cold Mountain* (2003). His elegant, understated score for *The Lives of Others* contributes greatly to the power of the film, which is evidenced in the various musical motifs associated with the characters and in the haunting, mournful piano piece "Sonata for a Good Man" in the seminal scene in the film.

16. Havel, p. 90.

—For Sarah Palmer, who visited East Germany in 1987—

PARADOX NEVERENDING: PSYCHE AND THE SOUL OF THE WEB: A CONVERSATION WITH DEREK ROBINSON

LEIGH MELANDER

The World Wide Web is a place (and nonplace) of paradox. It is an Indra's Net of jeweled global connectivity between autonomous individuals, an image of empowerment, interdependency, and communication, but with dark shadows of entrenched hierarchies, corporate commerce running amok, legal and illegal attacks on individual privacy. It generates both rhapsodic praise as a tool for re-inventing and re-imagining the world, and equally strong condemnation as an "addiction" that substitutes for the rewards and challenges of real life, a zombie-like virtual existence in the mind of the machine.

It offers some of the purest entrees into the world of ideas and some of the most egregiously crass mass media manipulation. It offers philosophy and pornography, side by side. The Web is a place where clever marketing can vault unknown individuals and companies to stratospheric fame and fortune overnight, while some of its most ingenious creative thinkers can stay anonymous, playing with ideas without finding the need to sing their own praises.

Leigh Melander, Ph.D., has a doctorate in cultural mythology and psychology, and is the Founding Fomenter of the Imaginal Institute, http://www.imaginalinstitute.com. Derek Robinson is a Fellow of the Imaginal Institute.

Derek Robinson is one of those thinkers. He taught Photo Electric Arts in the Integrated Media Department of the University of Ontario and researched technology for a "voice puppet" interface for people with severe motor deficits at the University of Toronto's Adaptive Technology Research Centre. He has engaged in extensive research in bioinformatics, an interdisciplinary approach to biology through applied mathematics, biochemistry, artificial intelligence, computer science, and statistics to make complex life sciences data more understandable, known most broadly through the Human Genome Project. His bioinformatics research was presented at the International Joint Congress of Artificial Intelligence in 1993, and the "coincidence sets" algorithm developed through that research was utilized as a core component of the bioinformatics software suite developed by Molecular Mining Corporation, Kingston, Ontario. With web luminaries Jason Classon, Stewart Butterfield and Caterina Fake, Robinson helped develop *Game Neverending*, which morphed into the popular photo-sharing site, Flickr, which allows people from all over the world to upload photographs and videos into virtual photo albums. He imagined early versions of "reciprocal syndication" — automated, live hyperlinks that connect web pages together, such as those found in social networking sites like Facebook, while a simple browser-based rich text editing demo he wrote helped define Web 2.0 (the re-imagining of the World Wide Web as a lateral, co-created medium rather than a static construct of owner-created websites that has birthed the explosion of all of the social networking sites like Facebook, MySpace, Flickr, Gather, and joint knowledge construct sites like Wikipedia) as a more democratic, two-way "read-write" medium, where the users are also the content creators. He is also active in the conversation about the next dreamed iteration of the web, the Semantic Web, which is building the technology necessary for computers to organize and share information based on linked meaning, allowing people to share content beyond the boundaries of software applications and websites.

Derek Robinson is his own dance of paradoxes: an imaginer of connectivity, an internet philosopher, a gentle anarchist who has been a witness to the birthing of several of the most creative technology applications in the last decades. His involvement with the philosophy of technology goes back to the mid-1970s when for a time he was, he says with characteristically self-deprecating Canadian wit, Marshall McLuhan's pet rock. And you have never heard of him.

For Robinson, that is as it should be. His world of technology is the world of ideas, of possibilities, and a humanistic connection that celebrates the dance between individual and collective without being caught up in the race for money or celebrity. He doesn't seem to mind their absence. For him, the point is interaction, much like in *Game Neverending* that he helped design, where no one actually wins and success remains undefined.

I met Derek about a year ago, online, through another colleague who was interested in online community. Over the course of that year, we have had many conversations about *communitas*, imagination, and the soul, and where they intersect with technology. Like the Internet and like psyche both, our conversations are spiraling and nonlinear.

The following is one of these conversations, conducted, appropriately enough, on Skype, the internet/phone system that removes the need for long distance phone lines and allows conversers to share voice, text, image, and even live pictures of one another as they speak. It is a short course on the history of the psyche of the internet, its goals and shadows, beginning with Bishop John Wilkins' and members of the Royal Society of London's efforts to catalog all of creation to the coming newest iteration of the Semantic Web, the next generation beyond Web 2.0—working towards making meaning of all of this information we are wildly posting and collecting, weaving context and interconnectivity of ideas. Intertwined with these underpinnings, we played with the question: where is psyche in the Web? How does it reflect soul and open us to new psychological possibilities?

We begin at the beginning, imagining the birth of the Web.

LEIGH MELANDER (LM): Where do you think the soul of the idea of the Internet was born?

DEREK ROBINSON (DR): I think some of its earliest antecedents were in the ambitions of 17th and 18th Century scholars and mystics to define a perfect or Edenic language—for example, Bishop John Wilkins' artificial language of self-illustrating words whose definitions or ontologies, what they mean, could be read directly from their syllables and graphic signs. The Royal Society and other communities in the early modern period wanted to catalog and map everything, everywhere. Leibniz had the idea for a synthetic logical language that would be so clear and so free of ambiguity that people could resolve their conflicts by sitting down and saying "Let us calculate." It's a beautiful, rational, idealistic, and probably impossible thought. But it certainly helped inspire the logicians and engineers who created the computer age in the mid-20th Century.

Umberto Eco's book, *The Search for the Perfect Language*, traces the history of this ideal. On the cover of the book is a picture of the Biblical Tower of Babel. The Web, in particular the Semantic Web project of Tim Berners-Lee who invented the WWW in 1991, aims to undo the curse of Babel: it aims to allow each of us metaphorically to speak our own language, while understanding the thoughts of those around us. It began as a utopian search for connection, towards understanding, overcoming human differences through knowledge.

(LM): In its earliest iteration, the Internet was imagined by J. C. R. Licklider as a "Galactic Network," in work commissioned by the American Defense Advanced Research Projects Agency in response to paranoia about the Soviet's success with Sputnik—the U.S. Military seeking ways to better its communications in the arms and space races and to develop a communications system that would outlast a nuclear strike. But then it fairly quickly moved into academia?

(DR): I think a great central archetype of the Web has been that of a global brain—this is from the title of H. G. Wells's book published in 1937, *The World Brain*. Wells was inspired by the work of European documentarians like Paul Otlet, a pioneer in what is now called information science, and by the new technology of microfilm, to imagine a worldwide effort to create a new permanent Encyclopedia that would unify all humanity, or at the very least preserve our common heritage should the rapidly approaching world war bring about the total collapse of civilization. This had also been a big part of the motivation of Leibniz and Wilkins and the other artificial language projectors, 300 years before.

One of the Web's shadows is the threat of oligarchic control: the ability of nation-states and/or corporations to eradicate the very concept of privacy. Like with what they've taken to calling "biometrics," the way our steps can be traced through stray bits of DNA, the way ants leave lingering trails of pheromones. A world without privacy. But there's also a way in which this is quite wonderful and liberating, too— "even the president must sometimes stand naked." At some point, people will have to drop the pretence and admit their incorrigible humanhood.

But mostly it's about making connections.

(LM): Why do you think these connections are important? Is there psyche in these connections?

(DR): Oh, yes—now the tribe is global. The effort is to connect the tribe. How can we reach out to one another, gaining understanding from each other's ideas and perspectives? And how can we archive those connections and conversations without exerting editorial control on which conversations are important? Is it possible?

What interests me about this is taking a lesson from anthropology —it's the anthropologists' dilemma, when they're out "in the field" in some remote settlement, recording stories, customs, and language, but their very presence threatens and hastens the destruction of the way of life they are recording. It becomes archival, something for the museum, the cabinet of curiosities—but in the same stroke, it also becomes something for all of humanity. Something is lost and something is gained.

But it's only gained if we succeed in keeping it—one of the challenges of digital media is that it is so fragile and transitory. Magnetic tapes from even 20 years ago, from remote-sensing satellites or the Voyager Mission, say, are already falling apart, the bit-rot is setting in —we don't have any machines that can read them, they've lost the Captain Marvel decoder ring, it's just jillion dollar garbage. If something is on paper, it might endure 500 or 1000 years, but digital technology changes so quickly we're losing much of what we've gained. Library card catalogs and newsprint archives which have served generations of scholars are destroyed and replaced by an expensive proprietary piece of software that'll be obsolete in five or ten years—people are being so shortsighted, it's like they don't care, they're not thinking, they're just doing a job. It's not like they're being paid to think...

But, digital media is noncommittal as to content. You can capture cultural memory in every sensory modality, at least in principle—we've got a ways to go on scents and tastes, but it's coming—the digital medium is incredibly omnivorous, vicarious, and precarious. That is its paradox: digital media provides us the opportunity, in its scope and possibility, to begin to archive cultural history and consciousness laterally, but the medium itself is so transitory.

I think that's interesting in itself. I remember a science fiction story from the 1950s, written by a librarian, where all of human knowledge had been committed to a little crystal about the size of a grain of sand —then of course they lose it, oops! Marshall McLuhan used to talk about how you only become conscious of something when you lose it. Only when you emerge from it into some other thing can you understand what was important about the first thing. This is an amazing psychological move. So the paradox circles back on itself— perhaps part of digital media's value, as well as its limitation, is its fleeting life cycle. Maybe it can help us to suss out what is important to us by illuminating what we have lost.

(**LM**): Circling back a little, that's one of the great critiques of the Web—the vicariousness—that we aren't actually engaging in anything, but are just receiving.

(**DR**): Yes. That's a great question. Where is the living there? Where is the being?

Having direct experiences, personal experiences, a sense of engagement is so much on many people's agendas currently; I think it is a quest for the spiritual. I think there is a convergence on what that sense of direct, nonconceptual, immediate experience means, where art, mysticism, and spirituality all collide. There is a phenomenology with this that plays very interestingly in the "nowness" of the Internet. You are there—you're eyeing it—it's some kind of shared moment.

Stewart Brand, who created the *Whole Earth Catalog* (which incidentally at one point in the 80s morphed into something called the *Whole Earth Software Review*) insisted that the modem was the most important development of the computer age. His gang really moved forward with the idea of the Web as a relational and psychological force—they were the "macramé and brown rice," counterculture types who were also developing video games.

They really created the first sense of virtual communities, which started with the old bulletin boards and now are the forums, listservs, and social networking sites of the Web. Personal computers became relay points for grass-roots, many-to-many communication.

(**LM**): What's next on the horizon with this kind of communicating?

(**DR**): I am excited about the imminent availability of multi-touch displays and the wall-sized flat screens that had been promised by our science fiction friends for a long time—an interactive flat surface where you can use fingers as cursors, with both hands, drawing things spatially in depth. And endowing computers with rudimentary senses, pattern recognition, eventually this will go far beyond anything we're seeing today, in the direction of sensory and cognitive enhancement or augmentation. Not quite sci-fi cyborgs, but when it happens it will seem so ordinary that we simply wouldn't see it in those terms. It's like, is Stephen Hawking a cyborg? In the 1990s, I was working on an assistive technology "voice puppet" for people with major speech disabilities; this was technology that required a kind of simple "mind reading" capability on the computer's part to read intentions from fairly subtle physiological clues. Some people find that scary.

Again, this is a sword with two sides—in the hands of the "evil oligarchy," it could be pure 1984—it could easily become the TV that watches you as you watch it. Piracy, child porn, terrorism, there will never be a lack of reasons for inviting the thought police to watch everybody's every word and every move. This global panopticon has grown up around us. But the flip side of the flip side is 100s of millions of cell phones with 100s of millions of video cameras built in, which make it much harder for governments to act in certain ways without raising an immediate global outcry. And I hope to see greater use of remote sensing and digital telemetry in the foreseeable future, documenting perfidious acts of corporate polluters, for example.

(**LM**): One of the paradoxes I'm caught by is the privacy issues that you're talking about in relief with the anonymity of the Web—with screen names, for example, you can be who you want to be.

(**DR**): I think this is one of the places where psyche can be most playful on the Web. It can shape the nature of our interactions and they can become more playful. We can have more of a sense of "putting on" a persona as a normal way of being, the way theater people do, the way performers do. I'm thinking of this generation of kids growing up with their online lives; there is no one more concerned with their authentic self than a teenager! But this kind of adopted persona can open up the multiplicity of that authentic self, allowing us to explore our multiple selves.

Of course, this brings us back to the question of spirituality. Which self are we talking about? Little self? Big Self? But there is more mutability, more flexibility.

This brings me to a fond, fond wish for the future of the Internet and how human beings relate interpersonally and intrapersonally.

(LM): A fond, fond wish! The best kind...what is it?

(DR): We've lived with bureaucracy since the time of Hammurabi, long ago and far away, when certain systems—empires, armies, priesthoods, book-keeping practices—first got established. The anthropologist Jack Goody talks about this in his book *The Domestication of the Savage Mind*, and Bruno Latour, the philosopher of science, always comes back to how long-lived certain cultural practices have been, these ingrained and unquestioned ways of being.

Our practices get coded—in archetypal ways—think of a Table or Grid of rows vs. columns, things against their qualities, and how this orthogonality or rectilinearity becomes part of how we view the world. There's the bureaucratic context—"bureau" means "table" after all! Tables are often hierarchical, like a book's Table of Contents, which is serial, linear, step-at-a-time, logical, "a thing either is or it isn't" kind of thinking. No ambiguity. Tables impose their own order, they demand there be no gaps, no overlap, they subtly coerce people into chopping up reality to fit the table's needs, not the human needs. Isn't that just like bureaucracy though? I mean, apart from all those good and wonderful things bureaucracy has done for us, of course! Like that bit in Monty Python's *Life of Brian*, about the Romans ...

And maybe they are only cultural habits because we've been inside our own culture for so long. We become a culture of certain practices, and those practices are dictated too often by the needs of bureaucrats, such as simplicity, non-ambiguity. It would be stunning, revelatory, if people could just get human with one another. If we could simply acknowledge the person on the other side of the table as human, going both ways, from both sides.

I think that the Web can help people do that, like in the title of the Richard Brautigan poem, "All watched over by machines of loving grace." It's this kind of Whitmanesque fantasy, an image of aroused multitudes who will, through the fierceness and purity of the fraternal love of human for human, beat these digital swords into ploughshares and so prevail against the air-conditioned nightmare of industrial civilization that the artists and poets have been railing, wailing, and howling against.

I worked in pattern recognition for years. There really isn't any technical obstacle to realizing Brautigan's dream. We really can all help each other, and the software could even help with it, but there are still those powerful forces of darkness and ignorance arranged against us. For example, there is constant pressure to make the web a place innately of capitalism. The major internet service providers are currently fighting to create a financial gateway for email delivery—under the guise of protecting us from spam, they're interested in selling email accessibility to their members to the highest bidder, thereby shaping who gets to communicate to whom, about what, and when. It's not a far leap for anyone in power to dictate the same thing—be it companies or governments, ideologues, or religious institutions. You can shut down the revolution that way, by shutting down ideas.

(LM): So this could be a revolution? What kind of a revolution is it?

(DR): Oh, sideways! Definitely lateral.

I spent a lot of time working with indexing, and where you'd find indexers was in the field of library science, which was divided into "lumpers" and "splitters" — cataloguers and indexers, which were like two different species that don't really belong on the same planet. Or it's like there's one schizophrenic little boy playing on the beach, delighting in building up sandcastles and then flattening them, smoosh. We have a psychological urge to build things, to see the splendor in connectivity, and a similar urge to separate or destroy. We get caught by the idea that these things are mutually exclusive.

But the index is about flatness, no hierarchy. You tear down the towers even as you build connectivity. This is something that the Semantic Web will have to deal with: how you assign connections and make meaning while staying in the anarchic splendor of everything being equal and equidistant.

I think this relates to psyche in a very profound way, seeing the mind as an associative matrix, if you like. This comes, of course, all the way from classical philosophy going back to Aristotle, up to the latest in cognitive science and neural modeling. The Web is this vast associative matrix as well. Look at Google—that's the power of the index, lateral connections, all edge and no center.

This is very profound, and certainly I'm not alone in noticing it, but if people actually get this ground into them from living with it every day, using Google, learning to think the way Google thinks, having it rubbed into our pores this way, maybe that could really change things, change the collective consciousness ...

(LM): This is the multiplicity of psyche?

(DR): Yes! And it plays out in an extremely important way.

We live, mostly, in a logical, linear, self-narrativizing, rationalizing, and objectivizing mode of cognition—this narrative that is, by turns, our guide and our pet. Sometimes we lead our little thought monkey, and sometimes it leads us. Most people are completely self-identified with it, even if many of them aren't even aware that it's there. It's so intimate, it's so much who we take ourselves to be.

But, it breaks down when confronted with the a-logicality and a-locality of a network. It gets shaken out of its self-absorption. Circular causality breaks the logical, rational, hierarchical, categorical mind. Not permanently, but long enough to stop and question "the general in the head," as Deleuze and Guattari put it. It challenges the linearity of general's logic: X is true, so it follows that Y is true. In circular causality, X is also true because Y is true!

In the history of ideas, it took an incredibly long time for people to get the idea of feedback. The great mathematical physicist James Clerk Maxwell wrote an essay in the mid-19th Century about feedback, and no one understood what he was talking about. It wasn't until the 1940s-1950s that people began to understand the idea. Now it's part of the lexicon, so that's real progress!

This is key—this is Indra's net. Everything is operating in relationship to everything else. We still have trouble with this. The logical, rational part of the mind sees it as vicious circularity that makes everything seize up and stop. Remember the Star Trek episodes where some planet-sized computer was going to destroy the USS Enterprise? But Captain Kirk would come up with some logical paradox, and the computer would blow its circuits, couldn't figure out how to deal with it. Our brains are the same way, they get caught here. Actually, I think that this is just about the only thing that logic is good for, convincing itself to commit *hara-kiri*.

Rudolph Arnheim, the art theorist, talks about this in a wonderful way, using colors. There's a logical paradox in how we perceive colors. The world that you see when you open your eyes is a bunch of color patches, even before the various shapes begin to articulate and mean something. Each patch of color gets its sense, the color it is, from the colors of its neighboring color patches. But those patches only get to be the colors they are, the colors the eye sees, from the combined effect of the colors of the color patches adjacent to them, and so on and so on. Ultimately, all the color patches depend on all the other color patches. Therefore, logically, it's a vicious circle, an impredicative definition that can't possibly work. Colors can't exist, and we can prove it. Yet there they are!

It's the same with the words in a sentence. The meaning of a sentence obviously depends on the meanings of the individual words that make it up, but each word can take any of several possible senses, and which of them is the correct sense depends on the meaning of the sentence where the word appears, the entire context—the hermeneutic circle. The mainstream of linguistics got stuck there for 40 or 50 years. They just said, "Semantics? We're not even going to go there." Caught in that reductivist science world view. Houses are made of bricks, bricks are made of houses. Except in biological systems and ecological systems and cognitive or semiotic or symbolic systems, bricks *are* in fact made of houses. Christopher Alexander talks about this at great length in *The Nature of Order,* and from the reception he's received it's obviously still an uphill struggle getting the message across.

People resist it because it threatens their sense of stability and security. There's no solid ground if everything rests on everything else and it all keeps shifting, the landscape keeps dancing, as Stuart Kauffman would say. Science has rediscovered the creative power of circular causation, mutual determination, self-organizing systems, over and over again—but knowing how things are, intellectually, isn't the same as getting it viscerally, in the bones and gut.

And, on some level, it's all semantics. Meaning is completely co-determined, relational. This is psyche, a move towards soul. Symbols have meaning because of their co-determined contexts. Archetypes as well. Charles Sanders Pierce once said humans are signs, we get our meanings from the people around us, their lives, acts, and words are living signs to us, as ours are to them. In the Web, particularly as we move forward to the Semantic Web, everything has this co-determination. The structure of the network animates and literalizes the archetype of circularity, the sacred hoop of humanity's ecological interdependence and interbeing. And it happens in this apparently disorganized, spontaneous, anarchic, zen, be-bop kind of way, without a bureaucracy telling it to be that way. So, there's a sense in which the dynamic connectivity of the Web really does furnish a pretty good model of the circulation of "thoughts" in the noosphere, Vladimir Vernadsky and Teilhard de Chardin's imagining of the coming global brain that is the next evolution past the biosphere, where the collective conscious begins to shape the world around us. Even if information scientists might still prefer to call this "citation indexing."

(LM):. Do you think this anarchic move is a soul move?

(DR): Absolutely! I think it's about intuition. How we're presented with, in the liminal ... the way things come to us, there's something on the other side that places things there, and then we can find them, if we have a relationship with the liminal. These things can be anything that exists outside the comfort zone of our constructed worldview and understanding, from ideas to belief structures to physics that we haven't yet comprehended. Anything! We can see these sideways, out of the corners of the eye. The things that get passed between belong to this circling, non-logical, non-rational way of understanding that arises from many things happening all together, from co-determination and mutual constraint.

Our stream of consciousness, consecutive, single-stepping rational mind, doesn't deal with this very well. And there is a reason for that barrier—well, many reasons—but one reason is that the things that entail multiplicities are happening on the other side. Outside of self-narrative focal consciousness. That's the work of consciousness, I think:

to shine light into this great creative darkness there. To go spelunking! And maybe the Internet is helping make that structure more apparent —that infinite sphere whose center is everywhere and circumference nowhere. It's all center, and at the same time it's all edge, and it's all the same place, nowhere and everywhere.

And I think we're reaching for it. For example, the Web is swallowing television completely. I was just visiting my brother, and he turned on the TV to see what stories *60 Minutes* was offering that night. As soon as he saw what they were, he turned to his computer to seek out his own sources rather than accepting the editorial vision of one news organization. He is literally seeking that decentralization, finding the center in the array of editorial voices that are speaking about one particular news event.

And again, this is a place where the corporate/governmental forces are fighting to define what we can gain access to. There's just a lot of inertia there, many people's livelihoods are wrapped up in certain obsolete ways of operating, the command and control mindset and division of labor, the institution of work—a lot of people are subjugated to that.

(LM): Can the anarchic revolution survive? Can soul survive in this battle over who controls the Web?

(DR): On technical grounds, resisting power, I think it can resist. The vulnerability is the ISP, the Internet Service Provider. There is definitely pressure right now for a wedge to be driven by sovereign governments in the service of corporate powers/entities. They're working to close it up and entrench for all time the Thousand Year Reich of continuous surveillance, the ultimate police state. There is new legislation in Canada, for example, to make it illegal to have anything to do with any technology, to have technical knowledge that could possibly be used to break digital rights management. It's Mickey Mouse, king of the world...where the freedom of the individual's computer mouse is dictated to by the corporate Mouse and all that implies.

On the other hand, like with the Great Firewall of China, people are having quite a bit of success punching holes in the wall, breaching the state censorship and evading their scrutinizers, being able to communicate anonymously and securely.

What we sometimes called "democracy" or the public will or consciousness can sometimes get aroused and "do something." That public opinion, the mass mind—no, not a mind—that great brute beast, the Mob, can make change happen. Why and when does change ever happen at that large level? What would it take to make a change on that level, at a time when it seems national governments are working towards an unlimited ability to spy on their citizens for their "own protection"? This is still very vexatious.

Salvation might come out of Africa. The power structures there are so screwed up, and that's where they've planted the one laptop per child program, with its integral networked wi-fi or mesh networking, where every computer acts as both a radio receiver and transmitter. It sidesteps the ISP problem pretty much, because they have no presence there, and therefore no power. This technology, which empowers each computer to be its own internet service provider, could be implemented around the world, and we will have made the ISPs irrelevant.

Everyone has or will soon have a cell phone, even in Africa. I think that's ultimately where the overthrow of hierarchy is possible—not laptops—the laptops will disappear into cell phones. And the Web infrastructure will eat the cell phone networks—within three years, mark my word, you heard it here first! — then the few rich guys who own cellular communications won't have a power source any more, because they don't own that infrastructure. No one owns it, unilaterally.

(LM): I know one of the things you've been working on is the ability for people to use their own computers to create self-regulated private networks. This could sidestep the ISPs as well, couldn't it?

(DR): Together with the mesh wi-fi, yes. Decentralization is inherent to the design of the Internet, making it very difficult for any combine or cartel or government to impose centralized control. Virtual private networks are self-elect communities, virtual constituencies that stand separate from the public net, whose participants can communicate securely and anonymously, safe from prying eyes, thanks to digital cryptography.

The present organization of the Web is based on semi-centralized server farms with persistent addresses, who you pay to host a web site for you, and the server computers are distinct from the "clients," our desktop or laptop computers we use to browse and instant message and do our email, and which tend to move around a lot and lack permanent addresses. The trick is to get every client computer to also act as a server to the computers it's connected to. That's how the Internet is *in fact*, however the client-server architecture has been layered over it, so now we have to layer another peer-to-peer layer above *that* layer.

The content of the Web—the text, images, and multimedia, the secure permanent archival storage of people's personal documents, and the indexing and search functions—all of this can and should be massively decentralized, massively replicated and encrypted, atomized, shared out as zillions of massively distributed fragments between everyone, everywhere. It's the natural architecture of the Internet—a massively decentralized, peer-to-peer digital network—and there are mathematical reasons, combinatorial reasons, why this architecture is so powerful. Abstractly considered, it's the same architecture that nature uses in immune systems, nervous systems, ecosystems, and the genetic, enzymatic, proteinomic dance-steps coded into our cells. And it's the multiplicity of the psyche as well.

And then people who belong to more than one community can intersect. That's the beautiful picture, the multiplicity of psyche again. It allows for local concerns, local issues, local solutions, and also global ones. The global is also local. It's all in the many-to-many connectivity. There's no top cop.

But an important thing, I think, is how it breaks public discourse into many local communities that partially intersect or overlap. People as connectors for other people. It's kind of like China, which has been held together by the gossips for 6,000 years. Everyone is informed about what's going on; everyone's business is that sweet little old lady's business. There's a recent book by Cory Doctorow, *Little Brother,* a novel aimed at the "young adult" market which spells out all the technical details behind making this work, it's this pulpit-thumping sermon on the necessity of mesh wi-fi, peer-to-peer networking, and cognitive liberty. Great stuff! So the picture is all these Little Brothers prevailing against the great, big, scary Orwellian Big Brother.

I am really excited, too, by the multi-touch tables. You could be with someone, with a group of people together, both virtually and physically, and blending the two. It seems wonderful, doable, and ties in with local power generation and distribution, the local economy, barter, micro-banking, home schooling, and so on. Locality is only going to get more important. The worst offenders for global warming are jetliners. It looks as though we're going to have to give those up. Blimps, maybe, or sail boats. It will be slower!

(**LM**): This reminds me of something I was thinking about speed and the Web—I was thinking that it is part of our growing addiction to all things fast. However, with this idea of slowness, I'm also realizing that it also invites a kind of slowness, of mythic time. I find that when I get into a forum that I love with people that interest me, I can spend hours reading, writing, and feeling fed without realizing it.

(**DR**): Oh, yes. And, at a slower pace, the world starts to appear differently. Marshall McLuhan, who had this wonderfully ironic and rhetorical way of looking at things from a vantage somewhere way back deep in the manuscript culture of the twelfth or thirteenth century, said that speed reaches such a pitch that slowness emerges as something exotic, to be nurtured and reveled in.

We're seeing that, in the Slow Food movement, the Slow City movement—I'd like the Quiet City movement! But there's a connection, between slow and still and quiet.

The Web can invite that. And, as you've found on the forum you frequent, it can open up very intimate, very democratic, very multiple ways of solving problems. While it has limitations because we're not in the same room, it also frees us up from bodies that react to other bodies in ultimately inconsequential ways that distract "mind essence."

(Though, in defense of bodies, I will say that 50 percent of Web traffic is pornography. I think it's all to the good! We are so gendered, so sexed, it makes so much trouble for us. I think the more sex that we can actually see, the more people may come to understand how in its thrall we are. Not that we need more Calvin Klein billboards in the world! But it's got to eventually dawn that there's no one to blame here—we didn't make these desires, they're just there—part of the territory. Bless Grandpapa Freud!)

But, about lateral communities. I was very impressed with a woman I went to for physiotherapy, very curious about this extraordinarily gentle approach she was taking. She told me that she and a group of online friends are discovering physiotherapy, articulating it, making it up as they go, discovering new facts about physiology and how the nervous system works. It's a true academy, with no professor leading it, no authority figure, but instead people—some of them academics and scientists, and others not—drawn together through common interest and love of learning.

This mythology of democracy fuels the Web. I heard a speech once to Google employees about all of the impeccable technical reasons why the only way forward to make efficient use of the technology is this absolute anarchic structure. This is the architecture that I'm working on in my own project. If we're lucky, this may be the way that it's done. Laughing at the clowns who want to control it! Who are these idiots?!

(LM): I've seen references to the Web as a literalizing of a global collective unconscious. Does this make sense to you?

(DR): Completely! And I think it can go much farther than it has. We've been waiting forty or fifty years for good speech recognition software. It's impending, and I think it will change everything. This goes back to the co-determination we were talking about earlier, the bricks and houses, parts and wholes. Speech scientists got stuck on the idea that phonemes logically must come before the words, because words are made out of phonemes, therefore the first problem to solve is disambiguating the phonemes. However, phonemes are actually much *more* ambiguous than words! Progress is being made—a lot of it was simply to do with memory, it requires very large databases containing vast numbers of specific instances of things, organized associatively by sounds, meanings, and contexts, every which way.

In the big, big picture, once there's good speech recognition and direct real-time translation, the curse of Babel will be undone, which may partially compensate for the thousands of languages and cultures lost to the centuries-long onslaught of globalization.

I think this is one of the places where human culture will thrive, and the collective unconscious will find new life. Of course, we'll have to do a lot of it over the dead bodies of lawmakers bent on protecting and enforcing copyright. But that is already unraveling, and people are saying we don't care, we like these movies, these books, these tunes. This is our culture, and how is this different from a public library? The stakes are for human culture. Most of the individual content creators actually don't receive monetary rewards, certainly not commensurate with the time they put into their work, which is always the great

argument for copyright. Take the music business, for example—
Courtney Love wrote an amazing article about copyright, artists, record
labels, and how the idea that copyright benefits the artist is nonsense,
it's all for the benefit of the big media combines.

And this brings me to another fond "liberty idea."

(LM): A fond liberty idea? This is even better than a fond, fond
idea…

(DR): It's the death of the expert. I would love to see the death of
the expert. Any human being, just as they are, with the natural
endowment of gifts and graces, ought to be capable of looking after
things more directly and naturally in areas ruled by what Ivan Illich
used to call the "disabling professions." Why do I need a doctor, who's
acting as a functionary on behalf of insurance and pharmaceutical
industries, looking at me like I'm a piece of meat while prescribing
some radical new drug or exploratory surgery or therapy? Help! I could
use a healer, but I don't need that! I wonder how much of a lawyer's
work could be replaced by access to a decent search engine and a library
of precedent cases. Or, the long-running conversation about vernacular
architecture and urban planning, how people have been building homes
and towns for centuries without explicit regulations and expert
interference? Looking at squatter communities, the *favelas,* shanty
towns, people who can't afford architects or planners, who don't need
bottled water and at some point may lose patience with governments
which continue to sporadically bulldoze their homes and communities.

What's exciting about this is people finding new ways of figuring
individual responsibility for themselves. This freedom comes about in
conjunction with caring for others, necessarily.

Using what Illich called "tools for conviviality," people together
are surely capable of solving the problems of the world. This seems to
me like it's the only way, because the world's problems are so pervasive,
so numerous, so massive, and they are always local and they're always
global. It's not that there's a lack of knowledge or solutions; there are
plenty of solutions, but they aren't being deployed, mostly, I think,
due to bureaucratic and professional structures left over from a different
time, a different world. This is Frances Moore Lappe's point about
global hunger. It's about organization and logistics, not about there

not being enough food. We don't have time any more for those kind of costly, centralized top-down ideologies.

And of course, the human soul is fed by the sense of active personal agency given by banding together, working together on things that matter directly.

We've got to be Taoists, I guess. The changes we require are going to be so radical.

(LM): And virtual communities can be part of the answer?

(DR): Utterly. We think about the Internet, on the surface, as being about efficiency and speed. But what it really brings us is the gift economy, new ways of being useful to our kind. Human beings fundamentally need to be useful. And play, we also need to play, of course. The Net brings new ways to play—with the clan and guild structures of online gaming communities, the game itself is, in a sense, only a pretext for community building, camaraderie, self-discovery of learning to work together as a team to achieve a common purpose. Except this isn't "work," it's play. But it might also provide a glimpse of what "work" may become in the kind of pluralist, decentralized, locally self-reliant but globally connected world that, with luck, might emerge from the present disorder.

But beyond that, there is something very extraordinary about things that don't become unvirtual—it's the big dreaming—the sharing, the viral connections, the soul, and the endless paradoxical knot of the mutual determination of the living signs we are.

Merleau-Ponty wrote about this. He said the fundamental thing about human cognition, human perception, is that it is, in the first place, about what other people are perceiving. We humans are so imbedded in this circularly dependent, multilateral, collective bringing forth of reality. This shared dream of purposes and values. The web weaves this in a remarkable way, and we're just on the edges of what that weaving can become.

Jungiana

Concerning the Training of Jungian Analysts: What is Possible and What is Not

ADOLF GUGGENBÜHL-CRAIG

Translated by Michael P. Sipiora & Eva-Maria Simms
with an Introduction by Paul Kugler

The following essay, "Concerning the Training of Jungian Analysts: What Is Possible and What is Not," was written by Adolf Guggenbühl in the 1970's and published in German in 1977. While certain aspects of the essay are dated, for example, referring to the requirement of personal analysts writing letters of recommendation for applicants, the overall essay provides valuable insight into many thorny issues that continue to be at the heart of depth psychology training programs. During his many years of involvement with the running of the Zürich Jung Institute, Guggenbühl struggled with the practical everyday reality of training Jungian analysts. The writing of this essay gave him an opportunity to

Adolf Guggenbühl-Craig was a Jungian analyst, lecturer, and author based in Zürich, Switzerland. He died in July 2008. An extended biography of him can be found in the "In Memoriam" to him on p. 1 of this issue. Michael P. Sipiora and Eva-Maria Simms are both Associate Professors of Psychology at Duquesne University, Pittsburgh, Pennsylvania. Paul Kugler is a Jungian analyst in private practice in East Aurora, New York and the author of several books and articles.

record some of his reflections on various aspects of the educational process, ranging from the criteria for the selection of training candidates and defining a curriculum of study, to the difficulty in objectively evaluating the success or failure of training analysis. In the end, Guggenbühl concludes, Jungian training institutes must struggle with the underlying tension between the necessary organizing "work of *Homo faber*, a busy ego," and the shadowy, more vexing claims of the soul, the human psyche.

The selection and training of Jungian analysts appears to be a more or less problem-free endeavor. The following selection criteria are, to be sure, well established: the training candidate is supposed to be mentally healthy, of slightly above average intelligence, and have a differentiated emotional life. A psychological aptitude—whatever that is—must not be lacking. Moral integrity is also a necessary requirement. There are certainly people who radiate a calming and beneficial energy, while there are others whose psychological presence is destructive. Undoubtedly, the training candidate should be one of those individuals able to exert a healing influence on others.

It need hardly be mentioned that a comprehensive general education must be a criterion for selection. And, since analysts are always expressing themselves in the spoken word, they should be articulate. Furthermore, because psychological life expresses itself through symbols, and the ability to comprehend these varies greatly from one individual to another, a gift for symbolic understanding has to be required. (I speak here of symbols in the Jungian sense, namely, evocative images that represent psychic phenomena, which can barely be grasped intellectually and rationally. For example, the picture of the Black Madonna in Einsiedeln or the black-haired girl in a man's dream are symbols of the dark aspects of the feminine, etc.)

The question of how to educate candidates selected according to the aforementioned criteria does not appear to pose too many problems either. The C. G. Jung Institute requires an academic degree and several years of clinical work. This guarantees a minimum of intellectual ability and psychological stamina.

The candidate gains an essential knowledge of her own psyche, of her unconscious, of her aptitudes, neuroses, and pathologies, through training analysis. A general theoretical knowledge of Jungian psychology and a comprehensive theoretical and practical knowledge of the areas of neurosis, psychopathology, and psychiatry must be acquired. Knowledge of the history of psychiatry helps her realize the historical relativity of psychiatric concepts. A substantial knowledge of the symbols and images of the unconscious, how they are manifested in dreams, figures, etc., is indispensable. The study of the history of religion, mythology, and the world of fairy tales helps the future analyst comprehend the archetypal background of the individual psyche's image world. Through supervised work with patients, the so-called "controlled analysis," the training candidate learns to apply her acquired knowledge and understanding. And finally, a written thesis teaches the future analyst to work in Jungian scholarship.

It would seem, then, that the selection and training of an analyst is relatively simple and without problems. Appearances, however, are deceptive. Why? We have to backtrack a little. The objective in the selection of candidates and their training is to know who will be "good" analysts and award them diplomas. Those who receive diplomas should be qualified to help people with their psychic difficulties.

The success of our training and selection resides precisely in the effective strength of the graduate's analytical and psychotherapeutic ability—which the diploma certifies—to bring about cures that are, in the Jungian sense, "good" or efficacious. There are certain prerequisites to the evaluation of this success. We should be capable of clearly determining the success of psychotherapy and analysis. Are there generally binding, testable criteria for measuring this success? Do we know, outside of our personal opinions, whether someone is an encouraging, "good" psychotherapist and analyst or not?

Why do we not take as the criterion for a successful therapy the simple disappearance of neurotic and psychosomatic symptoms? In most cases, patients decide to go in for analytical therapy because of the suffering that is brought by these symptoms. Unfortunately, practical experience often shows that when the patient's neurotic and psychosomatic symptoms disappear, the passions too are extinguished. The patient may become healthy, but banal and bored.

Is fitness for work and professional advancement a criterion? Did psychotherapy help patients progress in their professional situation and help them earn more money? Increased business efficiency cannot be the only goal of a therapy!

Should we make an effort to examine happiness as a criterion of success? Is the therapy really successful when, on the one hand, the patient has become happier, but on the other, the people around him are driven to despair by his joyful self-development?

What about the ability to adapt oneself socially, to be a popular and exciting fellow human being? And yet, the person is not only a *zoön politikon*, a social animal. Is a deeper grasp of the meaning of life appropriate as a criterion for the success of our work? But how are we to evaluate this "grasp"?

Should we employ all of these and even more criteria? And how do we weigh the relative importance of these criteria? Assuming that one, several, or all of the mentioned criteria, or even yet other criteria can validate the success of our work, who should undertake the evaluation? The patient himself? The analyst? An independent panel? Or all of them together? Evaluation of the success of analysis and psychotherapy is, at the present moment, extremely problematic and still in its early stages. Moreover, even if we were able to judge the success of psychotherapy, we still remain a long way from being able to discover which type of analyst, with which training, and selected according to which criteria leads to the greatest therapeutic success.

At this point we are at the crux of the issue. The success of psychotherapy and analysis is hard to evaluate objectively—except perhaps in extreme cases. The patient's suicide, for example, is usually understood as the definite failure of the therapy. Nonetheless, I have a talented, knowledgeable colleague who, after the suicide of a patient, wondered: "Perhaps the suicide was psychologically correct; perhaps the conclusion he imposed on his life made complete sense." Therefore I repeat: the success or failure of psychotherapy is difficult to evaluate objectively. Accordingly, it is still more troublesome to determine objectively if someone is a good or bad analyst—again, except perhaps in extreme cases.

Under these circumstances, how can we find out if our selection and training program are completely effective, somewhat effective, or entirely ineffective? Our ability to evaluate the effectiveness of our training work in terms of its results is quite limited. We cannot avoid the fact that tradition, and above all our fantasies, ideas, and reflections determine the selection of candidates and the training program. We put into practice whatever we imagine to be or think of as significant. It is important to recognize that fantasies, ideas, and reflections are extremely creative and just as sensibly realized as the results of statistical investigations. A great deal of our educational system—not only in the training of analysts—is based on unverifiable imaginings, mythologies, and reflections. I have, for example, still to come across any work that clearly demonstrates that mathematical instruction actually sharpens thinking, as is often assumed to be the case.

A lot could be gained from acknowledging how much in our system of educational—from primary school through middle school, and perhaps even through college—evolves from our fantasies, not from objective, verifiable realities. Our discussion about the design of education and the nature of educational institutions themselves would have a more playful and artistic character if we were aware of the role of the imagination in them.

We will probably never be successful in evaluating the outcome of our children's basic education. The images that guide the goals and methods of our educational system change at least every 20 years. In order to determine the worth of our efforts, we would have to conduct lifelong studies of people brought up in specific ways.

Let us return to our main theme. The selection and training of analysts is based, therefore, only to a small degree on experience. For the most part, it is really based upon our fantasies, ideas, and reflections. We need to examine whether these are convincing.

First the selection criteria: mental health, good intelligence, and a developed emotional life are required. It seems self-evident that a person who wants to help the mentally ill has to be herself mentally healthy. But is this really self-evident? In a variation on Goethe's statement: "Were our eye not like the sun, how could it perceive the sun?" we can easily say: "If we are ourselves not also mentally ill, how are we able to understand mental illness?" Don't we have some mental illness in ourselves, and if we fail to be in contact with this illness, is it then possible for us to understand mental illness and to help the mentally ill? It seems to me that our experience also indicates—even if it does not prove—that so-called normal, well-adapted people, who neither harm themselves nor the world around them, very often do not understand people who are ill. Perhaps we actually find access to the depths of our souls, to the unconscious, equally through our mental illnesses as through sound health. One could, for example, imagine selecting those individuals for training whose biographies reveal them to be very troubled—people who have found themselves by way of suffering personal problems and life crises. Indeed, the severe neurotic, even those who show psychotic symptoms, are perhaps as suited to the analyst's calling as so-called healthy individuals.

We often simplify our attitude toward this complex issue by saying: the future analyst should or may have thoroughly experienced even severe mental crisis, but she must have resolved her inner problems. Yet does the command, "have a mental problem, solve it," really have any value as a psychologically valid statement? Do mental problems ever get resolved? Or do they not simply become repressed or replaced by other problems, or become an inducement to psychic movement without really disappearing?

One restriction must be made regarding the "mental illness" of candidates. Those who want to become analysts only to heal themselves should be refused. No doubt we heal ourselves in a profound sense through all our professional activities just the same, whether we are active as physicists, farmers, city officials, school teachers, or whatever. But people who expect to be cured not through their own engagement in these activities, but on the contrary, expect a cure from their surroundings, are too narcissistic and rarely have the power to work a cure on others. The future analyst must not expect patients to help her bear her neurosis. Further, I believe that the candidate must not be dominated only by crises and illnesses; she must also have in herself ideas, images, and conceptions of health, strength, the intact family, a functioning society, etc. Otherwise, she later draws patients down into her own unbalanced chaos.

What can be said, from the experiential and reflective points of view, concerning psychological aptitude as a selection criterion? What is a "psychological aptitude" really? Is it that which we in ordinary language characterize as knowledge of human nature, the ability to evaluate the other quickly and practically—for example, what does he actually want of me? Or is it the ability to recognize and describe conscious and unconscious psychological connections theoretically? Time and again I have made the following peculiar observation: practical knowledge of human nature is not always linked with the ability to see psychological connections. We meet many individuals who are interested in psychology, who can formulate interesting psychological insights based on specific facts, individuals who are absolutely and unequivocally talented in recognizing enigmatic psychological connections, generally and in particular people. However, the so-called knowledge of human nature, the ability to instantly recognize and grasp what is right in front of them, is often lacking in precisely these individuals. They know very well how to evaluate a case, understand dreams, or see symptoms in connection with the unconscious. And yet at the same time they are unable to recognize whether the other person is lying to them or whether the feelings are genuine, etc.

It is also fruitful to divide up the so-called psychological aptitude in terms of conscious and unconscious. The conscious aspect is less problematic than the unconscious. Many people are capable, at the unconscious level, of extremely differentiated and profound perceptions of their fellow human beings. An unconscious psychological aptitude can be surmised from their psychologically efficacious, destructive, or constructive words and actions. These unconscious perceptions stand, depending on the circumstances, in the service of destructiveness or love, or both. Such people are able to hurt their fellow human beings severely or help them. The question is: how much of this unconscious aptitude can be made conscious without destroying it. If it remains unconscious and linked to aggression, it can make subsequent analytical and psychotherapeutic work more difficult.

It often seems to me that precisely among those interested in the profession of psychotherapy, one finds people who in every sense completely lack a psychological aptitude. Maybe this phenomenon can he explained through the need for compensation; many people admire their inferior function and wish to live according to it. Feeling types want to appear to themselves and the world as thinking types. Those without psychological talent want (in this sense) to do psychology. One recognizes such people in that they continually make use of psychological jargon and have a psychological label prepared for everything.

Moral integrity seems an undisputed selection criterion. Nonetheless, it is not certain whether a psychological aptitude, and above all psychological healing power, is always linked with moral integrity. Jung himself was of the opinion that the analytical profession should not be wanting in moral integrity. The analyst is really the medicine in therapy. Every medicine can, however, if given in incorrect dosage, act as a poison. The analyst should have the integrity required to honestly try to hold to the contract she has entered into with the patient. She should not take advantage of the patient either financially, emotionally, or erotically, even when the patient offers to let her do so.

The demand that a future analyst should have a true personal healing presence is by itself very reasonable, but this healing power can hardly be substantiated. Assertions about it are always based only on personal impressions.

A good general education and the ability to be articulate can at least be examined. On reflection, one is not able to say much against a good general education. A broad general knowledge, not necessarily in the academic sense, is certainly needed for the work of the analyst since she must be truly able to identify with people from all occupations, social strata, and cultures. An analyst must feel at ease with a biologist, a professor, and an unskilled laborer. However, the ability to be articulate, when carefully considered, can be called into question. The contact between psychotherapist and patient does not occur completely by way of speaking but partially via gestures, and above all through the direct contact of the unconscious of both.

The desire to be objective is always present when selecting candidates. We wish to avoid the personal factor in order not to be arbitrary. On this account, there is a tendency, which exists the world over, to insist on a good academic education as an objective criterion. The C. G. Jung Institute in Zurich insists on a general academic education. Other institutions are of the opinion that an academic education in psychology or medicine should be a prerequisite to being selected for the study of analytical work. In itself, the requirement of an academic education is nonsense. There are countless people interested in psychology who possess a knowledge of human nature as well as psychological aptitude, and have a healing influence on others, but have not been academically educated. Thus, through the requirement of an academic education, many talented therapists are barred from the analytical profession. But at least, the in-itself-objective criterion of a complete academic education guarantees—as said before—a minimal intellectual standard and is evidence of a certain stamina.

You see, now, the difficulty of the selection process. We are unable to know exactly whether it is right or wrong since we are never able to check its success accurately. Even our reflections about the selection are not uncontested and unequivocal. It is all the more important, then, that at least the training be set up so that it comes to achieve what we have in mind. Here, too, we are above all dependent on our reflections, fantasies, and ideas, and are not able to precisely evaluate the results of our efforts.

I daresay that it is hard to raise an objection against requiring a thoroughgoing awareness of one's own latent psychological difficulties, conscious and unconscious. This is certainly not only a matter of knowledge but more one of initiating psychological growth, of becoming whole by means of unconscious dynamics. The training analysis is an attempt to free the analysand from her defensive rigidity and to aid her passionate devotion to the power of her conscious and unconscious psyche, hoping she may continue this impassioned movement all through life. Further, I am of the opinion that it is an illusion—which comes from a colossal yearning to produce a healthy, sound world—to expect that in the training analysis anyone will be liberated from his or her complexes or is supposed to be made completely "unneurotic." The training analysis should lead the candidate to the root of her illness. You rarely remove these roots, yet you are able to help the candidate not become defensive and repress the particular pathology, but to be stimulated and moved by it.

I find it difficult to figure out whether our official requirements for training analysis realize or even approximate our intentions. Is a minimum of 300-400 hours, with two analysts if possible, the right amount to get the psyche moving? Why not 600? 650? 700? 1,000? Or are just 100 hours enough in many cases? Do our requirements paralyze us? What is the value of the training analysts' recommendations? How much of these recommendations are the expression of a counter-transference? Here my fantasies and reflections come to a standstill.

A student who will later have to deal with neurotic or psychotic people should acquire a thorough knowledge of psychopathology and psychiatry. This is part of his or her technical, professional training. One should, at the very least, be able to recognize and name the phenomena that one will later encounter. However, psychopathology and psychiatry must not be studied only for the job-related or technical reason of acquiring the necessary knowledge and skill to deal with sick people. They should also be studied because they provide us with unparalleled access to general psychological knowledge.

Many insights of modern depth psychology are obtained through psychopathology. In psychopathologies, the fundamental structures of mental life are revealed in extremely sharp, sometimes almost caricaturish, fashion. Working with delusions, for example, lets us better understand how the connection of so-called normal people to reality likewise takes place primarily by means of projections, that is, transferences of their own images. The life history we narrate is never a factual report, but a representation of our mythology, a poetic sketch of our life, which uses elements of reality but is not bound to them.

We can naturally assume that the future Jungian psychotherapist must be thoroughly educated in psychology in general, but especially in the psychology of the Jungian school. Almost as important as psychology proper are the fields close to psychology, such as mythology, religious studies, anthropology, the study or fairy tales, etc. Study in such areas develops a sense of the symbolic, without which I cannot imagine any analytic work. We also use the symbols from these fields to bring patients closer to the symbolic value of their dreams, fantasies, and symptoms. Yet here the student panics. Does she ever know enough? The symbols of the psyche are infinitely numerous. It can even happen that students let themselves and their patients be distracted from the central problems of the soul by a superfluity of symbols.

Symbols are effective—they can heal and order, but they can also overwhelm and destroy. They can stimulate the dynamics of the psyche, but their fascinating play can divert us from what is really important. Conveying the nature of the symbolic image is one of the most difficult and most important aspects of the training of an analyst. It is essential for the Jungian psychologist to learn to think and perceive symbolically. Not only is the ability to grasp the meaning of symbols taught in lectures on general psychology and related fields, but it is acquired especially through training and control analysis.

The archetypal contents of the unconscious are fundamental to Jungian psychology. Access to our inborn patterns of behavior, which we often find in symbolic images, is indispensable. Without symbolic understanding, the striving after this archetypal world becomes a literalizing idolatry;

images become confused with the gods they symbolically represent. Dream interpretation becomes the reading of oracles.

That the future analyst should know and must be thoroughly proficient in the specific material of her work is clear. She must, for example, be able to somewhat systematically interpret dreams, this *via regia* to the unconscious. She must especially be able to understand, as far as is actually possible, the unconscious' images in drawings, paintings, etc. She must learn to comprehend, relate, and illuminate the conscious and unconscious psychic life of her patients in terms of the concepts of Jungian psychology. How to acquire knowledge about the unconscious is not without its difficulties. Concepts, terminology, and ideas are of an entirely different meaning in Jungian psychology than in the natural sciences, which dominate our current thinking. Certainly we try to grasp something very real with our ideas and concepts, even the most real thing there is, namely, the reality of the psyche. But we always speak in *images*. Yet because of their previous training, many students tend to literalize these images. They believe, for example, that the anima is of the same kind of concreteness as a cat or dog. They do not see that the anima, the feminine aspect of the man, is only an image for something extremely difficult to grasp. All of our psychological concepts are merely attempts to lay hold of, by means of images, the continually elusive phenomena of the psyche. Many students learn how to interpret dreams carefully and systematically, and then they think that they can now understand dreams according to a set schema. They do not understand that dreams are symbolic images of the unconscious, which we animate through the attraction of other images. They do not understand that the mystery of a dream cannot be solved like a math problem or a puzzle.

We require at least 250 hours—often more—of controlled psychotherapeutic work. Why not 300 or 400? Why not 200? Carefully controlled work with a patient seems to me to be very important. Nevertheless, I am not excited by the exact specification of controlled patient hours and hours when one meets with the training analyst. I do not know of any other way, but I suspect much inevitable number magic lies behind the exact determination of the minimal number of hours.

Before continuing, I wish to review what has been said thus far: in order ensure that we give the diploma to capable and healing analysts, we should first select them according to specific criteria; and second, we should train those selected in a specific way for their profession. However, since we have so far been scarcely capable of determining objectively which kind of analyst is effective and which is not, who does a bad job and who does good, it is extremely difficult to test the validity of our selection and the success of our training. For this reason, the selection and training must be shaped first and foremost according to our ideas, fantasies, and reflections. However, these ideas and reflections are not unequivocal and without their problems; they are all questionable.

Here a small reservation: I personally think that in many cases I am entirely capable of judging whether a therapy was successful or not and to what extent our training and selection was bad or good. My colleagues too believe this about themselves. But this conviction is based on our subjective experience and relies only minimally on objective, statistically verifiable results. So it is that we often have differing opinions. But even when we have the same opinion, this does not objectify anything. It merely reveals that we come from the same fantasies and images. Perhaps in a few years or decades we psychotherapists will be better able to check the results of our efforts and then determine our selection and training programs accordingly. Even if this time does come and we have fewer difficulties with respect to selection and training, we would nevertheless still meet with enough problems and difficulties on the path to becoming an analyst.

Allow me to broaden these reflections that we might move them further. Although the current selection and training of analysts— Jungian or otherwise—seems to rest on a shaky foundation, it nevertheless appears to be extremely effective. This is so in a twofold sense. First of all is its external effect with respect to the outside world. The patients who turn to the psychotherapist for help experience the "well-trained" analyst as someone who really understands her business, who is serious and can help them. It is certainly not the patient's fault that it is so difficult to determine the success of psychotherapy. Patients want to have someone in front of them who has earnestly endeavored to acquire the knowledge and skills that will be of benefit to them in their suffering. The method and problems of the training are of no interest to them. What is important to them is that it happened at all and that it is "guaranteed" by a group of serious and intelligent people. Often, though, we encounter magical ideas here as well. Time and again there are patients who are conscious of the problems in the analyst's profession and training, but who nevertheless immediately trust the carefully educated analyst because of the training. Unconsciously such patients seem to take serious training as a ritualistic legitimization of the analyst's actions. Through her training the analyst has received a ritual certification for her work. She is an initiate and so patients trust her. In this regard, it is also beneficial when the analyst has an academic degree. This has a magical meaning for many people and reveals to them that the person concerned has undergone certain sacred rituals and is now capable of doing the work.

The fantasy of serious selection and training is effective not only with regard to the outside world. The analyst herself, because of her training, feels more competent to fulfill her task. But it is precisely she who should be aware of ambiguity and uncertainty throughout the entire training. All the same, she too has the impression of being ritualistically confirmed through a carefully thought-out training. Through certain ritual activities—such as attendance at lectures, training analysis, control analysis, examinations, a thesis, etc.—she has been admitted into the circle of initiates. She feels like a priest who has received his ordination. The idea of the Christian sacraments has become alien to the general consciousness of modern Europeans. Very few are still aware that through the ritual acts of the church a person is given something that he or she did not have before. As an example, not many people can understand that a baptized child—according to the ideas of the Christian church—has a different place in God's plan of salvation than an unbaptized one. This is the reason modern people experience and project the ritual significance of certain acts more outside of than within the Christian sacraments. That, for example, a trained analyst feels much more secure after having received her diploma cannot be explained through what she has learned and in what she has been trained. As long as our training still rests on such a shaky foundation, its ritual function is of the utmost importance for analyst and patient.

Our heartfelt desire is that future analysts achieve inner and outer confidence through their training, be it through the professional usefulness of the training or through its ritual value. They need this confidence and respect from themselves and from others because, in the end, they are always unsure of and partly unacceptable to themselves and the outside world. Why?

The human soul, as C. G. Jung understands it, is always a vexation, something that is feared and that one would rather avoid. All of us, analysts and non-analysts alike, are afraid of the soul. Yet it is just this soul with which the Jungian analyst is concerned. It is not the animal in us, the animalistic instincts, that shock us so deeply, but the humanness in us—the human knowledge of and anxiety about death. The animal, and in this sense the animalistic in us, has no anxiety about death because it does not reflect upon death. Connected with this is a "senseless" destructiveness, which is also specifically human—the human desire to kill and to sacrifice oneself. In their struggle with death, people try to pass death on the left, so to speak—or on the right, if you wish—in that they seem to drive themselves and others senselessly towards death. The formation of human consciousness includes a confrontation not only with death but also with suffering. Here, too, we overtake nature by time and again submitting ourselves—in obvious contrast to the animal—to "biologically" unexplained cruelty both passively as sufferer and actively as torturer.

Also specifically human is our all-pervading sexuality, which is not regulated by specific times as is the animal's and which has little to do with reproduction. In a mysterious way, it is connected with death. Orgiastic sexuality and death, sexual surrender and dying, are often psychologically close together.

The specifically human soul reveals itself not only in friendly love, relaxed serenity, and the enlightened structuring of life. It shows itself as well in the fear of and struggle with death, in fantasies of suicide and murder, in cruelty and orgiastic sexuality. All these manifestations terrify us profoundly. Jung shows that we human beings are driven to become conscious of the fundamental ground of our existence—not just in its comfortable aspects but in its uncomfortable ones as well. He also repeatedly describes how we attempt, individually and collectively, to avoid confronting those deepest levels of ourselves. To that end, here are only a few examples. The great events of our century are two world wars. Millions were killed during the First World War and millions let themselves be killed under the most horrible and unimaginable conditions. In the Second World War, millions of Jews were killed through a precise, well-functioning administration and many of them let themselves be killed without resistance.

Over and over again, we psychologists tend to shrink from a confrontation with these shadow aspects of the human soul by immediately explaining away or reducing the terrible. We explain the general destructiveness or cruelty in us as caused by a sick society, a disturbed relationship between mother and child, a perverted survival instinct, etc. Straight away the slightest hint of an explanation that splits off the destructiveness in humans from their essential being is enthusiastically latched on to as evidence for such a split.

So blind have we modern human beings become to the central aspects of our humanity that we are astonished when terrorism is once again in fashion. We provide superficial psycho-sociological explanations for the motivation of terrorists—bad living conditions, insecurity, political frustration, social injustice, etc. We downplay sexuality by presenting it as "something quite natural" and by reducing the bizarre multiplicity of sexual life to the "instinct of procreation."

For almost 2000 years the crucified, dying, tortured, suffering Christ, who died for love of humanity, has been the central image in Christianity's reflections and meditations. This should tell us something about human psychology.

C. G. Jung studied the "primordial foundations" of the soul. He speaks of the archetypal shadow in us, whose core is the murderer and the suicide. He also speaks of the *mysterium coniunctionis*, the unfathomable and eternally fascinating connection of male and female. He speaks of individuation as the passionate, almost instinctual search for meaning.

Homo faber, the skillful person who by technical means makes himself comfortable on this earth, is little threat. As for the *Homo religiosus*, who is a scourge to himself and his surroundings, it is his divinity and demons that frighten us. And it is in this sense that the better the Jungian analyst is trained and the more she has been formed by the spirit of Jungian psychology, the more of a threat she becomes to the surrounding world and to herself. The unconscious, repressed, superficial social collective wants to train the psychologist as a technical counselor for managing life problems. A psychotherapist and analyst should be someone who helps us to raise our children, to lead beautiful and honest lives, to be successful and well adapted in our jobs, and to use our sexuality to improve human relationships.

Here we touch upon one of the central contradictions in the training of Jungian therapists. An organized training, an institute, is plainly the work of *Homo faber*, a busy ego. Lecturers must be hired, courses organized, curricula drafted, and minimum hours fixed for training and control analyses. A Jungian training must provide its students with the technical and intellectual skills that will later enable them to become respected therapists who are able to help their fellow human beings live relaxed, happy lives and who can show them the way out of psychic difficulties toward well balanced existences.

If a Jungian institute merely trained those desired psycho-technicians who are able to restore a marriage, help parents raise their children, make a successful workforce even more successful, it would be fairly large and profitable. It would indeed make a happy contribution to the welfare of the whole. However, it would betray Jung and the human soul. It would become an instrument of resistance against the depth of the human soul.

A true Jungian analytical training must over and over again shake the confidence of its students. Only then can they stay in touch with their souls. The qualified Jungian graduate who is trained to be "confident" is a failure. Her confidence reveals that she has closed herself off from the soul and has become a self-deceiving *Homo faber* who frolics about in a wholesome, rational world. Uncertainty is often important to the patient as well. Certainly, it is nice to see a phobic who has been cured and leaves therapy without his fears; but has he confronted the deepest fears and hopes, the joys and sorrows of life?

Jungian analysts will always be a vexation to themselves and to others: they step out of line. They do not want merely to help their patients and the surrounding world develop successfully and healthily and live a happy life. On the contrary, the Jungian analyst wants to help her patients grasp the demonic and divine depths of their own souls.

Much has been said and written about the relationship between Jungian psychology and religion. I do not think that Jungian psychology gives religious answers. But in any case, it always touches those regions of the soul from which religious questions and answers emerge.

The training or our candidates should transmit a great deal of precise knowledge about psychology, mythology, the history of religion, fairy tales, psychopathology, psychiatry, etc. Experiences with the conscious and unconscious psyche of their patients, and—last but not least—with their own psyche, are fundamental. All of this is meaningless if it does not bolster and increase the desire of the candidates that brought them into training in the first place: the desire to be confronted, for the rest of one's life, with the uncanniness and grandeur of the human psyche, healthy and sick, even if this should bring shock and profound emotion, uncertainty and anxiety, faith and nagging doubts. The training of the analyst should not provide certainty and respectability; far more, psychotherapy and analysis call for *passion*.

WITNESS TO THE ANCIENT ONES:
AN "ENTERVIEW" WITH PATRICIA REIS

ROBERT S. HENDERSON

PATRICIA REIS is the author of *The Dreaming Way: Dreamwork and Art for Remembering and Recovery* (with Susan Snow), *Daughters of Saturn: From Father's Daughter to Creative Woman*, and *Through the Goddess: A Woman's Way of Healing*. She works as a psychotherapist and mentor in southern Maine. She has a BA from the University of Wisconsin in English Literature, an MFA from the University of California Los Angeles (UCLA) in Sculpture, and an MA from Pacifica Graduate Institute in Depth Psychology. Holding positions as faculty, lecturer, and dissertation advisor, she has facilitated many artists and writers in bringing their work to fruition, through, for example, Pacifica Graduate Institute, Vermont College, and John F. Kennedy University. She was one of the co-founders of The Women's Well, a spiritually-oriented educational program for women. Patricia also appeared in the film *Signs Out of Time,* a documentary on the life of Marija Gimbutas by Canadian film maker, Donna Read.

Robert S. Henderson is a Pastoral Psychotherapist in Glastonbury, Connecticut. He and his wife, Janis, a psychotherapist, are co-authors of *Living with Jung: "Enterviews" with Jungian Analysts: Volumes 1 & 2* (Spring Journal Books, 2006 and 2008). Volume 3 will be released in 2009. Many of their interviews with Jungian analysts also have been published in *Spring Journal, Quadrant, Psychological Perspectives, Harvest,* and *Jung Journal: Culture and Psyche.*

Robert S. Henderson (RH): How did you come to know about Jung?

Patricia Reis (PR): I first came upon Jung's work while I was working on a Master's in Fine Arts degree at UCLA in 1978. I was in my late thirties at the time and had just gone through a difficult divorce. The Master's degree was my way of "reinventing" myself. Little did I know how profound that process would be. I describe it now as a complete de-structuring and re-structuring of who I was—or thought I was. This transformation was accomplished through the art-making creative process.

UCLA is not exactly a warm, nurturing environment for one undergoing such an ordeal. But I persevered. The things that carried me through were living by the ocean, connecting with the Neolithic archaeologist, Marija Gimbutas, and the writings of Jung. The first book of Jung's I read was *Memories, Dreams, Reflections*. This is a wonderful work for anybody undergoing a large prompt from the Self —very inspiring and encouraging. Through Jung's work, I was able to name what I was going through. Later, my understanding of feminism made me take a more discerning and critical view of his work. But in the beginning, Jung's writing and thinking were very influential.

(RH): How have you come to understand the masculine and feminine in yourself?

(PR): I try not to think in these terms. I find most thinking on this terminology to be quite confused and confusing, at best, and derivative and disabling for women, at worst. Short of giving a whole treatise on the matter, I can say a few words about how I think about these things—and, believe me, I have thought a lot about this subject!

Basically I make a distinction between sex and gender. Sex—female and male—is a biological given, a physical reality with all its attendant sexual ramifications. (Of course, now with transgender entering the conversation, the subject gets even more interesting, more provocative, less rigid, more fluid.) On the other hand, gender—feminine and masculine—is not a given. These terms describe gender constructions that are socially and culturally determined. And this is where the water gets murky.

I have done a pretty thorough analysis of these notions in my first book, *Through the Goddess: A Woman's Way of Healing*. Suffice it to say, I do not ascribe to the idea of contra sexuality or the integration of the "masculine" as the *sine qua non* of women's individuation. What really irks me is when I hear women ascribe to their "masculine" side qualities that are seen as strong, decisive, intelligent, directed, brave, robust. To me, this sounds too much like giving one's power away, and not owning and claiming those qualities as potentially female.

It is too easy in our culture, which is still weighted toward privileging men's experience, for women to let men carry these very powerful aspects for us, or to ascribe them to the "masculine" side of ourselves without giving it a second thought. We have all grown up with socially constructed notions of gender—and it is no small work to deconstruct these ideas and behaviors in ourselves. The notion I find most helpful is one found in female initiations where a woman's power becomes "magnified" through the initiatory ordeal to include previously unexplored, unimagined, or even unacceptable attributes of strength and power.

(**RH**): For those who have been brought up understanding people as having a masculine and feminine side, your ideas sound very interesting. Speaking to both men and women, what are some of the important implications of your notion?

(**PR**): Well, first of all, the Jungian concepts of masculine/feminine are considered to be universal or ahistorical. They are not. These ideas grew out of the 19th and early 20th century family structure which reflected the gender stereotypes of the day (for white Western culture). Secondly, any of these ideas must be grounded in lived bodily experience, otherwise we continue to support a body/mind duality. Then, notions of masculine and feminine are not simply ways of speaking about the psyche, or even of the body/mind. The real implications are about power.

In the last twenty years, there has been an enormous body of work produced under the title of Gender Studies. Simply speaking, this body of work does for the idea (and experience) of gender what the feminist movement did for women and the civil rights movement did for people of color. It examines the power dynamic inherent in the dominant ideas of gender in our culture and then deconstructs them. In the case of gender, we have to realize that heterosexuality has hegemony and, in the past, has been compulsory.

With the outing and empowering of lesbian, gay, bisexual, and transsexual people we can no longer cling to tidy little categories grown out of our own gender insecurities. We have to expand our notions out to include the embodied and psychological experience of, say, a female-to-male transsexual person. When we start to apply the traditional masculine/feminine categories to that person, the whole idea starts to fall apart. Basically, I believe we are being asked to become more differentiated in our knowledge. It is a matter of having our ideas cohere to the multiplicity and diversity of human sexual experience.

(RH): Do you consider yourself a spiritual person? And what does that mean to you?

(PR): I do consider myself to be a deeply spiritual person. That said, I want to distinguish my spirituality from any particular religious tradition. My spirituality has evolved over time. As a child, I was raised as a Catholic. In my twenties, I converted to Judaism.

It was an effort on my part to "go back," to go more deeply into the source of religion as I understood it at the time. Then, for a while, I had no interest in things religious or spiritual. However, in my late thirties as I was studying art at UCLA, I began to learn about the neolithic goddess-worshipping cultures of Old Europe (2500-6000 BC). This coincided with my meeting and studying with the internationally known archaeologist, Marija Gimbutas, who pioneered the research on these cultures. As a woman and an artist, I was interested in making the connection between art-making, spirituality, and female imagery. I pushed my study further back in time and went to the paleolithic caves in the Dordogne Valley in France, looking for the "first" images made by humans (20,000 BC). They turned out to be female images, engraved on walls and carved in coal, stone, and bone! This was electrifying for me and laid a groundwork for the experience of female spirituality.

Because I am an introvert, I never joined any of the goddess-worshipping groups, although there were many in California where I lived at the time. And I wasn't interested necessarily in finding a paticular form of worship. But these cultures did give me a felt sense of ancient lineage. During those years, I was also doing wilderness vision quests in the Sierras, and I was powerfully grounded in those experiences where synchronicity abounds and dreams and visions occur. So all these experiences are layered in to form my own personal spiritual repertoire. I have an instinctive resistance to "organized religion," although I have sampled Hindu spirituality as well as Buddhist meditation. I would say now that the teachings that support me the most in my personal life and in my psychotherapy practice are the Buddhist teachings on suffering.

(RH): What have you learned about suffering?

(PR): Well, this is an enormous topic, and one worthy of many, many long conversations. I have had to really feel my way into the kind of answer that would be both spacious and specific.

The Buddhists teach us that life is really all about suffering and the alleviation of suffering. This teaching is not necessarily palatable to our "feel-good" culture. Nor does this notion represent what might be called a "depressive" position, i.e., focusing on the negative. In fact, I find the Buddhist teachings on suffering to be extremely liberating. More oppressive to me is the idea that we should not suffer (if we are on the right path, if god loves us, if we are really good, if we eat the right food, think the right thoughts, *ad absurdum*, etc).

The Buddhists also give us guidance on how to deal with suffering in our lives, and I find much wisdom to be gained from their perspective: for instance, the idea of the "poisons" or afflictions which infect us, i.e., attachment, hatred, ignorance, pride, and jealousy. Meditation practice offers ways of clearing these poisons from our minds and lets us see that we have a self that is capable of living without these afflictions. There is also a response to suffering which calls out for justice.

In my own privileged, white, western, educated, middle-class life it would appear that I have not suffered. But there are certain sufferings which are not readily apparent from the above descriptors. For instance, I was born a female into a culture whose institutions (religious, medical, governmental) denied women control over their own bodies in subtle and not so subtle ways. My personal experience with this was an illegal abortion (pre-*Roe v. Wade*) while in my early twenties in which I was badly abused.

I have subsequently worked for women's rights in every way that I can. In this country, I have worked with the suffering incurred by rape, incest, physical abuse, and other forms of domination. I have also made several trips to Bosnia and been present to the profound and unbearable suffering of the Muslim women during their recent war. From that experience, I found that the role of witness, being able to bear the intolerable, to breathe with it and into it, was a practice that was helpful and even potentially healing for myself and others.

Finally, from years of attending to my own dreams and listening to the dreams of others, I have developed a firm belief in what I call "transgenerational haunting," a term coined in the 1950s by two Fruedian analysts, Nicholas Abraham and Maria Torok. This is suffering that operates at the collective level.

I was born in 1940, right about the time that Hitler was beginning his rampage. I believe that I, along with others born during those years, carry a psychic haunting of what happened during that time.

I was born in America. And I have a deep feeling (in my DNA?) for the genocide of Native people that happened on our soil. I have worked with people whose ancestors were slaves and others whose ancestors were slaveholders. I do not believe we can escape this heritage of suffering. We can only work for justice, for understanding our human implication in these tragedies. The Buddhists believe that no one is free until everyone is free.

(**RH**): I can remember when we first met. It was in Santa Barbara at a conference to honor your mentor, Marija Gimbutas. You made an incredible presentation and showed many pictures of your art and sculpture. I could tell then that you are a deep artist. Do you feel your spirituality and creativity are connected?

(**PR**): Yes, I remember that event very well. I had presented a slide show of the evolution of my art work, which was really an evolution of myself as an artist, which was really an evolution of my self as a woman on a psychological and spiritual quest. So, indeed, those two streams, creativity and spirituality, flow deeply together.

As I mentioned before, Gimbutas's work fired my own imagination and was an important and grounding influence on my creative life. In those days, I had a burning desire to understand how image-making, spirituality, and female consciousness could be deeply and authentically expressed. That work culminated in a large installation of nine sculptures I called the Ancient Ones. I also wrote a poem that expresses who those Ancient Ones are:

> We say the time of waiting is over.
> We say the silence has been broken.
> We say there can be no forgetting now.
> We say
> LISTEN
> We are the bones
> of your grandmother's grandmothers.
> We have returned now.
> We say you cannot forget us now
> We say we are with you
> And you are us.

The poem has apparently had a wide circulation—and seems to speak to many people. It has most recently been published in Jane Ely's book, *Remembering the Ancestral Soul*, where I think it has found a good home. The sculptures themselves I let disintegrate back into the earth. They only exist now as a photographic image.

The process of making those sculptures and writing that poem was my first real experience of what I would call "co-creating with spirit." It stands as a benchmark for me, a point of reference by which I measure all my work.

(RH): Can you talk more about "co-creating with spirit?"

(PR): Well, this is something that happens when I get deeply involved in a project. It doesn't matter what the medium—art, writing, or even teaching. It is the experience of feeling that there is another energy beyond my own personal energy that is actively interested and participating in the work. Maybe it is energy that wants to take a form, or be given a form.

It requires a certain amount of ego-surrender, but not completely, so it is not like channeling, but more a move toward putting my ego in service of something. I have to move away from working from my will towards working in a state of open willingness; willingness to be influenced, guided, inspired, even directed. I don't really know "where" this energy is coming from—if it is actually some part of me or outside of me; sometimes, it is in the materials I am using if I am doing art, sometimes it is in the story I am telling if I am writing. I believe this also can happen in the consulting room, and then it comes as an energy field that is co-created by the two people. However it happens, it is precious when it does.

(RH): On a personal level, what has it meant to you to have an older woman, like Marija Gimbutas, be your mentor? What do you feel happens to a woman who does not have a mentor?

(PR): To answer this question I have to say that I have had three very important older women in my life—each one reflecting a different yet significant aspect of my life. I call them my Other Mothers. My own mother was a "good woman." She was a housewife, mother of six children, stable, hard-working, and devoted. But she did not ignite my imagination. So I was always on the look-out for these "Other Mothers."

The first one was my aunt Ruth, my mother's sister. She was a nun, a maverick, a deep mystic, and a free spirit. She lived her whole life as a nun from age 13. And yet she was one of the most liberated women I have ever known. I first learned of Teilhard de Chardin from her. In her later years, she was a Sandinista in Nicaragua. She practiced Liberation Theology and lived her life in service to social justice. We were very close, and I felt very held spiritually in her wide embrace. I am currently writing a fictionalized version of her life.

Then, when I was forty, I met two other older women. One was June Yuer. She was my Tai Chi teacher. But she was also an artist and sculptor. She lived in Los Angeles and had done 10 years of Jungian analysis and painted her dreams during that time. We became very good friends and remain so to this day, although she is now nearly 90 and we live far away from each other. She built herself an art studio when she was 75!

I met Marija Gimbutas while I was at UCLA in 1980. I became her archaeological illustrator, and I was also in her seminar for a number of years. I traveled with her as well. And, most importantly, she introduced me to James Harrod, my partner of twenty-two years. Marija was one of those "big" people who, just by being herself, had a tremendous influence on my life. She was a profound intellectual and deeply generous, a true scholar who was devoted to her life's work. Donna Read, the Canadian filmmaker, made a film about her life, *Signs Out of Time*. Jim and I are both in it.

I feel very fortunate to have known these women. Even though my own life path was different from theirs, I was able to expand into my own possibilities knowing there were other women, women I knew and loved, who had followed their heart, mind, and soul. Women who did not follow a prescribed pattern for their life.

Because of my experience, I am very conscious of how important it is for women to have at least one Other Mother. In some respects, it takes the pressure off the personal mother to be and provide all things for us—which they never can be or do. I am also aware, now that I am in my mid-sixties, of my position as an Other Mother for younger women. It is something I cherish. I don't think of it as "role model," which sounds rather dull. But more as being an example of someone who has tried to live her own life with as much integrity and passion as I can muster, regardless of the rather peripatetic twists and turns it has taken.

(RH): Fellini, the late Italian film producer, once said, in talking about his inspiration and creativity: "when I see a beautiful, sensual woman, I feel religious." As a spiritual and creative woman, have you had a similar experience, in the presence of a man?

(PR): It probably should not be surprising to me that such a brilliant man could make such a conventional and rather banal statement like that. I assume he is talking about a kind of muse, about what moves his creative energy, or in Jungian terms, his anima.

I think, for many women, it is more complicated. I wrote about the experience of the Muse for women in my book *Daughters of Saturn*. There I quote from the poet Adrienne Rich, who says, "a woman's poetry about her relationship to her daemon—her own active, creative power—has in patriarchal culture used the language of hererosexual love or patriarchal theology." In the last part of the book, I explore other possibilities, for instance, the goddess-muse and how she operates in women's creative expressions.

Again, I think the essence of this is about differentiating the many complex ways in which we can be inspired, both creatively and spiritually. I find that I am most deeply moved or inspired wherever and whenever I feel eros. This may happen while I am walking by the ocean and see the sunlight sparkling on the water or when I am snowshoeing on a frozen stream in winter. It can happen in the counseling room, in the energetic field between two people. It can occur while I am sitting with a purring cat on my lap. It can happen while making love, or making a fabulous dinner for friends. I understand that it is my responsibility to keep myself open for any and all possibilities for experiencing this divine, creative, and spiritual energy.

(RH): What have you found often keeps people from remaining open for any and all possibilities for these experiences?

(PR): The simple answer is the millions of ways we can distract ourselves. Beginning with myself, I find that I can most distract myself by those things that I think require my immediate attention—phone calls, emails, letters, my relationships, and all preoccupations about things in the future. These things often do need my attention, but most of the time not immediately. I tend to stay away from television and newspapers.

I prefer to get my information through several select magazines. I am deeply affected by events in the world. Fortunately, I am not one of those people who can lose hours on the Internet. Staying present is the primary practice for keeping the channel open both creatively and spiritually. Everybody finds their own way of doing it. Being conscious is a full time job! Most of us don't like to work full time. I need quiet, solitude, and preferably some contact with nature. I journal in the mornings and am attentive to my dreams. Walking is my best access point, especially if I am near water or the woods.

Basically, I think it is terrifying to be alive and awake for most of us. I think the poets, like Rilke, write about that. I am not exactly sure why this is so—maybe it has to do with death.

(RH): What do you suspect it is about death that makes being alive and awake so terrifying?

(PR): As you can see by the delay in my response, I had to really think about this question! I don't know if I can even approximate an answer—even though it is an important question, maybe even one of the most important questions. It is easier for me while I am sitting up here in Nova Scotia looking out on the great tidal basin with its red sands and deep blue incoming and outgoing tides—the highest in world they say—to begin to even think about this.

So here is what I have come up with so far. I think the death I am talking about is very specific, i.e., my death (or our very specific individual deaths.) When I contemplate that death of mine, the one that belongs to me alone, it feels very closely related to the creative process—in the sense that it is about my very specific relationship to life and the creative work that I do. This, of course, goes not just for me, but for everyone, but it is very precise, this particular life. And for my creative work to have any depth or meaning, for it to be based in reality, it needs to be unambiguous, at least as far as I can make it so. So the requirements for creativity are stringent, and I can't say I am always up to it! This is the great blessing of distractions!

I also think that age is a factor. It is not so easy to think you have forever to do your creative work when you are 67 years old! This is actually a help, in the sense that it sharpens the point.

(RH): Often we hear about "writer's block," and perhaps we could also say "artist's block." The creative process usually involves a lot of inner wrestling before something emerges. What have you found going on inside as you try to create?

(PR): I am put in mind, often, of the Martha Graham quote: "There is a vitality, a life force, an energy, a quickening, that is translated through you into action, and because there is only one of you in all time, this expression is unique. And if you block it, it will never exist through any other medium and will be lost." This quote implies that there are two things at work: a "creative block" which is something a person can do as a kind of resistance, i.e., "if you block it." It also implies another force, an "it" that is pushing for expression.

From this, I imagine there must be at least two kinds of block. One that comes from the ego and says things like, "Who am I to take up this project? It has all been done before. There are a million books (artworks, objects, etc.) in the world already, what could I possibly have to offer? People will think I am crazy," etc. etc. This kind of mental talk comes from a damaged aspect of the ego, a kind of wounded narcissism that can really stop somebody in their tracks. I, myself, am familiar with this kind of block, but fortunately do not suffer too much from it, though many people do. The prolific writer, Margaret

Atwood says, "Inertia is my constant companion, procrastination my household pet. If I am not eager and keen and resolved and strenuously bent, I find it very difficult to write at all." I resonate with that.

Then there is the kind of block that is actually more interesting to me. The block that is put up by the work itself. I experience this as another kind of resistance, not in myself, but in the actual thing I am trying to express. The energy stops flowing for some reason. Things dry up. Why? The stubborn muteness and silence of a work at this time can be eloquent! Pursuing the usual ego refrains is not fruitful. I have to interrogate the work itself. What is it wanting? How can I better get at it? Deepen it? What risks do I have to take in order to make the work come alive? Sometimes the work requires a rest, sometimes a dream appears that gives a clue as to its desired direction, sometimes I just have to throw it out and start over or begin working on something else. But it is all in the context of relationship—between me and the work, the work and me.

(RH): In your wonderful article, "Mnemosyne's Well of Remembrance" in Spring Journal's *Muses* issue (2005), you write that it is the work of the artist to restore memory. As an artist concerned with memory, how do you understand Alzheimer's and brain damage where the memory has been impacted?

(PR): I do not have a lot of direct personal experience with these conditions, although I have worked with people who have gone through this condition with partners and parents, and I was an adviser to a Pacifica student who wrote a wonderful master's thesis about living with her father through the various progressions of Alzheimer's disease. It is certainly an awesome experience since it challenges our cherished notions of personhood. Are we still who we were even when we can't remember ourselves?

My interest in memory is less concrete, maybe more poetic, or even literary—at least it has more to do with the levels of psyche that appear in creative work, in dreams, or even mysterious behaviors. I am most interested in what Abraham and Torok, two Freudian analysts writing in the 50's that I mentioned earlier, termed transgenerational haunting. This is memory that appears unbidden, returns as ghosts, as a kind of haunting. One of the best examples in literature is Toni Morrison's book, *Beloved*. But I have also seen it operating in clients who seem to be haunted by events that occurred in past generations, things they have no conscious memory of, except as lingering fears, terrors, or dream scenarios. Memory and its role in the human psyche is very deep and enigmatic. A great source for those of us who love to probe the mystery.

(RH): My brother has brain damage from a car accident, and his memory is considerably impaired. I have wondered a lot as to what, if anything, I can do to be of help to him. A good friend of mine suggested something which felt poetic. He said that my brother was "caught in a moment in time." Does that make sense to you, as you consider your interest in memory?

(PR): This feels a bit outside the interview process to me. But I want to respond on a personal level and say how deeply sorry I am for you and your family that this has happened to your brother.

Outside of the fact that the brain is one of the most amazing things and that people can recover all sorts of functioning, the issue of memory loss is one of the more poignant aspects of these injuries. Because our relationships are held together by a kind of consensus reality, it is very troubling when one person goes into another "reality" whether from brain damage or any other kind of dysfunction. We feel like our own grip on reality gets loosened. I imagine what we would want, if the situation were reversed, is that someone does the work of memory for us—re-members us, keeps an image of our wholeness in their minds, while still accepting that we cannot. This feels like heart-breaking work, but it is something that feels necessary. Memory does have to do with time. And, I suppose, there are realities that are not time-bound. So then we are in the Mystery.

(RH): In your own life, what are some of the ways you have found to stay in touch with the Shadow, or have you found the shadow stays in touch with you?

(PR): Short of dragging us into a discussion of the Jungian ideas around shadow, I would like to talk about something that arises in my work with women, individually and in groups. Christine Downing has written an excellent book, *Psyche's Sisters,* on the subject of the shadow of sisterhood. It occurs in women's relationships with each other where jealousy, envy, gossip, competition, and all of those other distortions of women's power drive emerge.

In some sense, you could say it occurs in the larger context of the shadow of patriarchy, because that is where women's power becomes suppressed. But I am talking about how women internalize that suppression by the things that we do to our own and often to our best: like cutting powerful women off at the knees, through poisonous language and perceptions, c.f. Hillary Clinton or Nancy Pelosi. Or, by "matronizing" each other by expressing concern and caretaking, all the while thinking and acting in disrespectful ways. Women know what I am talking about. Women with frustrated, suppressed, or distorted power drives are often more vicious and dangerous to each other than any threat that comes at us from men. I understand this from my own life when I thought I was powerless and acted accordingly.

My own personal power was infinitely more treacherous because I thought and acted as if I had none. This is not uncommon for women, especially of my generation. Often women hide their power, even from themselves, because the culture has deemed it unacceptable. I once had a dream that I owned a rather large snake that I kept in a briefcase! It has taken a lot of experience with self-expression to get into a better relationship with that snake by allowing it to freely and naturally move in its own way, unobstructed.

Another aspect that comes to mind is the way the collective shadow comes to women so often in dreams. Bag ladies, women in burquas, and prostitutes are representatives of how the collective shadow appears for women. But it can also happen that we as women cast into the shadow our most sacred and wise potential—our healers and high priestesses, our oracles, prophetesses, and visionaries. This seems to me a most critical work—to own and claim our potential, which is so needed in the world.

(**RH**): Last August (2006), you and eight other women had an incredible trip to the Arctic that included rafting down the Sheenjek River and encountering grizzly bears, bald and golden eagles, and even a musk ox. I remember after you returned you said that you did not want to come home. What is it about such an experience that captures you?

(**PR**): I am easily captivated by wild nature for a number of reasons, but this Arctic landscape did something beyond the usual. I will try to name some of the aspects that moved me so much. For one thing, this is one of the few places left on earth where a person may safely drink directly from a wild stream of water. And in this rare, pristine, and barely accessible landscape, there is no human imprint, only the tracks of grizzly bear, gray wolf, musk-ox, moose, and in late summer many thousands of caribou.

The work of bearing witness to creatures who do not converse in our tongue, to a landscape that speaks in the language of elementals, is wonderfully challenging. Then, there is the silence. The very absence of sound in a place like this is so profound that it becomes a presence, original and archetypal. Words cannot hold its vast innermost and outermost dimensions. What I thought was: "Here is the geography of hope."

Because I could see that there was a coherence to this place, an intelligibility, uncluttered and unimpaired. A larger order prevails— the sky, mountains, river valley, and the river—each element appearing with its own wisdom nature, its own life story that stands in relationship, in deep harmonious relationship, to every other element. Humilitas is a virtue one finds in oneself in this kind of place.

Human arrogance is laughable here. Vulnerability, respect, and patience are necessarily cultivated. It was surprising to find that the land is actually not formidable. It could contain us, even nurture us. By its very beingness, its evolutionary persistence, this place inspired hope. Immediately one is placed within the larger order of things; the land is simply and awesomely there, and we are in it. Over days, I found that the dignity of an unbroken land can be restorative, even healing. But seeking intimacy with a landscape such as this requires engagement, attention, presence—body, mind, spirit. And most importantly, it means ordering one's disarrayed interior to match the integrity of the land. There is a cleansing, purifying consolation to be had here.

All that said, you can imagine what it felt like to arrive back in our so-called civilization—so many cars, so much pollution, scented soap in the bathrooms! What are we thinking? Are we thinking at all? To experience a primal place undominated by human mind and hands, unbounded by human culture or custom, is a rare privilege because it gives such a profound perspective. It is also painful, in that our disconnection and manic flight away from the natural world is so extreme and allows all sorts of decisions to be made that only make the disjuncture more permanent. I must admit that I had an overwhelming feeling of misanthropy as I sat in the airport on my return. This, of course, abates over time. But the experience of the Arctic Refuge remains forever deeply embedded in my psyche.

(RH): In college when I worked at the Outward Bound School in Minnesota, Sigurd Olson, the late philosopher of that area, once told us as we were about to embark on a 21-day wilderness venture that once our souls relaxed, we would feel the old rhythm of the ancestors whose home was amongst the sun, moon, wind, and stars. Did you find something of that rhythm on your excursion?

(PR): Yes, that definitely does describe an aspect of it. I wonder about the expression "once our souls relax." Really, I think our souls are just longing for these kinds of experiences where we are placed within the larger order of things, where the human mind with its relentless pursuits cannot dominate. It feels more like the mind, in the Buddhist sense of the word, has to let go, be emptied, in order to experience that ancient and true rhythm and feel at home on the earth.

That means not only opening our hearts, but also confronting the myriad of fears and anxieties that are generated by being in such a place. Who are we when we drop our cultural accoutrements, when we enter, what is for us, now, the unknown territory called the "wilderness?" We still have a bit of the "conquering" mentality which arises out of fear. And most of us, unless we have been specifically trained, are completely unequipped to fend for ourselves in the wild. Even with the security of food and gear, there is still something to contend with —and I believe that it has something to do with the realization of how "small" our little spark of humanity is in the scheme of things—no more, no less, than the bears and the musk-ox, no more precious.

(RH): It has been great doing this "enterview" with you, Patricia. You are a most interesting and creative woman.

(PR): I have enjoyed the process immensely, Rob. The dialogue, as you have mastered it, is a great relational format that feels very free and spacious. Your questions and direction have given me a chance to think deeply about things, and the process has given me the space and time to work things out in what I hope are articulate and understandable responses. Thanks!

FILM REVIEWS

WALL-E. Directed by Andrew Stanton; original story by Andrew Stanton and Pete Doctor; screenplay by Andrew Stanton and Jim Reardon. Voices: Ben Brutt, Elissa Knight, and Sigourney Weaver.

REVIEWED BY GLEN SLATER

Wall-E's World

Who would have thought that the animation studio, Pixar, whose infancy was nurtured by Apple Computer's Steve Jobs and is now owned by Disney, would make a film that ponders the consequences of unchecked technology and the accompanying cultures of consumerism and built-in obsolescence? *WALL-E*, a story about a garbage-compacting robot left alone on an earth long abandoned by humans, does just this, suggesting critical reflection on the implications of innovation may be a more pervasive occupation than we think. Managing to provoke and entertain at the same time, this animated feature is not preachy, nor moralizing. Instead, it conveys its theme by opening a realm of aesthetic response, inviting us to contemplate life

Glen Slater, Ph.D., is a core faculty member at Pacifica Graduate Institute where he teaches in the Mythological Studies and Depth Psychology Programs. He has written several essays for *Spring Journal* and currently edits the journal's film reviews. Glen also edited and introduced the third volume of James Hillman's *Uniform Edition* of essays. He is the guest co-editor of this issue of *Spring Journal*.

on earth before and after the ultimate exchange of landscape for landfill. Think of the world after a century or so of ignoring all the inconvenient truths and you get the picture.

Make no mistake, WALL-E (Waste Allocation Load-Lifter: Earth Class) is one quirky, cute cartoon character, with enough of the orphan-turned-hero formula greasing his tracks to keep kids searching for his likeness on every happy-meal. But you'd have to be cynical indeed not to see beyond the bright packaging into a finely tuned tale for our times, the heart of which is not all that happy. Both the careful conception and the critical reception of *WALL-E* hint of a collective capacity to imagine a possible future in which the planet is literally trashed, a future where the most animated beings are automatons and humanity has fled the scene to become barely conscious lounge-lizards lying around on the outer space version of a giant cruise ship. In other words, the earth is dead and, psychologically speaking, so are the people. For a work aimed at a general audience, with refreshingly little reliance on cliché and astounding attention to detail, there's plenty of room for the imagination to enter the story from many angles. Both the narrative itself and its mesmerizing visual realization invite a deeper look.

The opening vision of skyscraping piles of compacted garbage channeling dust storms through a former metropolis is so vivid, so "real," that one is immediately taken by the premise. The scene may be centuries away, but somehow it's close to the bone. The trash is familiar and made more so as we follow WALL-E around for a day or two. So too his constant companion, a cockroach, which we cheer on through the close calls with every heavy flat object; suddenly that bottom rung on the ladder of life seems like a godsend. The absence of anything green in WALL-E's world is brought home in devastating fashion when we spy the fragile sprout of plant he tends in an old shoe—a bittersweet indicator of Nature's desperate struggle to survive our outsized carbon footprint. As the absence of green morphs into a palpable presence in the mind's eye, a sense of the vegetable soul enters. The whole effect of this earth-on-its-deathbed scenario is to conjure up a potent regard for any sign of life whatsoever. And before much of a narrative unfolds, we're drawn into the world of WALL-E in a way that makes what follows all the more compelling.

No doubt one level of this film is a contemporary eco-fable for children. However, beyond the uniquely rendered post-life planet, what punctuates the story for the rest of us is the clever interlace of themes with some psychological heft—loneliness, home, nostalgia, and becoming conscious, to name a few. Sprinkle in a thinly veiled satirical targeting of consumerism and corporatization and you soon forget this film comes from the same source as *Toy Story*. The specter of a government merged with the "Buy-N-Large" mega-corporation is perfectly placed as a sign of present times, so too the corny rationalizations from replayed speeches by a President who once presided over the catastrophe. While the film avoids heavy political statement, there's enough of a commentary on current socio-political events to generate the occasional smile of recognition.

Right alongside the contemporary mirroring, *WALL-E* finds its depth in the nuanced characterization of its leading man. After 700 years alone, the little robot has evolved a highly differentiated relation to his surroundings. Besides the dutiful compacting and stacking of refuse, quite a few bytes are dedicated to a pronounced curiosity for the odd things he encounters and collects—from Zippo lighters to a Rubic's Cube. WALL-E's cargo container home is stacked with this paraphernalia. In one early scene he attempts to master paddle-ball while watching a Betamax (!) video of *Hello, Dolly!* As songs like "It Only Takes a Moment" play in the background, the world of this trash-compactor with large (literally) reflective eyes reveals our world too. Watching WALL-E at home is a dive into our psychic dumpster, retrieving a sudden sense of attachment to those devices and gadgets we've all committed to the landfill. So the nostalgia button is pushed at the same time as activating that painful awareness of how much we've contributed to those towers of waste obscuring the skyline outside WALL-E's door. A capacity to evoke several emotional responses at once is but one achievement of the film.

Watching this robot negotiate his surroundings is a cinematic version of a one-man play, albeit without words; it's a gestural field with enough gravity to pull us to the core. If the protagonist's binocular-like head and mini-bar-shaped torso don't exactly invite our identification with him, by the time he starts rummaging through the artifacts in his bachelor pad, he might as well be a lonely Harrison Ford in search of love while setting out to save the world: We're hooked. WALL-E's isolation, his longing for companionship, and the eventual meeting and then pursuit of a soul-mate named EVE (Extra-terrestrial

Vegetation Evaluator) opens us to the most pressing psychological drives and beyond to ultimate values: Reversing human apathy and recovering *anima-mundi* become the goals here, goals that seem to grow organically as the action progresses. WALL-E comes to realize he's a tin-man with a heart, which he follows, transcending his merely mechanical origins and teaching his human makers a thing or two about what matters most.

On the level of pure narrative, there's little question that *WALL-E* is largely a love story. But it isn't that the robot courtship and consummation is an add-on to keep things lively. *This* relationship isn't the primary theme either. It's more that the romance mirrors the principles of interconnection and beauty that are intrinsic to the larger scheme. In so many works that explore the terrain of technology and psyche, the problem comes down to whether or not a sense of beauty and relationship can mitigate the objective eye that so readily separates us from surrounding matter. Like other humanoids of the fictive imagination that seem to embody the dismissed Eros of their makers— of which Victor Frankenstein's monster is the template—WALL-E longs for a companion, and when EVE shows up, there's no resisting her: A perfectly rounded, egg-like body, remarkably expressive blue-beamed eyes and a laser-beam that is unleashed like the sharpest of retorts, she is a spirited "woman" through and through. From a purely visual perspective, her pristine, angelic form immediately complements WALL-E's gritty, square lines. It's a syzygy (that will be) made in heaven.

EVE serves as WALL-E's Beatrice, as his portal to a higher purpose. She represents a largely forgotten project, sent by the off-planet humans to search for any sign of life back on earth. When WALL-E's shoe-plant appears, she hits pay dirt, locks the leaf-ling in her belly, and turns her attention to incubating a new dawn of existence. All WALL-E knows is he can't live without this woman. All we know is no one can. So he clings to her departing rocket like there'll be no tomorrow.

What happens back at the mother ship sometimes seems like a wonderful premise dutifully winding its way to a conclusion. But we gladly go along for the ride as WALL-E and EVE join forces to protect the new seed of existence from the autonomous corporate agenda of Buy-N-Large that is determined to suspend the animation and keep civilization on cruise control. The sight of oversized people with oversized beverages, glued to their individual TV screens, constantly on the move in their twentieth-generation floating La-Z-boys, is the fitting flipside of the scene back on earth, making the last half of the film simultaneously humorous and disturbing. Until our robot friends manage to find a human ally in the situation, it seems as if only they have both the conscience and the consciousness—not to mention the passion(!)—to crack open the collective apathy. So, ironically, it's the mechanized beings that carry the day for planetary renewal, bringing us full circle to the question of how we relate to our devices today.

In 1983's *National Lampoon's Vacation*, Clark Griswold (Chevy Chase) takes the family on a cross-country trip to "Walley World," an aptly rendered facsimile of Disneyland. After purchasing a brand new, quintessential, built-for-obsolescence family wagon for the journey, the ideal American vacation predictably unravels. Amidst the slapstick comedy and merciless sending up of consumer ideals, the accumulating sentiment is that "there's no place like home," and that simple, straightforward pleasures trump idealized, accessorized treks to entertainment Meccas. I can't help but connect the worlds of WALL-E and Walley. In *WALL-E*, beneath the spectacle of a deserted earth and the specter of generations slurping soda while circling Saturn, the very notion of "home" has gone missing from the human condition. WALL-E's world is a consequence of the failure to tend inner spaces and the endless attempt to fill these empty interiors with alluring but facile exteriors, which only results in dead things filling outer spaces. Deep humanity is squeezed from the picture and, in this vacuum of soul matter, corporate cogs and literal machines take over. This exchange of archetypal matter for material abundance may be checked by the gremlins on Wall Street from time to time, but the shift to sustainability and the accompanying recognition that biosphere and psyche are woven together still appears to be some way off. Yet the point seems clear: If life is a never-ending trip to Walley World, we'll all end up in WALL-E's world.

WALL-E and EVE's quest to return humanity to its roots is crafted with a dramatic exactitude that surpasses most big screen offerings and makes its underlying themes all the more pressing. Sparked by images that extrapolate current trends in such a unique, offbeat way, those who've seen or will see *WALL-E* are returned to a potent awareness of the earth as "Home" and reminded that the biosphere shapes and defines our being. A love of "things," of "objects," even those computers and gadgets that seem to have outgrown their usefulness, may be one key element of this relationship, which reverses the Cartesian divide in the psyche so often questioned when depth psychologists turn their attention to the adverse impact of technologies. Being endeared to this animated trash compactor with sad eyes is not only a result of effective characterization; it may also be in keeping with the reanimation of matter that is the undercurrent of this fable. Challenging our binge and purge lifestyles, *WALL-E* reminds us that what is desired and gathered sometimes consumes us, and what is dismissed sometimes redeems us.

FILM REVIEWS

Into the Wild. Emile Hirsch, Marcia Gay Harden, William Hurt, Catherine Keener, Vince Vaughn, Hal Holbrook. Directed by Sean Penn. Screenplay by Sean Penn, based upon the book, *Into the Wild,* by Jon Krakauer.

REVIEWED BY JOY GREENBERG

If the sign of a good film is one that you reflect upon long after leaving the theater, then *Into the Wild* qualifies, for it demands to be considered on many levels. On one level, Sean Penn revisions Jon Krakauer's book of the same title, which details the tragic story of Chris McCandless. On another level, *Into the Wild* works as a hero's journey as Chris is called to and embarks upon a spiritual quest. On yet a third level, Penn portrays the American landscape in such a way that it becomes more than a cinematic backdrop for Chris's adventures; it is itself a character. The often jarring juxtaposition of these three levels both exhilarates and disturbs the viewer, creating a vague unease that possibly may explain the film's mixed reviews by those who see Chris as a romantic, if misguided, *puer aeternus* and those who view him only

Joy Greenberg completed her MFA in creative writing with a focus in creative nonfiction from California State University Chico. Her memoir, *A Pause in the Rain*, details her marriage to Chuck Greenberg, founder and leader of the Grammy Award-winning band, Shadowfax. She is presently a doctoral candidate in the Mythological Studies program at Pacifica Graduate Institute.

negatively because of the emotional devastation his behavior wreaked upon his family. In fact, such conflicting reactions testify to the film's essential paradoxicalness, adding to its mystique.

Penn does not hide the textual origins of *Into the Wild*. In fact, he celebrates them, for watching the film is much like reading a book: The scenes are divided into "chapters" with subtitles and dates, often lending the impression that we are reading Chris's own words as he enacts the activities he describes. Indeed, Penn intercuts many of the scenes with what appear to be Chris's handwritten notes, letters, postcards, and journal entries, making clear that the film attempts to remain "faithful" to the known facts and artifacts of Chris's short life. Penn even includes a shot of Chris reading a poem to his sister in a scene that both reinforces the film's textuality as well as portends what is to come. When Chris comes to the line "you're going to do bad things to children," we become aware of a dark shadow lurking within the otherwise seemingly normal McCandless family.

Lest there be any doubt about the nature of Chris's quest, Penn has provided us generously with chapter titles: "My Own Birth," "Adolescence," "Manhood," "Family," and "Final Chapter—Getting of Wisdom." As he embarks on his journey, Chris clearly enters an initiation process—a rite of passage on his quest for self-knowledge. In so doing, we become privy to the events that have shaped his life, leading him to the point where he feels compelled upon graduation from Emory University with nearly straight As to give away his college fund of $24,000 to OXFAM, to cut up his credit and identification cards, to abandon his car, and to burn his cash.

It soon becomes clear that the root of Chris's desire for self-imposed exile extends far beyond ordinary (if it can ever be called that) adolescent angst: he holds a bitter grudge against his parents for exposing him and his sister, Carine (Jena Malone), to their often cruel confrontations. Penn uses the technique of voice-over effectively, which allows Carine to explain the family's background and the psychodynamics of the relationship between their overbearing father (William Hurt) who bullies them and their mother (Marcia Gay Harden). In this way Carine also describes how the parents forced her and Chris to watch them and even to take sides during a discussion of divorce, which they never actually end up getting. Such "witnessed violence" is bad enough, but even worse is the discovery during an earlier trip to California by

Chris that he and Carine are technically illegitimate, having been born before their father was divorced from his first wife. Carine reveals what she calls the "ugly truth [that] redefined Chris and me as … bastard children [of a] fraudulent marriage." Of course, controversy over parentage is a common motif of the divine child, and Penn's paralleling of Chris's life with Christ's is evident throughout the film.

Like Christ who retreats to the desert, Chris withdraws. He intuits that psychic healing begins in solitude. Penn wastes no time establishing that Chris intentionally chooses to be alone; the first lyrics sung by Eddie Vedder as the opening credits roll are: "Have no fear / For when I'm alone / I'll be better off / Than I was before." Chris's sense of alienation from his parents can be ameliorated only by physical separation. Cutting himself off from them is thus an integral part of his journey, as it is for all mythic heroes. As Campbell, Jung, and van Gennep remind us, separation is an initial phase of the monomyth, individuation, and rites of passage, of which all Chris's actions are emblematic.

Penn plays up Chris's congruence with Christ in the impression he leaves on the other lost souls he encounters throughout his journey, including Jan Burres (Catherine Keener). Burres' boyfriend, Rainey (Brian Dierker), perhaps expresses best Chris's effect upon others when he asks Chris, "You aren't Jesus, are you?" Penn bolsters this image repeatedly with shots of Chris on a mountainside standing with arms spread wide and floating on his back on the Teklanika with arms outstretched and legs together. Both scenes reinforce Chris's crucified-Christ image: Like Jesus, Chris is on a mission and will not be deterred; he has been *called*. He has embarked upon a hero's journey, except that unlike Christ, Chris represents the postmodern hero, "whose character arc is more nebulous and whose process shows a greater integration of unconscious factors."[1] In Chris's character we see a complicated collection of complexes that make him seem more *anti*-hero than hero.

While the stuff of many myths, heroes are unsupported by contemporary society, which cannot abide its individual members becoming too independent. Indeed, society imposes strict sanctions on those who dare to buck the system; individuation comes at high cost. Consider what happens to Christ, and Chris fares no better. In one chilling episode, Chris is caught train-hopping by a railroad-hired thug and severely beaten—one of the many trials that he, like all mythic heroes, must endure.

Not all trials are externally inflicted, either. Indeed, both Christ and Chris undergo *self*-imposed ordeals. In many ways, Chris's journey may be seen as a peripatetic purification. Feeling unclean after discovering the truth about the circumstances of his birth, Chris sets his sights on Alaska—one of the last remaining pristine frontiers—to "purify" himself and enter an Artemisian realm. Artemis beckons whenever the body demands a general purification, for the virginal goddess Artemis represents spiritual and physical purity. Chris's odyssey corresponds, therefore, to an attempt to rid himself of the negative notions he has of himself as a bastard child and to be reborn as a new man. He adopts an Artemisian spirituality reflected by his chastity and asceticism.

Such Artemisian sanctity has been demonstrated by the various ascetic traditions throughout history and is well known to monastics who believe that chastity is *de rigueur* for all who seek enlightenment. Seen this way, chastity "resembles the castration of the priests of Artemis, who emasculated themselves voluntarily to enter the service of the virgin Goddess, approaching her through mimesis."[2] Chris's chastity is portrayed most notably by his eschewing of love interests, including the 16-year-old girl, Tracy (Kristen Stewart), he meets at Slab City. Although she is quite eager to bed Chris, he turns her down, telling her she's too young; but his real reason, it seems, is that such intimacy is simply not a part of his ultimate goal of returning to Artemis. In supporting such a belief, Krakauer points to a sentence circled in Chris's copy of *Walden*, found with his remains: "Chastity is the flowering of man; and what are called Genius, Heroism, Holiness, and the like, are but various fruits which succeed it."[3]

Contained in Chris's pursuit of purification is his quest for truth, since part of his sense of defilement is based upon the elaborate lie foisted upon him by his parents about his childhood, which made him feel "his whole world turn [and] made his childhood feel like fiction," according to Carine. Consequently, truth takes on monumental importance for Chris, which is why he can't bring himself to forgive his parents for their duplicity. For it is one thing to make up the Tooth Fairy; it is quite something else for parents to pretend they met and married in college when in reality Chris's dad lived with his mom out of wedlock until after Chris and his sister were born, all the while being still married to his first wife and even having a sixth child with her. Chris makes clear what he thinks about deception while attempting to explain his position to Rainey: "To paraphrase Thoreau, 'Rather than love, than money, than fame, give me truth.'"

The conflation of Alaska with Artemis is apparent from the beginning of *Into the Wild*. Before the introductory credits even roll, a half-screen superimposition of Lord Byron's poem, "There is a pleasure in these pathless woods," appears over a backdrop of impossibly gorgeous Alaskan scenery and wildlife. The romantic tone of Penn's film thus is set, although kudos must go to Eric Gautier for his camera work that incarnates not just Alaska but all the locations, making them come alive along with the characters. The shots of glorious desert, mountain, prairie, and sea vistas go *beyond* scenery, and, in so doing, all of nature is personified. As Glen Slater says, "Personifying reminds us that psychic persons can't be confined to literal characters and that intelligence and agency can appear outside actual people."[4] In this film, place provides more than setting; it becomes a *character*. It embodies psyche. It is Artemis, and it is she who lures Chris—the unwitting Actaeon—to Alaska.

After spending several years on the road, making friends along the way, Chris discovers that separation from his parents alone is not enough to sooth the savage beast within—what is known clinically as a "negative introject." His meanderings around the continental U.S. fail to assuage the utter disdain Chris continues to feel toward his parents and all they represent to him, especially what he sees as their hypocrisy, disingenuousness, and filthy lucre. However, it is not just his parents Chris is at odds with; he is rebelling against a society that seems to encourage materialistic greed. He has nothing but contempt for material possessions and money, which, as he tells Wayne Westerberg (Vince Vaughan), "makes people cautious." If anything, Chris is the antithesis of caution. But then, he is a *puer*.

With what he considers to be thoughtful preparation, Chris eventually devises a plan for his Alaska adventure. Ginette Paris tells us:

> When social life absorbs one's energies completely, it is time to
> penetrate the deep forest of Artemis and allow nature to replace

> human relations. … [T]here is a very evident link between a life
> rich in relationships and the need for solitary retreat in which
> the ego receives no stimulation.[5]

As well as Chris relates to his new-found friends on the road, he finds
their presence a hindrance to his presence to himself. Consequently,
he becomes "attracted by the asceticism, simplicity, and naturalness
that characterize Artemis, [and] solitude appears as one of the ways of
entering her world."[6] Chris understands he must finally do what he
has been talking about for two years: go to Alaska.

That Chris chooses the deep woods as his final destination
underscores the symbolic significance of the wilderness forest, which
is not simply a miscellany of trees; it is enchanted. In other words, the
forest is a place where spirit is infused throughout and psyche's work
of transformation becomes possible, as we see in Chris's encounters with
the moose and the bear. This connection between forest and the
unconscious is confirmed by Heinrich Zimmer when he says that the

> enchanted forest [is] the dark aspect of the world [where] the
> elect, who survives its deadly perils, is reborn and leaves it a
> changed [person]. The forest has always been a place of initiation,
> for there the demonic presences, the ancestral spirits, and the
> forces of nature reveal themselves.[7]

It is this enchanted quality that comes from personifying.

If the allure of Alaska is in its Artemisian numinosity, such appeal
is countered by an inherent ominousness. In Chris's tragic moose
experience—filmed in slow motion that renders it mythopoetically as
ritual—may be seen the consequences of defying Artemis and portends
Chris's demise. Like Actaeon, Chris commits a cardinal sin against the
nature goddess: hubris. He assumes he is sufficiently prepared for his
confrontation with her, but he is not: The method of curing meat he
has learned about from a South Dakota hunter does not take into
account how the timing of the process differs in the Far North where
the longer summer days cause carcasses to rot faster. When Chris finds
his moose covered in maggots much earlier than his hunter friend had
predicted and before he has had the opportunity to finish curing it,
he is devastated, a mood only partially mollified by his observation of
wolves devouring the remains and so benefiting from his misprision.

It's one of four critical mistakes Chris makes that lead to his downfall, the others being his choice to go to Alaska in May when hunting and gathering are especially difficult, his failing to take into account the increase in water level in the Teklanika River during the summer which makes it impassable, and his failing to understand that the potato seeds he thought were safe to eat become toxic in the summer.

Also, like Actaeon, Chris paradoxically is transformed by his experience; the predator becomes the prey. Whereas Actaeon's metamorphosis is physical and he is changed into a stag, Chris undergoes a psychic transformation as he comes to understand better the contradictions of Artemis, the protectress and huntress, who gives life but also takes it away. Ultimately, like Actaeon, Chris's return— both literally and figuratively—is to the primal womb of Artemis, and it is she who presides over his initiation into the mysteries of her nature. Artemis's significance is that she "personifies a force which urges us to withdraw from human relationships and to seek elsewhere, in solitude, another kind of self-realization."[7]

Chris's journey comes full-circle when he arrives in Alaska. Convinced when he heads out that he must lose everything that connects him to his past, he apparently undergoes a change of heart while there and arrives finally to a sort of decision to go back. Evidence found with him in the old Fairbanks transit bus he inhabited during his months in the Denali wilderness includes a marked up copy of *Doctor Zhivago* in which he indicates his apparent readiness to return to civilization. At the top of the page on which the following passage occurs, he has printed NATURE/PURITY, and is so seemingly excited by what he reads that he has scribbled notes in the margins and underlined several places, according to Krakauer:

> Lara ... rediscovered the purpose of her life. She was here on earth to grasp the meaning of its wild enchantment and to call each thing by its right name .... And so it turned out that only a life similar to the life of those around us, merging with it without a ripple, is genuine life, and that an unshared happiness is not happiness. ... And this was most vexing of all.[8]

This passage is read as a voice-over, and the illuminating words— HAPPINESS ONLY REAL WHEN SHARED—written next to the above passage appear as Chris is writing them down. Whether Chris intended to renew family ties remains unclear, but he obviously felt a restoration of desire for some form of human company. The irony, of course, is that by the time he is ready to return to civilization, Chris is too incapacitated from starvation to walk out of the wilderness—a potent image of the spiritual pull going too far. Such paradox is the essence of the hero in that he can cope with the greatest perils, yet, in the end, something relatively insignificant is his undoing.

It is at this point in the film that Penn presents what is perhaps his most magical personification of nature: Chris is standing motionless, undoubtedly frightened but not outwardly so, as a massive Alaskan brown bear wanders by, its hulking body just inches away. The animal is momentarily curious but not really threatening, and Chris bears the beatific expression of one experiencing *satori* as he stands perfectly still, eyes locked with the bear's. Is he hallucinating from hunger? Possibly, but it doesn't matter, for it demonstrates the way in which cinema transcends literature; we see what Chris sees. We see Artemis in all her glory. Artemis, the bear, creates soul movement in Chris and through him in us, the viewers, as well.

In so doing, Penn's effort succeeds in ways that the book cannot. Krakauer may only surmise that Chris's experience is similar to his own while scaling Devil's Thumb, an Alaskan mountain ascended by only the hardiest of climbers. While Krakauer does a capable job telling what it's like to come face to face with Artemis, the film *shows* us by simply focusing on Chris, whose look conveys fear and rapture simultaneously—the primordial kinship with all creation that Actaeon's fate personifies.

Into the Wild exemplifies cinematically how wilderness works as a metaphor for the unconscious. Moments like Chris's encounters with the bear and moose are virtually impossible to articulate in words, yet are essential in communicating the paradox of Artemis—that she is exquisitely sublime and simultaneously dangerous—for they allow us, the viewers, to experience vicariously what the on-screen character feels. We understand better what Chris senses because we see it on his face. Indeed, it emanates from throughout his entire body, whereas words like "beatific" or "sublime" or whatever other adjectives might be used simply cannot convey the same essence of meaning. In Chris's emotive expression, then, we feel the movement of psyche—both his *and* ours. That Chris fails to survive Artemis's "deadly perils" does not diminish the implicit heroism of his quest. In his contacts with the animals, plants, and landscape, which Penn meticulously films in their actual settings, Chris finds the Artemisian spirituality he seeks.

Into the Wild shows us that for all his blundering hubris, in the end Chris gains a wisdom many never experience though they live far longer than Chris's 24 years. Despite what must have been an agonizing death, his final message, written on a piece of paper and attached to the bus, seems almost upbeat, considering the circumstances: I HAVE HAD A HAPPY LIFE AND THANK THE LORD. GOODBYE AND MAY GOD BLESS ALL![10] Such remarkable sanguinity is borne out by what is perhaps one of the most breathtakingly beautiful death sequences ever seen in a film. The final scene begins with a montage of Chris with family and friends, which could have come off as a maudlin cliché of "life passing before his eyes," but is edited so well as to allow us to feel more than sympathy for him—we see Chris's journey as something to which he has been called. In the words of Carine, "everything he is doing has to be done."

Following the montage of his past, the film cuts to Chris as he writes "happiness only real when shared" in *Doctor Zhivago*, as noted above. The next image is a sustained spiraling from tight close-up outward that cuts back and forth between the sun and Chris's face as the life ebbs from his body; yet the look on his face is of utter peace, "serene as a monk gone to God,"[11] or in this case, Goddess Artemis. This crane shot astonishes in how it manages to remain focused on Chris's ecstatic expression as our view spirals slowly away until the window of the bus frames Chris; then the whole bus comes into view, until it is a mere speck in the forested landscape. In such a juxtaposition of camera angles, Penn forces us to acknowledge that life is all about perspective.

As with Christ, there is at times a compulsory madness involved in dying a worthy death, in which the ego-driven part of the self is sacrificed through its transformation. Through the integration of the three layers of biographical narrative, hero myth, and personifying in *Into the Wild*, we reach an understanding of just how powerful is the eternal lure of Artemis, the ancient goddess of nature, whose message we ignore at great peril. Like Actaeon, the hapless Chris learns Artemis's lesson the hard way and pays with his life. Yet his final moments, like virtually every scene, are rendered so aesthetically that it is possible to appreciate Chris's demise, tragic though it is, as paradoxically blissful.

Through Chris we become visually intimate with the search for self and depth. It is a journey that can take place only by going *into the wild*.

NOTES

1. Glen Slater, "Archetypal Perspective and American Film," *Spring 73, Cinema & Psyche* (2004): 17.

2. Ginette Paris, *Pagan Meditations* (Dallas: Spring, 1987), p. 133.

3. Jon Krakauer, *Into the Wild* (New York: Anchor, 1997), p. 66.

4. Slater, p. 7.

5. Paris, p. 134.

6. *Ibid.*, p. 135.

7. Heinrich Zimmer, *The King and the Corpse—Tales of the Soul's Conquest of Evil*, ed. Joseph Campbell (Princeton: Princeton University Press, 1973), p. 181-82.

8. Paris, p. 129.

9. Qtd. in Krakauer, p. 188-89.

10. Qtd. in Krakauer, p. 199.

11. *Ibid.*, p. 199.

BOOK REVIEWS

Bill Plotkin. *Nature and the Human Soul: A Road Map to Discovering Our Place in the World.* New York: New World Library & Sydney: Finch Publishing, 2008.

REVIEWED BY DAVID TACEY

The Ecological Soul

Ecopsychology is one of the most important disciplines of our time. As I understand it, it has emerged from the works of Jung and Hillman, and has followed their passion for discovering psyche in the world, and not merely inside the human mind. To this day, the core work in this discipline is and remains *Ecopsychology: Restoring the Earth, Healing the Mind,* edited by Theodore Roszak, Mary E. Gomes, and Allen K. Kanner, with forewords by James Hillman and Lester R. Brown.[1] This book deserves to be more widely read, since it brings together the insights of several related disciplines: ecology, depth psychology, psychoanalysis, theology, philosophy, and theoretical sciences. These disciplines are brought together in service of the challenge of our time: healing the earth and healing the psyche.

Bill Plotkin has contributed a seminal new work to this field, although his book is more narrowly focused than the text edited by

David Tacey, Ph.D., teaches depth psychology and literature at La Trobe University in Melbourne, Australia. He is the author of eight books on Jungian psychology, cultural studies, and religious studies. His recent books include *The Spirituality Revolution* (New York: Routledge, 2004) and *How to Read Jung* (New York: Norton, 2007).

Roszak, *et al*. Its attention is on the developmental implications of ecopsychology, and how as individuals and as a civilization we must work toward an ecological stage in our evolution. Plotkin has spent 30 years working on this project, and his new book is a crowning achievement of a career dedicated to soul in its human and "more-than-human" dimensions.[2] Writes Plotkin:

> The human soul, like any soul, cannot be separated from nature. Our souls are of nature. If psychology is the study of the human soul, then an integral psychology must be an ecopsychology or, better, an eco-depth psychology.[3]

Although this book is too long (I would have preferred it to be half its present 515 pages), it gives a wonderful overview of the daunting task ahead for consciousness and civilization.

I appreciated the recognition that mainstream psychologists and others might continue to dismiss this emphasis on "soul" as a marginal if not eccentric activity: "Soul has been demoted to a new age spiritual fantasy," comments Plotkin wryly.[4] How true this is. If students want to study soul in Psychology Departments at our Universities, they are still derided as advocates of the New Age. To fill his work with soul, Plotkin has not only drawn on Jung and Hillman, acknowledged masters of the field, but he makes use of soulful literary resources such as those of poets David Whyte, David Wagoner, Rilke, Mary Oliver, and others. These are wonderful additions, as they break up the intellectual labor and introduce lightness of touch and intuitive knowing. He also makes extensive use of Thomas Berry, Brian Swimme, David Abram, and a host of others who are working in the related fields of ecophilosophy, ecotheology, ecocriticism, deep ecology, social ecology, and eco-feminism. Plotkin's background is in psychology, but he has read widely for decades, trying to understand what has gone wrong with our world and how to set it right.

Plotkin proposes a way of progressing from

> our current egocentric societies (materialistic, anthropocentric, competition based, class stratified, violence prone and unsustainable) to soulcentric ones (imaginative, ecocentric, cooperation based, just, compassionate and sustainable.)[5]

In a sense, this is the utopian dream that has fostered many ideologies of social liberation, including Marxism, socialism, humanism, and even liberal-minded capitalism. Each of these ideologies wants to see a more just, fair, equitable, and compassionate society, but of course the dream is so often far from the reality. Often in instituting the social dream, the program of reform itself becomes the nightmare, the source of fascism, dictatorship, militarism, and tyranny. The sad history of Marxian communism is a stark reminder of how the dream can turn bad, and those who seek social revolution end up embroiled in new and extreme forms of oppression.

Nevertheless, the vision of ecopsychology and Bill Plotkin is unique insofar as it proposes a form of social revolution based on the idea of re-enchantment and spiritual recovery. Instead of overcoming our alienation by the revolution of the proletariat, the eco-psychological program is to overthrow the alienation engendered by a split-off ego-consciousness that is divorced from the totality of life. This is a revolution in consciousness rather than in social system or reform. Here the idea is to attempt to recover our ancient, lost primal relationship with the cosmos in general and with the natural world in particular. Plotkin's premise is that "nature, including own deeper nature, soul, has always provided and still provides the best template for human maturation."

Jung himself wondered if that primal connection with nature was lost forever, or if it was merely temporarily eclipsed in the industrial modern age. In the last year of his life, Jung wrote:

> Through scientific understanding our world has become dehumanized. Man feels himself isolated in the cosmos. He is no longer involved in nature and has lost his emotional participation in natural events, which hitherto had a symbolic meaning for him. Thunder is no longer the voice of a god, nor is lightning his avenging missile. No river contains a spirit, no tree means a man's life, no snake is the embodiment of wisdom, and no mountain still harbors a great demon. Neither do things speak to him nor can he speak to things, like stones, springs, plants and animals. He no longer has a bush-soul identifying him with a wild animal. His immediate communication with nature is gone forever, and the emotional energy it generated has sunk into the unconscious.[6]

> The symbol-producing function of our dreams is an attempt to bring our original mind back to consciousness, where it has never been before, and where it has never undergone critical self-reflection. We *have been* that mind, but we have never *known* it. We got rid of it before understanding it.[7]

One need only place these passages beside contemporary ecological writings as in this quote from Annie Dillard to realize to what extent Jung has prefigured, and perhaps influenced, the present preoccupation with the resacralization of nature:

> It is difficult to undo our own damage, and to recall to our presence that which we have asked to leave. It is hard to desecrate a sacred grove and change your mind…. We doused the burning bush and cannot rekindle it; we are lighting matches in vain under every green tree. Did the wind once cry, and the hills shout forth praise? Now speech has perished from among the lifeless things of earth, and living things say very little to very few.[8]

We seek to "undo our damage," and we are not even sure how to go about it. Working at the purely external or economic level on climate change and environmental matters is not enough. It helps a bit to attend to things from the outside, but since the real problem has to do with our psychological attitude and an absence of sacred feeling, I doubt the capacity of secular governments and well-meaning agencies to resolve the "environmental crisis." Plotkin keeps emphasizing this in his book, and the source of his inspiration comes as much from Thomas Berry as it does from Jung. In his influential book *The Dream of the Earth*, Berry wrote:

> We must go far beyond contemporary culture [to find a solution]. None of our existing cultures can deal with this situation out of its own resources. We must invent, or reinvent, a sustainable human culture by a descent into our pre-rational, our instinctive resources. Our cultural resources have lost their integrity. They cannot be trusted. What is needed is not transcendence by 'inscendence,' not the brain but the gene.[9]

To put this another way, one cannot resolve the ecological crisis using the same mental approach that created it in the first place. If we work within the same-old dualism of living human subjects and dead external objects, the crisis is merely perpetuated. Something further is needed, and that something is a recovery of the idea of the sacredness of the earth and the exterior or "outside" nature of the soul, which Neo-Platonism calls *anima mundi*. As Hillman wrote, we need to experience "the return of the soul to the world."[10] We need to avoid the Cartesian dualism which turns the world into cold objectivity and allows only the human world to be potentially ensouled. We need to recover our "pre-rational, instinctive resources," which is precisely where Berry and Jung join forces and concentrate on the re-enchantment of reality. The alchemists used to say, "The greater part of the soul is outside the body." If we continue to treat the world as "outside" the soul, we continue to perpetuate the problem. This idea is found in the writings of late Jung, which move beyond his earlier, purely "clinical" model in which soul was only felt to reside within the person.

What is fascinating about this debate is that the cure of neurosis and the solution of the ecological crisis turn out to be the same thing: the recovery of the primal bond with reality. Thomas Berry wrote that ecological healing on the planet could occur only when the world is no longer experienced as a "collection of objects" but as a "communion of subjects."[11] Healing occurs when we no longer experience ourselves as strangers in the world, but when we see ourselves as living subjects in a dynamic community. This is the formula that underpins the creation of human community, and it is the formula at the heart of the ecological vision. But this is the same formula for the healing of consciousness. The ego cannot realize its true nature, until it experiences a relationship with a larger reality. The ego "comes home" when it glimpses the *other* who is its origin, which Jung calls the Self. Thus the idea of well being, in biological-environmental and psychological-spiritual terms, is ecological. We feel better when the sense of wholeness is restored to our broken psyche and our broken world.

Although Jung often claims that our bond with primal nature is "gone forever," I don't think we should take him literally. After all, his own work is predicated on the possibility of recovering this relationship. The late work on synchronicity, in particular, assumes the possibility of recovering awareness of a primal bond that we have lost, but which is nevertheless still present, although we might not perceive this at a conscious level. As Jung says in the same essay, "Since energy never vanishes, the emotional energy that manifests itself in all numinous phenomena does not cease to exist when it disappears from consciousness."[12] What is lost to awareness falls into the unconscious, from where it has to be recovered, by hard labor, effort, and creative endeavor. The emotional, psychic, and spiritual connection with nature can still be brought into consciousness, so long as we have the courage to sacrifice some of our rationality and egotism, which keeps it at bay and prevents it from making its necessary return. We cannot make way for the spiritual communication with nature unless we make room for it in the psyche and prepare a place for it in the hierarchy of our knowledge and education.

What Plotkin, Berry, Jung, Macy, and everyone writing in this field accepts is that the recovery of the primal bond is no easy feat, but involves risk, challenge, and effort on the part of the ego. The way down is the way forward, and there is no easy "new age" formula that is going to bring soul back into the world, apart from the difficult task of encountering the unconscious and facing the forces within the psyche. When the ego realizes it is not the master of the house, when it sees that it is part of a greater whole, then we recover the bond that brings healing. But the ego has to sacrifice to allow this rebirth to take place. Are we prepared to make the necessary sacrifice?

This is the question with which Plotkin is concerned. Are we able to mature beyond egocentric formations of personality, to the soulcentric formations in which the ego allows itself to take a secondary place and allows other voices to appear? To renounce control involves risk and anxiety, but it is anxiety located principally in the ego, which Freud reminded us was the "seat of anxiety." If we remain anxious and bound by ego, the breakthrough into the larger reality can never take place, and yet, in our secular and anxious age, who or what gives us the courage to take this plunge? How can we "Let go and let God," if God is dead? Thus it seems that ecological conversion is at the same time religious conversion. One begins to doubt that a purely secular consciousness can enable the healing of planet or self that we are looking for in ecology and depth psychology.

Plotkin emphasizes Hillman's point that the confinement of soul to the human being has been responsible for the despiritualization of nature. In *We've Had a Hundred Years of Psychotherapy and the World's Getting Worse*,[13] Hillman argues that egocentric psychology perpetuates the ecological crisis by its denial of soul in the world. To walk again in a sacralized universe, we need to feel that we are walking through the soul of the world. Soul is "returned" to the world, but it never left the world. Only our error and misperception allowed us to experience the world as hollow and lifeless. When we revise our philosophy and epistemology, we will arrive at a poetics of being in which the idea of a sacralized universe can be represented to our thought, and experienced in our bodies as the foundation for the animated life in creation. In this way, we no longer inhabit a dead, alien landscape, and the earth becomes alive with the presence of the sacred, and the order of things is restored.

Plotkin believes that our current widespread egocentricism is a symptom of arrested development. We are arrested at the stage where the ego differentiates itself from the unconscious and from other people, and lives in the illusion of its separateness. The bulk of his new book is dedicated to tracking the "stages" of psychological development, and in giving descriptions of each stage, with thoughts and exercises for how we can move from one stage to another. While I agree with the general idea of our arrested development, I have doubts about the effectiveness of plotting the course ahead with maps, lists, progress indicators, design tools, a "five-faceted wheel of life," and so on. Plotkin has a Ken Wilber-like fascination for charts, diagrams, hierarchies of values, pyramids of knowing. I find this tendency to lay it all out and chart the course to be frustrating and overly literal.

Plotkin states: "My foremost goal in this book is to support people in reaching stage 5."[14] Really? I thought it was to open them to soul. I don't think the move from egocentric to soulcentric can be understood by charts and maps, but perhaps that's just a personal preference. Perhaps it works for some readers, but it puts this reader off, just as Wilber's obsession with this methodology has put me off his recent work. To me, the shift from ego to soul requires intuition, imagination, courage, and faith. If those elements are missing in our culture or religion, then we have to find them within ourselves, and this is an extremely difficult undertaking.

But Plotkin is correct in assuming that modern Western society requires not just more information, but an initiation into a new state of being. He argues that "this knowledge has been at the heart of every indigenous tradition known to us."[15] I fully agree, and this comment reminds me of a conversation I had with an Aboriginal man one day in central Australia. I was only a boy at the time, and I happened to chat with an old man who was walking along a dirt pathway. He said his name was Warren and he told me: "You whitefellas are a curious people. It seems to us blackfellas that you are not initiated." He went on to explain that "we black people don't even know who we are until we go through initiation, and discover something beyond ourselves at our core; an ancestor spirit." "White people," Warren said, "seem to live like grasping and needy children." He said we seem to expend all our efforts on accumulating material goods and items, as if these had enduring value. "For Aboriginal people," he said, "the important things are not those things." He asked if my white culture had any ceremonies to break open the childhood self, and to reach beyond it to an ancestral core. I mentioned the Christian ceremonies of baptism and confirmation, which intended precisely what he was indicating. In these ceremonies, Christians claim to give up their worldly identifications, renounce the evils of the world, and devote themselves to a higher purpose in God. "Those ceremonies," Warren said, "must not work anymore; otherwise you white people would act differently."

NOTES

1. Theodore Roszak, Mary E. Gomes, and Allen K. Kanner (eds.), *Ecopsychology: Restoring the Earth, Healing the Mind* (San Francisco: Sierra Club Books, 1995).

2. David Abram, *The Spell of the Sensuous: Perception and Language in a More-Than-Human World* (New York: Vintage Books, 1996).

3. Bill Plotkin, *Nature and the Human Soul: A Road Map to Discovering Our Place in the World* (New York: New World Library & Sydney: Finch Publishing, 2008), p. 32.

4. *Ibid.*, p. 6.

5. *Ibid.*, p. 3.

6. C. G. Jung, *The Collected Works of C.G. Jung*, trans. R. F. C. Hull (Princeton: Princeton University Press, 1952/1958), Vol. 18 § 585.

7. Jung, *CW* 18 § 591.

8. Annie Dillard, *Teaching a Stone to Talk* (London: Picador, 1984), p. 70.

9. Thomas Berry, *The Dream of the Earth* (San Francisco: Sierra Club Books, 1988), pp. 207-208.

10. James Hillman, "*Anima Mundi*: The Return of the Soul to the World," in *Spring Journal* (Dallas, TX: Spring Publications, 1982).

11. Berry, *Dream of the Earth*, p. 2.

12. Jung, *CW* 18 § 583.

13. James Hillman and Michael Ventura, *We've Had a Hundred Years of Psychotherapy and the World's Getting Worse* (New York: HarperSanFrancisco, 1993).

14. Plotkin, *Nature and the Human Soul*, p. 48.

15. *Ibid.*, p. 3.

BOOK REVIEWS

GLEN MAZIS. *Humans, Animals, Machines: Blurring Boundaries.*
SUNY, 2008.

REVIEWED BY MICHAEL MELCZAK

D r. Mazis's new text, *Human, Animals, Machines: Blurring*
Boundaries is a syncretic work that explores the relationships
between humans, animals, and machines.

The title of the work comes from a conference held in Stanford in
1987, and presented in publication as *The Boundaries of Humanity:*
Humans, Animals, Machines, edited by James J. Sheehan and Morton
Sosna. Dr. Mazis notes difficulties with boundary formation evident
in the text, and seeks to engage with these difficulties as well as move
beyond them (p. 7). His work draws from numerous fields to complete
such a task.

The central argument of *Humans, Animals, Machines* is that,
traditionally, we have approached these three domains as distinct and
separate entities. In the course of Chapter 1, Dr. Mazis unpacks his
central thesis, which he then strikes clearly and concisely at the
beginning of Chapter 2: "It is a mistake to define humans, animals,

Michael Melczak, Ph.D., is a psychologist and researcher. He received his
degrees in clinical psychology from Duquesne University and is a researcher and
project evaluator at the University of Pittsburgh. His academic interests include
depth psychology, phenomenology, and cultural studies.

and machines as three separate kinds of entities, for there are mechanistic dimensions of animals and humans, as well as animal dimensions of humans, and, in some ways, even of machines." (p. 21) The remainder of the text is a careful and thoughtful exploration of the ways in which the boundaries between these domains are not as clear as we have thought them to be. The three realms, Dr. Mazis contends, "can only be thought through together." (p. 6) More accurately, the reader is called upon to recognize the similarity-difference dance of these realms.

Dr. Mazis describes his method as phenomenological. A stated goal is to "get beyond the dualisms…and take in the world in meaningful and less fragmented ways." (p. 15) He asks the reader "to be patient in considering the course of the book and what it allows us to see together." (p. 11) Accordingly, the tone of the subsequent work is welcoming and inviting. Personally, I prefer the types of books that allow for wonder as well as question, those that allow the divergence of thought towards broader understanding in addition to convergence of central purpose. With this book, I found myself making many notes in the margins, perhaps as a function of reviewing, but also perhaps to dialogue with the material in a meaningful way. In this regard, the phenomenological method serves the reader well.

There are two main streams of thought apparent in the text: traditional phenomenological philosophy and post-modern philosophy, the latter specifically detailed through the use of the language of complexity theory and complex adaptive systems. With regard to phenomenology, Dr. Mazis draws on the work of Heidegger, but it is the influence of Maurice Merleau-Ponty that is most notable. Indeed, there are numerous references to Merleau-Ponty throughout the text, and Dr. Mazis does well in explaining and expanding upon Merleau-Ponty's work. He does not simply parrot Merleau-Ponty, but appears to channel his spirit in generating his own original work: one trajectory of the thesis (the interplay of humans, animals, and machines) is to elucidate embodied existence in the "surround," the "meeting ground for energies, meanings, and common identities." (p. 240) The post-modern thinker Donna Haraway is another generative figure in the text, and Dr. Mazis draws inspiration from her thought as well.

Because a main theme of the text is the blurring of boundaries (and the negotiating of boundaries), the language of complexity theory and complex adaptive systems is used throughout (at times, "taken for granted" or as a Husserlian "natural attitude"). Thus, the reader will encounter the themes of "emergence," "zones of complexity," and "open and dynamic systems." Illustrative of the "taken-for-grantedness" of this language is the use of "feedback," commonly invoked in the parlance of our times. Complexity theory itself emerged from the field of physics and is now gaining momentum as a theoretical underpinning for the whole of science. In brief, complexity theory approaches all systems as living, non-linear, indeterminate, and unpredictable. There are patterns, to be sure, but in the dynamic interplay of life and interrelationships, new forms bloom; chaos, in the mythological sense, is creative. Chapter 4, "Greater Area and Depth," articulates these ideas in an understandable way.

Of course, there is much more to *Humans, Animal, Machines* than Merleau-Ponty, Haraway, and complexity theory. Dr. Mazis draws from sources such as theology to modern quantum mechanics, from artificial intelligence to zoology. Each field is brought into a rich dialogue with the central thesis, and numerous examples are used to illustrate main points and ground complex philosophical thoughts. One need not be an expert of any single discipline to appreciate the story, or stories. For example, one will read of the touching encounter between Cog, an artificially intelligent robot, and a professor at Harvard Divinity School, and the competitive encounter between IBM's Deep Blue and chess champion Gary Kasparov. Additionally, there is the story of Michael Chorost, who at age 36 became deaf, was fitted with a cochlear implant, and reflected on his lived experience as being "part computer." There is a tragic story in the conclusion about the destruction of elephant culture and community—and their own reluctance to go quietly into that good night. Each story invites the reader to reflect on the relationships among humans, animals, and machines that wax and wane like moons and cast varying lights on our life in the world.

While some thinkers take up phenomenology as a "merely" descriptive approach, there are nonetheless social, political, and ethical implications derived from the method. Dr. Mazis calls on the reader to develop a respectful appreciation of the other, whether that other is human, animal, or machine. The human being is not at the top of a hierarchy, where animals and machines are inferior or subordinate, but the human, the animal, and machine are interrelated within the world. There is no segregationist metaphor of separate but equal, or even a modification of separate and equal. Rather, there is an explicit appeal for harmony amongst all things, "natural" or "man-made." Indeed, one of the questions raised is to what degree it is beneficial to think of the world in terms such as these. Such questioning invites us to re-imagine and re-arrange social and political structures towards a community-based ethic where humans, animals, and machines are not exploited for their use.

One critique of the text pertains to sentence construction. At times, there are some difficult passages to traverse. A generous reader may take some of the more ambitious passages as the freeing float of ideas, a flitting over the philosophical flowers of thought. Others may find the construction more cumbersome. An example:

> What emerges as common in understanding humans as beings-in-a-world who first comprehend themselves and the world through the embodied sense of a situation, animals as having a sense of their surround, which leads them to take specific foraging and navigating actions, and intelligence in machines, insofar as it might emerge from being embodied and learning through meshing with the environment, is that the three realms can be seen as inseparably part of what is around them and taking in the larger sense of the world. (p. 58)

Given the proposed inseparability of the animal-human-machine, such sentence composition seems appropriate. That is, one gets the sense that if one is to think of the inseparability of these entities, it becomes important to convey such ideas without short, Hemingway-esque sentences with well-defined punctuation. Ultimately, the readability of the content will depend on the experience and appreciation of style of the individual reader.

The readers of *Spring* are likely to read *Humans, Animals, Machines* for either personal enjoyment or for scholarly pursuits. The text would be appropriate for graduate students and even advanced undergraduate students, provided appropriate supplementary materials are offered in conjunction with the text. The lay reader with specialized knowledge or interests in any or many of the fields so referenced would also be a good audience for Dr. Mazis's text.

In sum, *Humans, Animals, Machines: Blurring Boundaries* is an intriguing work and due attention and respect has been given to the topic. Admittedly, I was unfamiliar with Dr. Mazis's prior books. Based on my reading of this book, I am sufficiently interested to explore those as well. I am sure the interested reader for whom this book is an introduction to both the author and the topic will be inclined to do the same. Additionally, the reader may find the referenced texts to be worthwhile for deepening the understanding of Dr. Mazis's work.

BOOK REVIEWS

Notes from the Seminar Given in 1936-1940 by C. G. Jung. Edited by Lorenz Jung and Maria Meyer-Grass. Translated by Ernst Falzeder with collaboration of Tony Woolfson. Philemon Series. Princeton and Oxford: Princeton University Press, 2009.

REVIEWED BY SYLVESTER WOJTKOWSKI

If you expect this volume to be a long lost, recently recovered major Jung work you will be disappointed. It is not an hermetic time capsule arriving to us seventy years later with undiscovered treasures, but a belated translation of a German edition of 1986; and only the first of two volumes. It is significant as an initial volume of the Philemon Foundation's effort to publish Jung's complete works. The cover, depicting a dancing child in the flowering meadows, is a major improvement over the shades of *nigredo* of various English editions of the *Collected Works*. It is as if in the alchemy of publishing, this Jungian work has reached the stage of *cauda pavonis*, or peacock's tail.

Imagine late thirties in Zurich, when heavy clouds of fascism darken and storms come: the Spanish Civil war, the Anschluss of

SYLVESTER WOJTKOWSKI, Ph.D., is a Jungian analyst in private practice in New York City. He is a founding member of the Jungian Psychoanalytic Association (JPA) and a graduate of the C.G. Jung Institute of New York. He received his doctorate in Clinical Psychology from the New School. He has been a teacher at the C. G. Jung Foundation for Analytical Psychology. He gives workshops throughout the country on the Jungian and Archetypal Psychology.

Austria, the take-over of Czechoslovakia, the invasion of Poland, and later of Benelux, France, and England. In those dark, critical times members of the first generation of Jungians gather to discuss children's dreams. On the surface it seems like a Swiss Magic Mountain, isolated from real life and where personal complexes and archetypes are carefully examined while valleys of Europe are inflamed by collective complexes and archetypal passions. You will not find here Jung's reactions to social-political conditions; those are in evidence in his Nietzsche's Zarathustra project given alongside these seminars. What we find here is solid grounding in his method of dream interpretation and Jung at his most pedagogical, developmental, and sexual (not to say Freudian) mode. The format includes a presentation of the dream text and interpretation by one of the participants, followed by Jung's analysis[1] and general discussion. Among others, students include Markus Fierz, Margaret Sachs, Ilse Berg, Liliane Frey, Hans Wespi, Walter Huber, Hans Baumann, Marie-Louise von Franz, Emma Steiner, Cornelia Brunner, and Jolande Jacobi. The presented dreams are not really children's dreams; but are mostly adult recollections of childhood dreams, with an occasional dream of a child-friend of one of the participants. The seminar notes give a rare insight into the dynamics of prominent Jungian figures in the presence of the master. Here they are seen simply as diligent students imitating Jung who in turn praises, corrects, and criticizes them. Like "the snake biting its own tale" (p. 71), Jung fertilizes the simple dream material with his own attention, illuminating the archetypal cosmos of the dreamer.

In our times, when mainstream child psychology has abandoned its psychoanalytic origins and is mostly interested in behavior modification, or worse in medicating unwanted behaviors, it is really refreshing to return to the roots and see all child activities symbolically, no matter how bizarre and revolting. This book should be required reading for all "providers of children services."

The seminars offer Jung's most radical assessment of the ego:

> It was the error of the nineteenth century to say: The center of the world is the ego. The ego is, so to speak, a clown acting as if it were a leading actor. At best it wants what happens anyway. And we are always talking about how we'd want this or were able to do that. But the conviction "The will can achieve

> anything" is merely a superstition of the ego. We want to see
> ourselves as having supernatural powers. (p. 134)

This remark is now more pertinent than ever. Technology has given the ego power to fulfill all kinds of wishes, no matter how damaging to the inner and outer environment.

It is instructive to read these seminars to gather Jung's understanding of child psychology, which is elegantly paradoxical. "We cannot credit a child with the psychology of an adult, however unconsciously the child already has all the psychology of the adult," he writes. (p. 20) Even seventy years later, reading Jung requires us to abandon our preconceived ideas and think anew about the child's psyche. It may come as a surprise to Jungians that a lot of material in the book has to do with sexual development. True to form, it is a Jungian view of the purposive movement from the nutritive stage of libido to the sexual one. Although Jung can sound positively Freudian in his comments, like when he interprets the "smoking red sealing wax sticks" as a phallic symbol, he does it in a distinctly "Jungian" way: "Even if the sealing wax sticks didn't have a sexual meaning from a start, one could be led to the same assumption from the mythological context." (p. 34)

Jung has his own profound understanding of object relations. When a neurotic child demands a single person to meet all her needs, Jung says:

> all hell breaks loose. One has made that person a part of one's
> psychological sphere, and he becomes a pawn in one's
> psychological chess-board, until he complains and
> misunderstanding arises. That is why one often keeps people at
> arm's length because otherwise one would simply become a
> psychological object in their psyche. (p. 40)

Jung's thinking about childhood trauma includes both outer and inner factors. Jung thinks of external events as fateful occurrences whose impact on the psyche needs to be assimilated, because what they bring in is a necessary aspect of unfolding of the individual's nature. Although Jung acknowledges that an impetuous father can traumatize his young daughter, he believes that her inner world has impact as well. As she dreams of him as a giant, Jung sees that the child needs to integrate that impulsivity in her own personality:

> It does not matter in the slightest whether this once came into
> her from the outside, or whether it was there from the beginning.
> If it is in her, it has to be accepted. We can never avert such an
> affect by eliminating it. The dreamer will be truly healed only if
> this natural force is assimilated. (p. 390)

Even around a topic as serious as the childhood trauma, Jung shows
his lighter side and enjoys provoking his puritan audience: "I myself
have seen my father naked more than once, and I was not traumatized
by it." (p. 111)

Jung analyzes how a constellated archetype (i.e., activated in the
unconscious of the child) can lead to peculiar and repulsive behaviors,
like when a privileged four-year-old eats excrement. These unseemly
behaviors carry symbolic meanings of search for the original unity, a
need for protective wholeness, and are an expression of "infantile
autoeroticism" that should be tolerated. (p. 38) Jung's view of a toddler's
masturbation is ahead of his times and of ours as well. He sees it as an
attempt at self-fertilization, to transform oneself, an important step
towards fertilizing others. He denounces educators who see such
behaviors as markers of conscious sexuality.

Given the contemporary cultural identification with the mother-
child archetype reflected both in the inflated impact of early object
relations on adulthood and the preoccupation with [over]education of
[privileged]children, Jung's voice still sounds like compensatory
correction for current collective attitudes:

> the mental functioning of human beings is not something that
> each individual has to learn anew for him-or herself.... It is not
> the school that brings this about. On the contrary, we have to be
> careful that the school does not destroy the natural functioning
> of the psyche. (p. 133)

He articulates an important idea missing from object relations: "We
always have to be aware of the fact that children also contain a future
personality within themselves, the being they will be in the following
years. The children already live in the tomorrow, only they are not
aware of it." (p. 50) As a child psychologist Jung is not developmentalist.
He does not value school education and believes in the entelechy of
basic natural endowment:

> On the whole, it does not matter if the child has had this or that education, or was exposed to this or that influence. In a way, there is no development of personality. It has always been there, only not in an empirical sense, but invisible, as potentiality. Education can do little more than polish the surface, or also change it a little bit, but the basic nature is not touched by it. We cannot add to it or take anything away. Education is nothing but a differentiation to a specific goal. (p. 181-182)

For all his critique of education, Jung, usually a psychic and social elitist, is an egalitarian in the pedagogic realm: "It makes no sense to harbor illusions about the human condition. I am all for sending kids to public elementary schools, therefore, by no means to the exclusive private schools, so that they can ingest the necessary dirt." (p. 213)

What is most valuable in this book is Jung's unwavering emphasis on the psyche, an attempt on depth understanding of *each and every* behavior. This is a foundation that depth psychologists should abide by constantly. In the age of Attention Deficit Disorder (ADD) even some Jungian analysts take the condition for granted, accepting a vague neurological explanation of the syndrome. It is as if we have forgotten that school is a necessary but often difficult change for children, and it is not because some children's brains are wired differently that they have difficulty in adapting (It is a truism to say that each child has a unique neuronal map.) Here Jung's voice can act as psychoanalytic epistrophe. Talking of a distractible child having trouble concentrating at school, Jung says:

> The process of the development of consciousness includes the danger that sometimes splitting phenomena between the consciousness and the fantasy world occur. This manifests itself in children's being 'in the air,' unable to pay attention. They are really devoured by their intuitions. (p. 134)

He believes that the child's ego needs at its disposal instinctual energy which comes from fantasy but entails danger of losing consciousness through identification with fantasy figures. Jung even offers a piece of practical advice on how to deal with the child overcome by regressive fantasy:

> We have to pay attention to the child and try to stabilize his or
> her consciousness. The child should draw to make fantasies
> concrete; the freely floating danger will thus be made concrete.
> Writing and drawing cause certain cooling off, a devaluation of
> the fantasies. (p. 87)

In the 1930s Jung's view of fantasy has still not reached his final appraisal,
and he considered fantasy pathogenic: "The child is letting herself get
lost tenderly in the fantasy. That is why we say that fantasizing is
unhealthy. That is right; it is indeed unhealthy. What is unhealthy is
the moral aspect, for we lose our capacity to decide." (p. 81)

However, sometimes Jung's symbolic understanding of human
behavior breaks down and concrete explanation follows. A beating is a
beating is a beating. When a nine-year-old dreamer threw her money
away and brought her mother a couple of stones instead, she promptly
got thrashed. Jung's comment is not metaphoric on account of either
the beating or the tool used: "[The Dreamer] relinquishing a bit of
consciousness, [is] coming home in a new state that just earns her a
beating." "With this beating, the disruption of the conscious state can
be reversed again. This is a kind of talion, an 'atonement,' to make her
become one again with her body." (p. 82) "The mother is the counter
tendency. Her example, indeed, shows how one should be conscious.
Because the child goes too close to the abyss, she is beaten." [p. 97]
Here maternal unconscious beating the ego into consciousness is not
just a figure of speech[2] but a mother hitting her daughter with a
switch. At times Jung's uroboric tale [or is it "tail"?] carries him too
far:

> We must not necessarily think that dreams have a benevolent
> intention. Nature is kind and generous, but also absolutely cruel.
> That is its characteristic. Think of children. There is *nothing*
> *more cruel than children* [emphasis mine], and yet they are so
> lovely. (p. 159)

Jung can also sounds horribly or charmingly (depending on one's
view of gender relations) old-fashioned: "Woman is man's fate.
Otherwise he is suspended in the air and has no roots." (p. 55) or
"Why so many men are so unconditionally enthusiastic about the
war, because finally they can—'thank God'—swear, hit, and be real

men. For how can one be a man in a pussyfooting, moralistic society?" (p. 355) However, our reactions to Jung's sexist or misogynistic comments say more about our cultural complexes than Jung's view of gender, which was quite progressive for his times. Still, the book contains enough interesting and inspiring material to warrant keeping on your Jungian shelf for archetypal reference.

NOTES

1. On two occasions Jung himself presents original dream material.

2. It goes along with Hillman's idea that heroic consciousness is produced by violence See: "The Great Mother, Her Son, Her Hero, and the Puer," in *Fathers and Mothers*, ed. P. Berry (Dallas, TX: Spring Publications, 1973/1991), pp. 166-209.

BOOK REVIEWS

MONIKA WIKMAN. *Pregnant Darkness: Alchemy and the Rebirth of Consciousness*. Nicholas-Hays, 2004.

REVIEWED BY VERONICA GOODCHILD

A rare sensibility inhabits the pages of Jungian analyst Monica Wikman's alchemical book, which makes it compelling for both seasoned clinician and interested layperson alike. Wikman explores the psychological/somatic processes of death and rebirth based on Jung's alchemical model of the psyche and breathes new life into this model with contemporary clinical examples and some deeply moving dreams illustrating her themes throughout the text.

I was immediately struck by the title of this book. Both the "Pregnant" and the "Darkness" suggested an emphasis not only on the processes of transformation rather than some end result, but also the importance of descent and the dark night of the soul as indispensable

Veronica Goodchild, Ph.D., is a professor of Jungian and Imaginal Psychology at Pacifica Graduate Institute. She has been a Jungian psychotherapist for over twenty-five years. She is the author of *Eros and Chaos: The Sacred Mysteries and Dark Shadows of Love* (Nicolas-Hays, 2001), and of a forthcoming book, *The Songlines of the Soul: A New Vision for a New Century*, that explores the implications of Jung's psychoid archetype from synchronicity to UFOs and Crop Circles, and further to the mystical cities of the soul.

for the renewal of life energy and creativity, and for which Jung's psychology provides such a unique context.

Wikman's book begins with her own brief account of her spontaneous and immediate healing of an aggressive stage IV ovarian cancer that she had suffered with for over four years and that had almost killed her. At the moment when the illness was finally declared terminal, she let go and surrendered to death, but not before raging at the universe for her profound disappointment and despair. This painful lament or heart-felt confession opened up a series of visions that Wikman refers to as taking place in the psychoid realm, an intensely felt psycho-physical level of consciousness beyond the collective unconscious. Jung began to name and explore this psychoid realm when he was forced to revise his notion of the archetype with experiences of synchronicity and other paranormal phenomena, but this late work of Jung's has not been moved forward significantly by many Jungian scholars or analysts. Wikman bravely pursues and explores the intense landscapes of this psychoid realm that she knows first hand from her experience of them. Apart from Jung's own visionary and imaginal experiences recorded mainly in *Memories, Dreams, Reflections*, the theologian and philosopher Henri Corbin perhaps comes closest to these domains when he describes the real (not fictive or imaginative) landscapes of the soul as psycho-cosmic imaginal geographies. In my view, Jungian psychology has neglected the reality of the imaginal domains in favor of an emphasis on symbolic interpretations, so it is refreshing to read Wikman's own and her patients' accounts of such subtle body experiences and their central place in the processes of initiation and transformation.

Wikman's contribution to our understanding of alchemy, therefore, is firmly grounded in the psyche-matter mysteries that so preoccupied the alchemists and for which the traditions of alchemy and the alchemical processes of transformation and transmutation provide a symbolic and experiential system. The recognition of the divine inhabiting the soul in the human physical body is at the center of this mystery and its exploration at the heart of its teachings. *Pregnant Darkness* is divided into two parts tracing the initiate's journey into this profound mystery. Part One, "The Nigredo and the Rising of Lunar Consciousness," is a journey to the source of living waters. Through acknowledging and opening to our wounds we experience a shamanic death—the alchemical *nigredo*—and open to the heavens and hells of deep subjectivity and archetypal reality; not, as Wikman writes, a journey for the faint-hearted. Here, Wikman, following Jung, stresses the importance of the human relationship between analyst and analysand over theoretical constructs as the necessary container for psychological dismemberment and the terrors of insanity that often accompany these darknesses and conflicts. A favorite clinical example in this part of the book is of a woman whose over-identification with independence and achievement led her away from her own feminine nature and instincts. Eventually a dream vision of an illuminated fairy queen arising out of the earth with other fairies all sitting on dew drops on blades of grass which become crowns leads to an experience of the healing light to be found within nature herself. The woman "*felt the experience* of the divine incarnating into matter." (pp. 55-62) Wikman masterfully amplifies the details of the dream vision noting especially the four main problems that Marie-Louise von Franz suggests alchemy addresses to help us all deal with the limitations of our Christian mythic inheritance: the value of the feminine erotic mystery; the elevation of the individual in relation to the uniformity of the mass; the problem of evil; and the reconciliation of opposites. An essential focus in Part One of the book is how the *nigredo* leads to the development of a religious attitude that comes with exposure to the dark subtle depths of the soul.

Part Two, "The Albedo & Rubedo: Rebirth of Consciousness, Shining Renewed," focuses on how the development of a religious attitude needs to be sustained by daily practice and dialogue with the unknown mysteries of the psyche as they appear in dream, vision, encounter, and relationship—relationship with others as well as in our experiences of nature. Wikman addresses both resistances to this process and the dangers of approaching transpersonal forces with the ego inflation that can result. She also witnesses the healing restoration and renewal of freedom and life that our odysseys can awaken for us. One of the things I found to be most valuable in this part of the book is the author's focus on how the religious attitude finds its true home in the awakening of the heart and the development of our capacity to love. Insight and conscious realization are steps along the way but not the *telos* of the alchemical *opus*. Rather, individuation is a process of moving from understanding with the mind to embodying the felt instincts of the heart, and this is one way in which the divine seeks to manifest in the human soul. Wikman writes: "The mental work and understanding feeds another mystery, the mystery of the heart, where the being of light resides." (p. 161) Alchemical work changes us, and these changes must inform the way we live with ourselves, with others, with the divine, and the world around us. In other words, the processes of transformation bring up the ethical consideration of how to live from the perspective of the wisdom revealed from the deep psyche.

Another important contribution in Part Two is how we discover what Wikman, following Jeff Raff, calls the Ally or Guide from the psychoid dimension of the psyche. Through the example of a patient who had had abdominal surgery early in life that led to her inability to bear children, and her powerful dream and active imagination, Wikman shows "the immediate experience of the divine in relationship with the generative psychic-emotional-physical wound, and in relationship with the path of individuation." (p. 186) We read how in the dream the patient's body becomes the landscape of earth, and how her belly becomes a lotus with water in the middle that draws the divine figure from the sky world through love and mutuality. Dreaming the dream forward in active imagination, the patient experiences a beneficent snake-like dragon lover that descends from the cosmos beyond our known galaxy and opens her belly revealing it to be like the mythic crack in the earth between the worlds in Celtic mythology. Her "being open to cracking open" also cracks open the sky, allowing this guide to descend to earth. The ally reveals himself to be a fierce protector of all that she loves and of her particular path in life. She feels an ecstatic exchange of breath with this companion-lover, a breath that melts away all cares and falsities bringing a "profound communion between cosmic being and human being" that awakens her soul and simple humanity. Furthermore, Wikman's example also demonstrates how our connection through our own woundings with the divine, personified as protector and companion, not only helps transform us but also helps transform the divine as well, in this case revealing how the god-image is changing in the patient's life. This deep connection to the guide gives us the confidence to sacrifice outworn modes of being and to become more real and to foster our lives as "carriers of living water" so central to alchemy. Furthermore, this spiritual contact gives rise to a deep erotic instinctual part of the psyche that with awareness can regulate both rapport and distance in our relationships and, as an inner helper, fuels our capacity for spontaneity, vitality, and creativity. (pp. 185-188)

We live at the end of an age and see death and destruction all around us. However, at the same time, we also live at a time when profound unitive levels of experience are arising in the human soul as well as in nature. For example, on the collective level, I have long been intrigued with how these psychoid levels of the world soul seem to be manifesting as "new creations" in the universal form of UFOs (from above) and Crop Circles (from below), initiating dramatic changes in consciousness for those who take such events seriously. These manifestations are not only symbolic of the emerging unity of psyche and matter (which they are) but they are also real expressions of the psychoid archetype. It appears as if what the alchemists called the *unus mundus* or one world is constellating today in an attempt to reconcile opposites and to seek balance away from divisive and devastating conflicts toward healing, wholeness, and Eros consciousness. Wikman's book assists us in recognizing and contributing toward this healing and wholeness in the individual human soul. Following the ancient alchemical mysteries, she shows us how the *imaginatio vera*—the *true*, spiritual or visionary imagination—is the organ of knowledge located in the heart, that assists in co-creating a new level of consciousness beyond opposites through direct experiences of the psychoid world. Such subtle experiences from beyond the archetypal domains give us glimpses into an interconnected and multidimensional universe fashioned by the deep mysteries of love.

BOOK REVIEWS

LAWRENCE COUPE. *Beat Sound, Beat Vision. The Beat Spirit and Popular Song.* Manchester University Press, 2007.

REVIEWED BY SUSAN ROWLAND

There are secret histories. Even in the most flagrant and ostentatious of arts, popular music from the 1960s, there are secret, because unconsidered, affiliations and invocations. There are secret histories folded up in words as the etymologists and the rhetoricians knew. So what does it mean that "Beatles" contains "Beat" as in Beat poets? There are secret histories and histories of secrets, as Laurence Coupe shows in this stunning and authoritative new work. His book on the Beat poets, popular music, and the *secret traditions they espoused*, encompasses mythology, Zen, the perennial philosophy, and a quest for the sacred.

Truly, Coupe here manages that most taxing of intellectual and spiritual demands, to sieve the authentic art from the poetry and music of the 1950s onwards, from the debased and darkened counter-culture that came to surround them. Few have tried so scrupulously to rescue the human desire for the sacred, as manifest in powerful 20th-century

Susan Rowland, Ph.D., is Reader in English and Jungian Studies at the University of Greenwich, UK, and author of *Jung as a Writer* (Routledge, 2005). She was chair of the International Association of Jungian Studies, 2003-2006.

medias. Few have so brilliantly evaluated the Beats' poetry and later songs' genuine challenge to conventional norms that promote war and consumerism. Coupe recognizes the fragility of the Beat legacy in the face of a capitalism that is capable of mimicking its harshest critics and seducing the Beat poets' work with money and celebrity. So *Beat Sound, Beat Vision* brings new clarity to the understanding of figures such as Jack Kerouac, Allen Ginsberg, Alan Watts, Bob Dylan, The Beatles, The Incredible String Band, Gary Snyder and Eco-Zen, Jim Morrison, Leonard Cohen, and Joni Mitchell. Without ignoring personal difficulties, *Beat Sound, Beat Vision* restores to these important artists their roles as visionaries, harbingers of myth, whose art brings the quest for the sacred to the modern age.

For what unites these experimenters in poetic and lyrical form, we learn, is the three meanings of "beat." Firstly, the Beat poets such as Kerouac and Ginsberg were inspired by the musical "beat" of bebop and jazz. Secondly, they were concerned for the poor and dispossessed. Only those who were dead "beat," were the true inheritors of the third meaning of "beat," the beatific vision. For as Coupe, a major theorist of myth has shown elsewhere (particularly in his bestselling *Myth*, published by Routledge), the Beats, all of them, are spiritually descended from William Blake and his very specific attitude to the divine and myth. Unlike those poets and philosophers who allegorize myth to produce abstract truths or knowledge, Blake sees the sacred as existing in a dynamic, dialogical relationship with the profane. So Blake is one visionary where shamanism enters the poetic tradition. Blake's works seed in literature the shamanic notion of myth as a shaping spirit of the imagination. Myth in this way is the means by which the profane world reveals the sacred.

After Blake, it is the Beats, in poetry, novels, and music who most espouse the imagination as the route to spiritual joy. Their use of myth is as the visible sacred potential of the fallen post-Eden modern world. What unites Blake and the Beats is the belief in the imagination as visionary. What unites their *writing* is a common dipping into much older scriptures of myth, alchemy, Eastern religions of Hinduism and Buddhism, Zen, Tao, and even Christianity. I say, "even" Christianity; for those Beats for whom the conventional Christian religion remains significant, such as Kerouac and Cohen, it is not the established religion of doctrine and code. Rather Beat Christianity is a fluid myth capable of joining and enlivening other major religions such as Buddhism. It is open to being "re-written" in order to feed the starved contemporary imagination.

Crucially, the Beats try to stay close to, imaginatively at least, the dead beat, the marginalized and ignored by mainstream society in America and Britain. Marvelously, Coupe can illuminate both Dylan's "Tambourine Man" and The Beatles' "Eleanor Rigby" by showing how the personification of the art's capacity for vision, the tambourine man, is also marginal, alongside the emptiness found in the "lonely people." Coupe does not shun the despair, pain, and disillusion found in both the Beat poets and the song writers. However, he does show that the correct framework of interpretation remains the mythical capacity to evoke the sacred from the profane, even when the profane threatens to drown the suffering artist.

A final layer of cultural potency for this movement proves to be perhaps the most coherent incarnation of shamanic practice known to modernity, that of Native Americans. Gary Snyder and Joni Mitchell are only the most persistent of Beats who have portrayed Amerindian culture as something buried under modern America. This is both a reference to the cruel persecution of Native American practices in the past, and of a sense that the only true spiritual tradition for America is that of the people who know how to live *with* nature instead of *on* it.

Beat Sound, Beat Vision is a work of tremendous cultural imagination itself in revealing the vertical and horizontal paradoxes of the Beat vision. Reaching back into ecological myths of a sacred feminine earth, forward to condemn capitalism's destruction of it, outwards to recognize, honor, and mourn the other Native American culture, *Beat Sound, Beat Vision* brings a healing scholarship to the complex, corrupted yet still vibrant picture of popular culture of the last fifty years. All those who seek to belong to the truthful in our own age, who seek art that offers a sense of the sacred to the collective, all of us should read this book.

UNIVERSITY OF
CALIFORNIA PRESS
JOURNALS + DIGITAL PUBLISHING

Psychology

JUNG JOURNAL

EDITOR // Dyane N. Sherwood

Jung Journal: Culture & Psyche is an international quarterly published by the C.G. Jung Institute of San Francisco, one of the oldest institutions dedicated to Jungian studies and analytic training. The journal was founded in 1979 by John Beebe under the title, The San Francisco Jung Institute Library Journal. In 2007 the title was changed to reflect its evolution from a local journal of book and film reviews to one that attracts readers and contributors from the academy and the arts, in addition to Jungian analyst-scholars.

WWW.UCPRESSJOURNALS.COM

New York Center for Jungian Studies
*Seminars and Study Tours
in Extraordinary Settings*

Join us in Ireland
for our

NINTh ANNUAL

JUNG
IN IRELAND

"The ARChETYPE OF home"
A Seminar
Dublin & Galway
March 26 - April 2, 2009

"a STUDY/TOUR IN
CELTIC MYThOLOGY"
Sligo & County Mayo
April 19-26, 2009

Open to the general public and Mental Health professionals (C.E. credits available).
To register, or for more information, please contact:

The N.Y. Center for Jungian Studies
Tel: (845) 256 0191 or e-mail: Jofisher@nyjungcenter.org
www.nyjungcenter.org

DARK LIGHT OF THE SOUL

by Kathryn Wood Madden, Ph.D.

ISBN: 9781584200659 ∞ Price: $25.00 ∞ 272 pages

Dark Light of the Soul explores the inner journeys of Jacob Boehme, the seventeenth-century Protestant mystic, and C.G. Jung, the twentieth-century depth psychologist. Each was concerned with the immediacy of experience, yet comprehended the importance of spirit as a transforming presence in human life. Kathryn Wood Madden connects the experiences of these two pioneers, focusing on a "ground of being that contains all opposites in potentiality." She examines those experiences from the perspective of depth psychology and religion, offering meaningful insights for anyone on a path of inner development, as well as for professionals in clinical settings.

"Readers will be grateful to Kathryn Madden for her clear discussion of Jung"s and Boehme"s experiences of and reflections on the nature of unitary reality. Her clinical insight and spiritual response to the otherness that addresses us from this depth, brings light to the life of our souls." —**Ann Belford Ulanov**, Ph.D., Christiane Brooks Johnson Professor of Psychiatry and Religion, Union Theological Seminary; psychoanalyst in private practice, and author of The Unshuttered Heart: Opening to Aliveness/Deadness in the Self (Abingdon Press, 2007)

"In this beautifully crafted book, Kathryn Madden shows how traumatic breakdown may turn out to be the first step in a psychological/spiritual breakthrough to a deeper "unitary reality" that supports us all. By exploring the breakthrough experiences of C.G. Jung, Jacob Boehme, and her own clinical cases, she shows how psychotherapeutically mediated contact with this "ground of being" (both immanent and transcendent) can make all the difference in the healing of trauma." —**Donald Kalsched**, Ph.D., author of The Inner World of Trauma: Archetypal Defenses of the Personal Spirit (Routledge, 1996)

About the Author:
Kathryn Madden Ph.D., is a licensed psychoanalyst, a Diplomate in AAPC, and has served the past 10 years as President and CEO of the Blanton-Peale Institute in New York City. Kathryn has a background in clinical work, teaching, writing, lecturing, and professional theatre. She received her M.A., M.Phil. and Ph.D. in Psychology & Religion at Union Theological Seminary under the tutelage of Prof. Ann Belford Ulanov. Kathryn is the Senior Editor of *Quadrant: Journal of the C.G. Jung Foundation for Analytical Psychology* and the Executive Editor of *The Journal of Religion & Health: Psychology, Spirituality & Religion*. She has written extensively on the subject of depth psychology and religion and frequently lectures at international conferences. She maintains a private clinical practice of Jungian orientation in New York City.

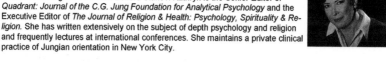

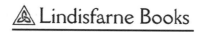

To order, please visit www.lindisfarne.org

Jungian Odyssey 2009

Photo Max Weiss, Courtesy Hotel Waldhaus

International English-Language Conference & Retreat

Destruction and Creation

Facing the Ambiguities of Power

June 6–13, 2009
Hotel Waldhaus
Sils Maria, Switzerland

- In the breath-taking Engadine Valley

- Site of Friedrich Nietzsche's summer-work on *Thus Spake Zarathustra*

- Historical Guests at the Waldhaus include CG & Emma Jung, Thomas Mann, Rainer Maria Rilke, Hermann Hesse

- Odyssey Speakers
  Keynote: Paul Bishop, PhD
  Special Guest: David Tacey, PhD
  Josephine Evett-Seckers, MPhil
  Murray Stein, PhD
  Mario Jacoby, Dr. phil.
  Kathrin Asper, Dr. phil.
  Ursula Wirtz, Dr. phil.
  Urs Mehlin, Dr. phil.
  Kristina Schellinski, MA
  Dariane Pictet, AdvDipExPsych
  Andreas Schweizer, Dr. theol.
  Raffaella Colombo, MD
  among others ...

PRESENTED BY **ISAP**ZURICH
INTERNATIONAL SCHOOL OF ANALYTICAL PSYCHOLOGY ZURICH
MEMBER SWISS CHARTA FOR PSYCHOTHERAPY
AGAP POST-GRADUATE JUNGIAN TRAINING

Hochstrasse 38 • 8044 Zürich • Switzerland
T +41 (0)43 344 00 66 • office@isapzurich.com

info@jungianodyssey.ch

www.jungianodyssey.ch